Birth Mother

Birth Mother

The Story of America's First Legal Surrogate Mother

Elizabeth Kane

HARCOURT BRACE JOVANOVICH, PUBLISHERS
SAN DIEGO / NEW YORK / LONDON

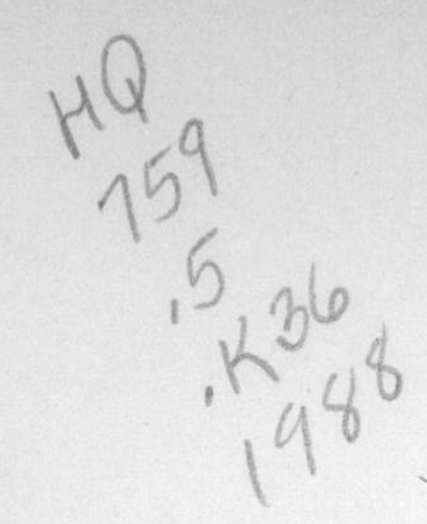

Library of Congress Cataloging-in-Publication Data

Kane, Elizabeth.
Birth mother.

1. Kane, Elizabeth.
2. Surrogate mothers—United States—Biography.
I. Title.
HQ759.5.K36 1988 306.8 [B] 87-23810
ISBN 0-15-112811-1

Printed in the United States of America
Designed by Ann Gold

First edition

A B C D E

To my Sunday's Child, my son

ACKNOWLEDGMENTS

For two years the manuscript for this book crossed the Atlantic numerous times to reach my friend Adam Hart-Davis in England. He will never realize the depth of my appreciation for sharing his knowledge and skills. From the very moment he began working on the 750-page journal, he never stopped believing that it would become this book. To my mentor and friend—thank you, Adam.

To my husband, Kent, who stuck it out in the last eight years. For listening to me for hours, for never losing faith in my ability to author this book, even when I was ready to quit, thank you for your loving patience and encouragement. Aside from Kent's moral support, his contributions are quite tangible here: every photograph not otherwise credited is his.

I am proud of my children Julie, Laura, and Jeffrey for their loving understanding and for defending me in ways only children can. Their loyalty was a stabilizing force as I wrote and rewrote.

The support and knowledge I have received from my fellow members of the National Coalition Against Surrogacy, especially from Gena Corea, will never be forgotten.

To my literary agent, Denise Marcil, for her perseverance—thank you.

To Marie Arana-Ward, senior editor at Harcourt Brace Jovanovich, for her foresight, expert editing, and love for this story—I offer my heartfelt gratitude.

To Alison Ward and Mary Beth Whitehead for guiding me back to reality—bless you both.

To my sensei, Steve Mott and Jim Price, for teaching me to stand firm in the face of adversity and for reminding me again that courage must come from within—lessons that will remain with me for life.

To my dear friend, Susan Finzen, thanks for holding my hand and cheering me on at all the right times.

Without the help and love of every person mentioned here, I would not be the person I am today.

AUTHOR'S NOTE

Although I have chosen to author this book as Elizabeth Kane—the pseudonym I used as a surrogate mother, and the name that has always been used for me in the press—my real name is Mary Beth. Therefore, in scenes with my family and friends, I am Mary Beth. All names in this book are real, except where I felt a change was necessary to protect the privacy of the individual.

In writing this book, I have relied heavily on my diary. The original thoughts, often naïve, are represented as I wrote them at the time.

Introduction

I cannot remember if the sky was bright and sunny or dreary and gray above the autumn leaves. I lost my sense of awareness during the twenty-six-hour labor on that Sunday morning, November 9, 1980, and I lay on the delivery table hardly feeling anything as the doctor sewed me back together. My newborn son—pink-skinned and perfectly formed—lay peacefully in the arms of his new mother, not in my arms.

I was a substitute. A surrogate mother. The scene was to be my reward for the giving of life, the moment that was supposed to hold me together for years to come. Eight and a half months earlier I had signed a contract promising to produce a healthy child, in exchange for a fee. I had just fulfilled that contract.

A dainty blonde woman, voguish even at that early hour, held him gingerly, as if unsure of the feel of his tiny body. Her husband was the father of my son, and he pressed against her shoulder to gaze at his child's face. Hesitantly he stroked the top of the baby's velvet head with one finger, as if the touch would shatter a dream and his male child would vanish instantly.

Baby Justin. At that moment I thought it would not matter to me if I never saw him again. I had vowed not to intrude on their lives or to cast a shadow on their happiness. It had not once entered my mind that, even though the doctor had physically disconnected us in cutting the umbilical cord, I would be attached to this child by a heartstring for the rest of my life. I know now that our judicial system might be able to take a baby from a woman's arms, but it can never remove that child from her heart or memory.

A crisp morning in November 1964 in many ways is the beginning of this story. I lay on the delivery table, little more than a week after my twenty-second birthday, following the instructions and gentle encouragement of a stranger—a masked doctor from the free clinic for unwed mothers. After a final, heroic push, he held high a dark-haired baby girl and then had her whisked from the sterile room. For four days in the hospital I held her and studied her every feature, awed by the strong resemblance to her handsome, dark-haired father, with whom I was in love. We had planned to marry. Weeks after I learned I was pregnant, I neither saw nor heard from him again. I left town and found a job babysitting for a family who opened their home to unwed mothers. After the birth, I named my little girl Heidi Marie and spent those first four days of her life calling everyone I knew, investigating ways I could keep her with me. When I ran out of ideas, I made the only choice I thought I had: I would give her up to a family that could love her and offer her the security of a home. My last phone call was to an adoption agency.

I never forgot my firstborn, yet I learned not to dwell on her absence. I never had any illusions that I would see her again. I was young, afraid, and desperate to begin anew, forget my tainted past, and someday marry a man who loved me enough to share his name. On June 25, 1966, I married Kent, and somewhere between the wedding ceremony and the reception, I began to hope there would be other children to love some day. And there were.

I was secure in the knowledge that I could survive the loss

of Justin because I had been able to endure the loss of Heidi. I am confident that the loss I underwent early in life was even a kind of reassurance to the surrogate clinic and the contracting couple who would receive my son. And then there was the fact that I would conceive Justin by insemination from a syringe filled with semen from a stranger; the coldness of the procedure convinced me I would feel nothing for the baby. I signed a contract believing that. How could I possibly know that this deep deception would surface slowly in a whirlwind of emotions for years to come? At some point after the birth of my surrogate child I realized I had two choices: either to survive or to succumb to an overwhelming grief at the loss of two children at very different stages of my life. This is the story of my determination to survive.

Chapter II

February 1967

Our car stopped near the quaint little ski lodge, a rustic building nestled in the mountains. Chandelle sat by the window of the small foreign car, staring blankly at the fiercely swirling snowflakes. Clad in ski clothes, she hugged her knees to her chest and spoke in a voice that was hardly a whisper. "I was sure this was it, Mary Beth. Ten days late." Her voice rose to a wail. "Ten days. God knows I didn't want to get my hopes up again, but I had all the symptoms this time." Chandelle's eyes welled up with tears, and now I barely heard her speak. "I was going in for a test as soon as we got back from this ski trip."

"Are you sure it's not a miscarriage?" I asked hopefully.

"Stop trying to be nice. I haven't even conceived. How many years have I been through this? Over and over again!" She dropped her head to her knees and began to sob.

Finally she raised her eyes to the gray skies and shouted, "God, what's the matter with me? Craig deserves to be a father."

She turned toward me. "Have you ever seen him with a little kid? When we were dating, he used to love to come to my house. With eleven brothers and sisters, every mealtime was like a reunion. We'd talk about all the kids we would have after we got married. Craig wanted one right away, by our first wedding anniversary. Did you know he was an only child? When he was a little kid, he promised himself someday he'd have six kids. Now look at us. I can't even give him one." She turned toward the front seat and cried hopelessly.

"Chandelle, don't." I patted the shoulder of her ski jacket in a feeble attempt to cheer her. "You'll have children someday. Just be patient."

"Don't talk to me about patience. We've tried for over a year, the tests we're going through make me feel like an animal in a laboratory, and on top of all that, all I ever hear from Craig's parents is, 'Are you pregnant yet?' Now they're starting to wonder whose 'fault' it is. Don't talk to me about patience. I'm sick of all of it." She spat the words and I cringed inwardly.

I ached with sympathy, but I also worried that Chandelle might ruin this ski trip. We had all looked forward to that weekend for a long time, but she was in despair and I knew her mood would be infectious.

I watched Craig and Kent throw snowballs at the car windows while they plodded toward us through the mounting drifts.

"We're all registered," Craig called, his smile brilliant. He was always cheerful. I began to wonder if he knew how Chandelle felt. Something, a glint in his pearly-gray eyes, told me that he did and that made him even more determined to let his enthusiasm make up for her dour expression.

"I can't wait to hit that powder in the morning," Kent shouted through the wind and swirling snow. He turned up the collar on his black quilted ski jacket and walked around the car to unclamp our skis from the rack.

"Okay, everybody. Out of the car. Let's get this luggage inside, find some chow, and hit the sack," Craig bubbled. "I'm going to be the first one on the slopes in the morning."

His childlike delight was so overwhelming, we all laughed

with him. I unfolded my legs from the tiny backseat of the sports car. We had been cooped up for seven hours getting to these mountains. I stood, stretched my arms wide, and inhaled the sharp, cold air.

Now I stood in the snow next to the car and peered through the open door. "Chandelle? Come on." I spoke gently. "Let's have a good time. The fellas have been looking forward to this trip for weeks. The snow is perfect. Please?"

The misery in her face made me draw back when she finally turned to respond. "You have a good time. I'm not skiing." The words were a hoarse whisper.

The tiny split-log cabin Kent and I shared was surrounded by silence from the continuing snowfall. Kent awoke in the night, groped toward the bathroom in the dark, unfamiliar room, and returned quickly to burrow into the warm feather quilts, the same kind my grandmother used.

His activity roused me from a restless sleep. "Kent?" I spoke into the darkness.

"Hmmm?"

"I want to talk to you."

"We have to get up early tomorrow," he muttered.

"I want to have a baby."

He yawned, then grunted. "You're always saying that."

"This time I mean it," I persisted.

He turned toward me, propping himself up on one elbow. "We just got married."

"Not just. Seven months is not just."

"It is to me. You know we're saving for a house. And I wanted to trade in the Corvette for one of those new Firebird convertibles." This was news to me. He studied me quizzically. "Why do you want to have a baby?"

I looked away quickly, unable to talk about the new fears Chandelle's infertility had begun to stir inside me. "I just do, that's all. I love babies."

Kent snickered. "So did my brother's wife. They ended up with five kids and three miscarriages. She was always pregnant. He ended up losing his place at the kitchen table." He looked at me a moment. "That's the last thing we need right now."

A small seed of panic was planted. "What do you mean?" My voice sounded tinny in my ears.

"Well, I don't know. It's just not something I've ever thought much about. I don't know what the rush is."

"The rush? You're thirty-two years old and I'm twenty-four. If it takes me a year to get pregnant, you'd be over fifty by the time the baby graduated from high school." I made an effort to control the impatience in my voice.

"It won't take you a year to get pregnant." Kent tugged the quilt. "Do you mind if we discuss this another time?"

I put my hand on his shoulder to stop him from turning away. "Wait. I have another question. If we try for a year and I can't get pregnant, can we adopt a baby?"

He sat up, staring at me openmouthed. "Are you kidding?"

"No, of course not."

"Why would I want to raise someone else's kid?"

"What kind of an attitude is that?" I retorted in disbelief, remembering I had given up Heidi for adoption.

"Well, the way I look at it, I'm not that wild about having a baby of our own right now. But if there's something wrong with you and you can't get pregnant, I'm sure not going to adopt someone else's kid."

"What's the difference?" My voice began to rise at the reality of what he was saying. "A baby is a baby."

"Oh, no, it's not," Kent's voice rose, too. "I want my kid to have my blood in his veins. It's not something I can put into words, but when I look at the boy, I want to know that he has my name and that he's part of my family. Not some stranger's."

"But after we had an adopted baby for a few months, he'd

be your son and you'd never remember he was adopted," I argued.

"Oh, yes, I would. Maybe it's a matter of pride and maybe other men don't feel that way, but I do. I'm not gonna raise someone else's kid. You never know what you're getting. I wouldn't even consider adopting." He flopped down, turned his back to me, and pulled the quilts up over him.

Silence. Dead, thick silence that hurt my ears. These were things we should have discussed before the wedding. I always assumed we would have a large family. Kent used to joke about his brother's five children and, in the same breath, insist he never wanted a large family. But I never dreamed he felt this strongly about not wanting children at all if we couldn't have our own.

The knot in my stomach began to grow. I felt that if I didn't become pregnant soon, I would never be anything more than the medical secretary I was. Since playing with dolls as a child, I had envisioned my adult life as one of wife and mother. Now I couldn't imagine going through an entire lifetime without children.

Kent slept peacefully beside me in the small cozy room while my thoughts flew in all directions. I worked in a large medical clinic where we saw hundreds of patients each week. The cabinets were jammed to overflowing with files that recorded the events of their lives. The births and deaths, minor illnesses and major operations. Some of the people whose names were in the files had become my friends.

I remembered rejoicing over a positive pregnancy test with a hopeful woman and imagining her joy when she went home to tell her husband the news. I saw many women come into the office month after month, their babies growing from embryos to fetuses to newborns. I saw how much the children added to their lives. Each new baby seemed wanted and loved.

I remembered the few patients who were pregnant and

single. No girl ever spoke about abortion but went instead to live with a relative in another city or to spend their last months before the baby was born in a home for unwed mothers. Because of these girls, adoption was possible for young childless couples like Craig and Chandelle.

In the office I had seen women tortured by symptoms of false pregnancy too often not to know the private hell that followed each barren month. I knew Chandelle well enough to understand she needed to be a mother to feel like a successful wife to Craig. She seemed to have everything else. She was lovely, with intelligent brown eyes. She and Craig had a small apartment with expensive new furniture, and they had a new sports car. They were well on their way to achieving everything they had always wanted and dreamed about. Yet it meant nothing without a child to share it all. And finally I understood why.

A vision of my great-aunt Esther sitting in my grandmother's living room came before me. She was one of my favorite relatives, my mother's aunt. Financially secure, well-dressed, widely traveled, and intelligent, Aunt Esther had never had children. Now in her early sixties, she was widowed, and alone.

Many times I had asked my mother why this refined, affectionate woman had remained childless. My mother did not have an answer for me. In all those years Aunt Esther had never discussed her barrenness with anyone in the family. It was easy enough to see her pain in her middle and later years. She joined family gatherings with my grandmother's children, including my mother and her children. After a holiday feast, we would fill the kitchen with happy chatter while we washed dishes and the smaller children indulged in wild, noisy games. Although my aunt was too gracious to curse fate, I did it for her many times.

I decided that night at the ski lodge that it was time for

me to become a mother. I would not spend the rest of my life watching other women enjoy their roles as mothers and be a bystander myself. I would not live vicariously through my sister Kathy and the children she would have some day.

I smiled peacefully to myself in the darkness. "Next month," I said aloud.

"What brought this on?" Kent's voice jumped from the darkness, startling me.

"What?"

"All this baby stuff. Are you tired of working or what?"

"No. You know I love that job. Besides, our office is only a block from the hospital. It would be the perfect place to go into labor with five doctors in the building," I chuckled.

Kent spoke to the moonlit window. "I wonder whose fault it is."

"What do you mean?" I feigned ignorance.

"Craig told me about Chandelle. He feels pretty bad. I just wonder what's wrong with her."

"Why do you say that?" I reacted defensively. "It could be Craig."

"Never." Kent sat forward on the soft mattress to add emphasis to his statement. "I've known Craig for years. He's the most healthy, athletic guy I've ever known. Really happy-go-lucky, you know? You can tell just by looking at him there's nothing wrong. He's too masculine. It has to be his wife."

He slid back down, pulled the soft quilt over his shoulders, and prepared to doze off again. He had already shut me out.

"Good night," I murmured to the wall. There was no reply.

I tried to visualize my calendar at home and wondered when the next ovulation would take place.

Kent's voice rang in my ears: "I don't want any kids after I'm forty. Once I hit forty, you're getting your tubes tied."

I shivered in the dark and wondered if, after I had given up my first child, I might never have another again. I tried to shut out these thoughts and my fear of having to face the future alone. I turned to the mound of Kent's body.

"Will you care if I'm a Chandelle? Will you care if I can't have children?" I murmured softly.

Chapter 2

December 1979

Within eight years I had given birth to three children—two girls and a boy—the first only ten months after our ski trip. My calendar had not betrayed me. I was stunned temporarily by a miscarriage between the second and third pregnancies. I recovered quickly, but the loss of that child stayed with me.

Kent and I were then looking forward to our fourteenth wedding anniversary as we settled into the routine of caring for a large house and yard in a lovely, quiet subdivision of a small midwestern town. We had an assortment of cats, dogs, goldfish, gerbils, and mourning doves that come and go over the years in a typical American household with children.

Craig and Chandelle were eventually able to adopt a son and later a daughter, but Chandelle's desire to become a biological mother was never fulfilled. Without warning she was forced to undergo a complete hysterectomy in her late twenties. I ached for her, and not one day went by that I ever took my small children for granted.

By that time, my immediate family was feeling the ravages of infertility. My sister had tried for ten years before she was able to conceive a child. In the years that followed, she was unable to have a sibling for that child, and her anguish was all too apparent. My brother and his wife had wanted children immediately after they were married. An antique crib stood in their house year after year, waiting to be filled as they struggled to overcome their infertility. Two of my dearest cousins were infertile. Conversations at family gatherings were consumed by talk of fertility tests, production of ova, motility of sperm, the emptiness of a family without children. I would feel suffocated by their desperation, guilty about my own fertility. By then, I had been pregnant five times. Why had I been blessed and they cursed? The question was often on my mind.

One night, after looking in at the children—Julie, Laura, and Jeffrey—I settled into bed with Sunday's *Peoria Journal Star*. A glass of chablis was on the nightstand, and the television played softly. I opened the paper to the second page. The dateline was December 2, 1979. A small article leapt out at me.

> Unable to have children of their own, a Louisville couple are trying to become parents with the help of a paid surrogate mother, according to their attorney and their physician.
>
> Under the arrangement they would seek, the husband would father a child with a woman by artificial insemination, the *Courier-Journal* reported yesterday in a copyrighted story. The woman would be paid to carry the child to term and then give it to the couple.
>
> Katie Marie Brophy, the couple's attorney, said she believes that—if successful—it would be the first time a child has been born by a paid surrogate in the United States.
>
> The couple want to remain anonymous for the time being, Miss Brophy said. They are looking for someone willing to take part through a classified advertisement that began running Nov. 24 in the *Courier-Journal* and the *Louisville Times*.

> Miss Brophy and Dr. Richard M. Levin, a fertility specialist, said the prospective parents are in their early 30s and have been married for four or five years. They have one adopted child.

I read the article again and again, hoping to find more information buried in those few short paragraphs. I began to consider the possibility of having a child for them. What would Kent think of the idea? Would I be able to predict his reaction, even after all those years of living with him? Suddenly a feeling swept over me—a knowledge that I would have a child for this man and woman in Kentucky.

January 1980

It had been six weeks since I had seen the news item and responded to Attorney Katie Marie Brophy. One January afternoon while I was getting ready for work, I received a telephone call from a Dr. Richard Levin of Louisville asking if I was still interested in becoming the surrogate mother for the couple mentioned in the article.

The pounding of my heart thundered in my ears as I tried to sound casual on the phone. Our brief conversation ended with my promise to discuss a surrogate pregnancy with Kent and to call Dr. Levin within a day or two. His warm Kentucky drawl was sparked with enthusiasm for the surrogate project, and it gave me new courage to talk to Kent that night. Dr. Levin had seemed taken aback when I told him Kent knew nothing of my desire to have a child for another woman. He urged me to broach the subject immediately.

Around nine-thirty that night I pulled into our icy driveway and sat in my old Ford. The warmth of the heater comforted me and kept the January wind at bay. I had spent the four hours at work rehearsing the words over and over, altering the lines constantly. How could I tell Kent that our lives were going to change? I shuddered from tension rather than from the cold and took a deep breath as I left the security of my car.

The porch light seemed less inviting than usual. The sidewalk leading to our front door was snow-covered and slippery. When I looked up, Kent's broad shoulders filled the doorway. He wore his usual big smile. I stepped quickly into the dimly lit living room. The soft lights enhanced the antique furniture we had begun to collect.

"Hi. How was work tonight?" Kent asked cheerfully. He asked the same question every night. I wondered if he ever listened to my answer.

"Slow. January blahs, I guess." My voice seemed hollow. Would he know by looking at my face that something was on my mind? How could I live with a man for all these years and still have secrets from him? It was the first time I could remember keeping anything important from him.

Our communication had been breaking down as the years passed, with each of us taking the other for granted. But we still loved and, equally important, liked each other.

I wished at that particular moment I had not waited six weeks to discuss the surrogate pregnancy with him. Would he resent my secrecy and let that stand in the way of his decision?

I stalled for time. "Let me check on the children. I'll be right down. Make me some hot chocolate, would you?"

"Sure. Want something to eat? A sandwich maybe?"

"I'm not hungry."

I started up the carpeted stairway leading to the four bedrooms. I couldn't stand the thought of food. I'd had enough difficulty trying to explain a weight loss to Kent those past weeks. Soon he would understand why ten pounds had mysteriously disappeared from my already slender body.

I peeked into Jeffrey's room, where my cherubic son was in his red football pajamas, blankets thrown to one side. Even at three, he was still my baby. I kissed his round, pink cheek and put his stuffed duck back into his curved fingers. The girls slept soundly in their rooms, and I pulled the blankets snugly around their shoulders.

I crept back down the stairs and went into the bright yellow kitchen. Kent handed me the drink, smiled, and started to speak. His gray eyes glinted and his jaw tightened. "What's wrong?" he asked.

I clutched my cup for security, not hesitating for a moment. "There's something I have to talk to you about. Let's go downstairs." I looked past his face when I spoke and stared at the clock on the wall without noting the time.

He followed me silently down to the basement family room, paneled and thickly carpeted in a rich rust color. I curled up in the large rocking chair and somehow found the courage to blurt the words I had rehearsed all evening.

"Kent, I want to be a surrogate mother. I want to have a baby for another couple."

His eyes widened in disbelief but I continued quickly. "I received a telephone call today from a doctor in Kentucky about a letter I wrote six weeks ago. I told him I want to have a baby for a couple who can't have children."

I squirmed with apprehension. Had he heard what I said? Would he understand? I had been thinking about the idea every day for weeks, and by then the subject seemed familiar. I knew Kent would need time.

The silence began to bother me. I bit my tongue to keep from saying things I knew I would regret later. I met Kent's gaze and waited. When he finally spoke, he was calm. "Who are they?"

"I don't know. They just need a baby."

"You're crazy, you know that? That's the dumbest thing I've ever heard in my life."

"Kent, let me explain. You know this is something I've wanted to do for years—"

"It is?" he interrupted sarcastically.

"Yes!" I spat back at him. "You remember after Julie was born, I mentioned to you many times how wonderful it would be if I could have a baby for Craig and Chandelle. At that time the idea seemed remote, there were so many problems—"

"I vaguely remember," he interrupted again, "but I never thought you were serious."

"How could you think I was joking?" I leaned forward in the chair, pleading with him to understand. "I've talked about having a child for our friends and relatives who can't have their own many times in the past years. You know that."

I was furious with him for taking my feelings so lightly, but forced myself to remain calm. "Let me explain something. Remember when we used to talk about my having a baby for someone else? Ten or twelve years ago? You used to worry about how I would conceive and about the legalities. You also used to worry about what other people would say," I reminded him. "But now Dr. Levin said it's done with artificial insemination in his office. I won't even meet the father of the baby. It's so simple." I smiled exuberantly.

Kent slammed his hand onto the arm of the chair. "Absolutely not! Mary Beth, you've come up with some strange ideas in our thirteen years of marriage. Maybe some of them weren't so strange to you, but they were to me. I'll admit, I am a rather conservative person."

"Rather?"

"Never mind. The point is, this idea is really off the wall. If you think for one minute you're going to talk me into this, think again." By then his face was crimson, right up to the top of his bald head.

"Just listen to me a minute," I said urgently. "Let me tell you more about it."

"No." Kent gripped the arm of his chair. "No, you listen to me." He pointed a stubby finger into my face and leaned forward in his chair. "You are a very persuasive person, Mary Beth. You've talked me into a lot of things over the past thirteen years. But this is one thing I will *never* agree to. You might as well forget the whole thing right now. And I do mean right now."

The realization that the conversation was over came like a slap in the face. I retreated to the living room, hiding behind the newspaper to sort my thoughts. Soon the words in front of me began to blur. What could I do to convince him? I knew he could not be pushed, but if I moved slowly, it could take months. There wasn't that much time. There were two people in Louisville waiting for Dr. Levin to find them a surrogate mother. I had to be the one, at any cost! I had to find a way to break through Kent's resistance. I didn't know how, but I would find a way.

Kent crossed the living room and fell heavily onto the floral-patterned sofa next to me. I feigned interest in the newspaper. He stared at the large spider plant across the room that I had failed to water again. I waited for him to complain about the drooping plant. Anything to break the silence.

I resisted the urge to shriek at the injustice of his attitude. Instead I controlled my emotions, knowing that anger would put Kent on the defensive. The paper crumpled loudly in my lap. "I know this is a shock to you, Kent. I've had six weeks to think about it. Give yourself at least a few days before you decide, and I promise, I won't bring it up again until you've had a chance to digest it."

With a familiar, impassive expression on his face, Kent stood abruptly and headed toward the stairway to our bedroom. I followed him without a word and undressed quickly. We climbed into our king-size bed and lay stiffly, unable to make any kind of physical contact. Not even something as simple as brushing my arm against his.

I fell asleep instantly in the awkward silence, emotionally exhausted from the tension and excitement that had started with Dr. Levin's phone call. But a few hours later I was awake and alert. I listened in the darkness to the hum of the furnace. Kent's quiet, even breathing told me he was not plagued by insomnia. Hadn't he lain awake at all, thinking?

I recalled with pleasure the surging excitement I felt back in December when I had read about the need for a surrogate mother. I had waited expectantly each day for the mailman to bring an answer to the letter and photograph I had sent to Attorney Brophy. Then the phone call had come, surprisingly, from a doctor whose name I had not remembered from the news article.

A sense of anticipation filled me as I thought about the possibility of carrying a baby for another woman. Why should Kent object to my growing a perfect child for her? The child would belong to the father from the day of insemination. I would simply grow the baby for him and return the child at the end of nine months. Didn't Kent realize what it would mean for this couple to have a baby that belonged to them? Why should they be forced to endure a lifetime of childlessness when I was willing to help them? He must be made to understand. If I were donating a kidney or a cornea to a person in need, would he be shocked and forbid me to help?

I sat up and shook Kent gently, getting no response, then grabbed his arm and shook him roughly. "Kent. Kent. Wake up."

"Huh? Huh? What's wrong?" He lifted his head from his pillow and turned toward me, groggy.

"Sit up. I want to ask you something." I nudged him again. "Come on. Wake up," I demanded.

He looked at me and blinked sleep from his eyes.

"Did you change your mind yet?" I asked.

He lifted a hand and rubbed his eyes. "What?"

"Please wake up. Have you changed your mind yet? Can I have a baby for these people?"

"No!" he shouted before he rolled over, his back to me once again. I knew we had reached a dead end. I lay under the heavy red blanket for a long time and watched a sliver of light penetrate the edge of the sheer draperies.

The early morning hours were filled with the frenzied routine of getting the children ready for school—helping them find shoes and searching for milk money before they missed the school bus. Why was it that one shoe or one schoolbook always seemed to disappear while we slept?

Amid the chaos Kent and I avoided each other and spoke politely only when necessary. The children never seemed to notice the tension that filled the kitchen, and when Kent kissed me good-bye at the door, it was more out of habit than anything else.

I made the beds, collected wet towels from the bathroom floor, and washed clothes the girls had thrown into the hamper after wearing them only a few hours. My mind whirled. How could I convince Kent, my conservative, insurance executive husband, that I must be allowed to have a child for a couple I would never meet? Why did it mean so much to me? I seemed to be filled with almost an insatiable hunger for this pregnancy.

Jeffrey's voice invaded my thoughts. "Mommy, read." His chubby arms struggled with a dozen Golden Books that slid to the floor as he crossed the living room. He left a trail without noticing the diminishing number of books in his grasp.

"Okay," I sighed, hoping *The Saggy Baggy Elephant* would take my mind off my obsession.

I read one story after another in a monotone that Jeffrey didn't seem to mind, while my resentment toward Kent began to grow. How dare he control my life! Damn him for shattering my dream! I pounded the arm of the sofa in frustration. Jeffrey tugged with quick jerks at my arm. "Mommy! Read!"

Before long we heard Julie and Laura cross the front lawn, shouting happily to friends as they made arrangements for after-school play.

"Hi, Mom. Do I have a piano lesson today?" Julie burst through the front door, her blonde hair blown around her round face by the wind.

"Hi, Mom. What's for supper? I'm starved," Laura demanded cheerfully. She slammed the front door behind her, and the antique picture in the hallway swayed with the vibration.

The chicken roasting in the oven soon filled the house with a pleasant aroma and warmth while outside the temperature plunged near freezing. I watched the kitchen clock move toward five o'clock. How should I act when Kent walked in the front door? What should I say? If he refused to talk to me at all, it would be useless for me to persist.

Cold air invaded the kitchen, and without seeing or hearing him, I knew Kent had come in. The cheerful bobwhite whistle he used to announce his arrival home each night was not to be heard. For the first time I could remember, he entered our home quietly.

"Hi," I said meekly as he laid his hat and coat on the green overstuffed chair. Then he turned toward me and the grayness of his face startled me. He looked ten years older, as though he had aged in one afternoon. He brushed past me without answering and walked up the stairs. I followed him. In our bedroom I lowered myself onto the bed, waiting for him to speak.

"I couldn't keep any of my appointments today. While I was driving to see my first client, I realized it would be impossible to talk." His voice was a monotone.

"What did you do?" I moved close to him now.

"My mind wouldn't function. I drove to the office instead and stayed there all day with the door shut doing paperwork."

He gazed at the carpet while he spoke, shoulders hunched, utterly defeated.

Guilt swept over me.

"My whole body aches," he continued. "I'm so tense I feel like I have the flu."

He turned, staring at me, as though he had never seen me before. His face was tight and ashen. "I can't understand what would possess you to do a thing like this for people you don't even know. What difference could it possibly make to you if they ever have a child or not?"

"Who cares if I know them or not?" I shot back. "I want to do this for the childless couples of the world. For the pain and anguish our friends have suffered because they're infertile. You know what they've been through. You've seen it. If I can spare one couple that trauma, that's enough for me."

Kent struggled with his feelings. I could see he still did not understand. He looked sick and spent. A chill shot through me at the thought that he could have a heart attack here and now as the result of my selfishness and stubbornness.

Did I have a right to persist when I knew how repulsive the idea was to him? I suddenly realized I had asked too much. What gave me the right to ask my husband to watch me grow large with another man's child? Kent had always been proud of my slim figure that had not changed with the births of our own three children.

I felt ashamed for asking him to make this sacrifice. I put my arm across his back and held him. "Kent, if you honestly feel you can't handle this, if you're going to hate me for the way I'll look or be ashamed of me, I won't go ahead with it. I'll call Dr. Levin in the morning and tell him I can't do it. I just can't hurt you this much."

His relief was so instantly visible that it stunned me. Before my eyes, the lines on his face seemed to disappear and his natural color returned. Within minutes he looked like the man I knew.

The realization of how much Kent had suffered that day hit me like a stiff left hook. I rushed from the bedroom before he saw my tears and returned to the kitchen to baste the chicken. Something inside me died at that moment. My dream was over. The child was not to be. The needs of the couple in Louisville would have to be met by a woman whose husband was able to understand her desires.

I mashed the potatoes with a vengeance. Kent had been victorious. How did he always manage to get his way in everything? Was it the silence that made me concede each time?

I sat mutely through dinner, passing gravy and listening to the children chatter about school. My throat clamped shut, but I tried to force down enough food to keep the children from noticing something was wrong. Kent kept his eyes glued to his plate and avoided mine. Before long the girls sensed the tension and grew quiet. I wanted to explain but couldn't. If a forty-five-year-old man could not understand my desire to have a baby for a childless woman, how could I expect my ten- and twelve-year-old daughters to comprehend it?

The meal was barely tasted by any of us. Only Jeffrey cleaned his plate.

Kent cleared his throat loudly and all eyes turned to him. "My secretary, Becky, gave notice today. She's quitting in two weeks."

I was startled at the news but did not question him further.

"Why is she quitting, Daddy? Is she the lady with the hair down to her butt?" Julie asked eagerly. Her green eyes glistened with curiosity.

"Yeah, she does have long hair but I think it's only to her waist. She's having a baby in six weeks."

I jerked my head up, hoping to meet his eyes. The thought of Becky glowing and radiant with pregnancy filled me. Then my spirits collapsed. My fork clattered noisily onto my plate and I ran from the table, grabbing blindly for a coat from the closet to throw over my lightweight sweater.

Icy rain greeted me when I ran through the front door, and I could hear the children calling after me, panicky at my unexpected behavior. It hurt me to leave them, but I fumbled with the keys and slammed the car door to lock out the rain and the sound of their high-pitched voices. I quickly shifted the car into reverse and backed out of the driveway. Between my tears and the rain pouring from the black skies, I could hardly see the winding road ahead of me, guessing instead at each familiar curve.

Within minutes I was rational enough to realize I would be killed or kill someone else if I didn't stop. I slowed the car to a halt on a nearby residential street with vast, lovely lawns. A soft glow came from the kitchen of a beautiful and expensive home, and I wondered about the family sitting inside. I envied their peaceful dinner and the normalcy of their lives.

The rain continued to pour in miniature rivers down the windshield while I sat in the car and howled like an animal. When the tears and the pain had subsided, all that remained was an empty pit. I tried desperately to see both sides. Was Kent worried about the reactions of friends and neighbors, relatives, the girls' classmates and teachers?

Now I would have to find the words to tell Dr. Levin I would not be the surrogate mother he was looking for.

I drove home slowly and stopped in front of our house, looking at it as if I were a prospective buyer. It was a lovely brick home on a quiet cul-de-sac. But what good was it if the family inside was so unhappy? Suddenly I hated the sight of the white pillars, red brick, and perfectly landscaped lawn. I stayed in the car until the damp chill drove me inside.

I stood quietly, listening to the sound of clinking glassware as Kent loaded the dishwasher. Finally he spoke without looking up. "I'm glad you're back. I want to take Julie to the piano concert at the Peterson Theatre tonight. You and I had tickets, but I asked her if she wanted to go and she does."

"Well, then. It's a good thing I came back when I did. I certainly wouldn't want you to miss your precious concert." I stood with hands on hips, waiting for a reply. He wiped gravy stains off the yellow tablecloth and remained quiet.

"Is that all you have to say?" I demanded.

"Yup." He bumped past me and went upstairs to dress. I glared at him, filled with rage. At that moment I wished bitterly I had married someone closer to my own age. A younger man might have understood my feelings.

In all our years of marriage, Kent had made all the decisions. He made feeble attempts to include me so I wouldn't feel slighted, but we both knew he decided where we would vacation each year and where we would live, how our money would be spent and when we would buy a car. And this house! He never had wanted my input but had treated me more like a child than an equal partner. Well, what did you expect, Mary Beth? That marrying a thirty-two-year-old bachelor set in his ways would be a sharing relationship? My father had warned me over and over while I dated various men, "Marriage is not a reform school. What you marry is what you get." That night I realized how wise he had been. If only I had listened!

I remembered how, as a newlywed, I would hand Kent a paycheck every Friday to bank for a down payment on a house. He would give me an allowance, and I felt pleased with the amount of five dollars a week. Yet I had always admired friends who could convince their husbands to do things and persuade them the idea had been theirs all along. I strained to remember the few feminine tricks I had read about or heard about from friends. I prayed for the right words to come to me that night.

Several hours later, long after Laura and Jeffrey were tucked in, Julie, our eldest, burst through the front door and pounded up the steps two at a time.

"Oh, Mom, you should have been there," she babbled breathlessly. "It was beautiful. I would love to be able to play that way someday. I wonder how many years those guys had to take lessons?"

I listened to her happy chatter for a while longer, then shooed her off to bed with the reminder that the alarm clock would still ring at 6:15 A.M.

Kent undressed for bed, concentrating on the small color television in the corner of our bedroom. I gathered the newspapers that were spread across the blankets and sat straighter against the pillows. "Kent, there's something I have to say to you." He seemed unaware of my presence. I began to breathe slowly and deeply, knowing anger would close his ears faster than anything else. I continued, aware of the trembling in my voice. "I just want you to take a minute to remember all the times I have supported you in our thirteen years of marriage. Remember when Laura was two weeks old and Julie was nineteen months? You came home from work and were so filled with excitement. You had taken a new job in Wisconsin Dells. Even though you had known about it for weeks, you had never mentioned it until that night. Remember how I packed everything without a word of complaint—the baby, a toddler, and a huge house full of belongings? We left our lovely first home and moved into a tiny, old, rented house. Do you remember that first winter? We had seventy-two inches of snow, I didn't have a single friend, and the closest relatives were hours away. Both babies were sick and in the hospital that winter with those terrible viruses and high fevers. It was a nightmare for me. Did you ever hear me complain?"

"No." His answer was almost inaudible.

"Do you remember when we moved again two years later because the job hadn't worked out the way you had hoped? We went through the same thing. But that time I spent a month alone with the girls while you started your job three hundred fifty miles away. I never let you know how discouraged or lonely I was. What a mess it was trying to pack and cope with two toddlers in that summer heat."

Kent lowered himself onto the edge of the bed, clad in navy blue pajamas, and looked directly at me as I spoke. My courage began to grow.

"Do you remember the time you spent one thousand dollars taking flying lessons? I didn't care about the money, but I was scared to death you'd never walk through that door again. I sat in the house with two little kids every weekend while you drove out to the airfield alone. How do you think I felt the day you soloed? I never prayed so much in my life. You never knew that, did you?" He shook his head once, as though in a trance, before I continued. "Do you know why? Because I knew it was a dream you had had for years, and I never once stood in your way. I did everything I could to encourage you to fly. In fact, I've encouraged you in everything you've done since we've been married. I grew up with the idea that it was a wife's duty to follow her husband without a word of complaint. 'The man is the boss.' 'The man makes the decisions.' That's how I was raised. Well, you've pursued your dreams and hobbies and your career. And in the process I've moved from one house to another, from one city to another, leaving behind family and friends I had grown to love because I felt I didn't have the right to stand in your way."

Kent said nothing, but I had a small feeling that he was listening and that I was getting through.

"This is the first time I've ever asked you to support me in something *I* want to do. Something I feel so deeply about that it's part of my very soul. If I'm not allowed to have this baby, to take advantage of this opportunity to do something I've thought about for years, I know I'll regret it for the rest of my life. I would never forgive myself. Or you."

Kent pulled back the blankets and climbed into bed, being careful to stay on his side of the mattress. I fell asleep with the conviction that he would not stand in my way.

He left the house early the next morning as I busied myself with the children. I knew he had left by the slam of the door behind him. I could only guess what he was thinking.

Maybe he was upset because I would be carrying the child of another man. Would it seem like adultery to Kent, even though the man was a stranger? Did he understand the process of artificial insemination or realize that doctors had been carrying out the procedure for decades? Did he know there was no sexual involvement? I wondered if he realized that every year thousands of women with infertile husbands received semen from a paid donor. If the feelings and egos of men were important enough for society and the medical profession to find an acceptable solution for male infertility—artificial insemination—then why not for female infertility? What help was there for a woman if the situation were reversed and the wife was sterile? Surrogate motherhood was the logical solution. Why couldn't he understand that?

I knew the only biological difference between a stranger donating sperm and a stranger donating an ovum was a matter of time. A sperm donation took fifteen minutes; my involvement would take nine months. But the end result was the same. A new family. I had to make Kent understand that the only obstacle was the opinion of society, and I was sure then that that was his biggest fear.

I sat in my sunny kitchen and waited for Jeff to get home from nursery school. I had promised Kent I would call Dr. Levin that day. But what would I tell him about Kent's reaction? Thoughts of the last two days of distress and thirteen years of petty resentments flitted through my mind like butterflies. Was this pregnancy so important to me that I would sacrifice my marriage?

I only knew nothing in the world would stop me from having a child for that man and woman in Louisville.

"Girls," I called into the dining room, where they had littered the table with books and papers. "It's almost five o'clock. I want to talk to your father when he gets home.

Take Jeff down to the family room and watch television. You can do your homework later."

"Woweee!" they shouted in unison and began to shove each other down the stairs.

"Me don't wanna go," Jeff wailed, hanging onto my leg.

"Okay, you can help me by putting out the silverware and napkins."

Kent's tires crunched on the snow and ice in the driveway. I hurried to open the front door and we stood facing each other awkwardly.

"Daddy!" Jeffrey jumped up and down as if on a trampoline, whining for attention. "Mommy bought me a new car." He waved a tiny Hot Wheels in his fist.

Kent went into the kitchen, tossed ice into a glass, and barely glanced at his son. "That's nice, chief." He absentmindedly stroked the top of Jeff's head. Satisfied, Jeff trotted into the living room to play with his car.

I poured chablis into a favorite antique wineglass and followed my son, my heart banging furiously. Should I just come right out and tell Kent that I would have the baby whether he approved or not? How would he react if I defied him and where would I go from there? My chest tightened and a silent prayer formed on my lips. "Dear God, please help me to say the right words. Please open his heart and mind."

Kent stood before me, still wearing his three-piece navy suit. I noticed the buttons straining on his vest. He sat down on the carpet next to Jeff and picked up the miniature red convertible. He turned it over and over in his hand. "Mary Beth." The sound exploded in my ears, and wine sloshed over the edge of my glass onto my slacks. "I've given your idea a lot of thought today. To tell you the truth, I haven't thought of much else while I drove around the city from one agent's office to another. If you want to have this baby so badly, if it means that much to you, go ahead. I don't have the right to tell you what you can and can't do with your body or your life."

"But I have to say," he continued, "I don't agree with what you're doing. I still don't understand why you want to have this baby, but I do love you. And because I love you, and because you'll do it anyway, I'll support you and help you in any way I can."

I felt that if I spoke, I'd destroy the magic. I only prayed silently, "Thank you, God. Thank you."

Hours later, when the children were asleep, Kent and I lay in bed and snuggled against each other for the first time in days. Yet we were wrapped in private thoughts.

I had to think of a way to make him understand. His permission wasn't enough. I had to dispel his negativity about the pregnancy.

I propped myself up, interrupting Johnny Carson's monologue.

"Kent?"

"Hmmm?"

"Remember when we were first married and when we were dating? On weekends we would drive to Elkhart Lake for the Road America races."

"Yup."

"You love fast cars. You told me once you used to fantasize about driving in a race with your Corvette. Now just think a minute." I leaned closer to him to emphasize the word *think*.

"Pretend that A.J. Foyt called you and said, 'Kent, I want you to be my partner in the Indianapolis 500 next May. It'll mean time away from your family while you train, and there will be a certain amount of danger involved. But I really think we can win this race together. Talk it over with your wife and call me back in a few days if she agrees to it. Then we'll draw up a few legal papers, get both your signatures, and get started with the training. It's a big race and it's not too far off. I'm really counting on you.' "

Kent looked over at me and blinked, and I kept talking as fast as I could before he could interrupt. "I know a race like that would fulfill a lifetime dream of yours. You know that I love you, but I'd be scared to death to let you go. I hate fast cars. My first reaction would be no, absolutely not. But do you know it's because I love you that I would never ask you to turn him down? It would devastate you to miss an opportunity like the Indy 500.

"I'll admit it. I wouldn't pretend to understand why on earth you would want to risk your life to do something as crazy as drive a car in little circles at two hundred miles an hour. I would even think the children and I meant nothing to you if you considered it. But I'm not a man and I can't begin to understand a man's dreams. I wouldn't have the right to say no to you. Even as your wife, I wouldn't have that right. I would have to let you follow that dream! Kent, please—this is my Indy 500."

Chapter 3

<u>*February 1980*</u>

I had gone back to working part-time selling cosmetics in a local department store more than a year before and soon found, despite my ambivalence at having to leave Jeff with a sitter, that I enjoyed the contact with my coworkers.

At work one morning I brought up the subject of surrogate motherhood to a small group of women ranging from a twenty-two-year-old to a divorcée in her mid-forties. They listened while I discussed the article I had seen in the newspaper, and I avoided any hint of my involvement.

"How repulsive! How can you even talk about such a thing?" asked Terry, the mother of a small son. The general reaction of shock and distaste had eroded my confidence by the time a male colleague joined the group. He was a tall, attractive, athletic man in his early thirties, with a pleasant personality. He clasped his hands behind his back and thrust out his chest like a rooster amid his flock. "I think people who are infertile just shouldn't have children. They should accept the fact like any other handicap. I think people like that should take up a hobby to occupy themselves. Like golf. Having a child for someone else is immoral." He rocked back and forth on his heels, a smug smile on his face. I glared at him and bit my tongue. Everyone in the store knew that he slept with anyone who would have him, despite his young pretty bride. Who was he to speak of immorality?

Kent's and my interviews with Dr. Levin were scheduled for the following week. They were to include psychiatric examinations, medical evaluations, and legal consultations. I was apprehensive and, during that week, lost another five pounds. I slept sporadically and woke often in the middle of the night. I prayed that I would have the strength to face the possibility of rejection in Louisville.

It was two days before our trip and the children had yet to be told. I was alone with them one night while Kent traveled on business.

I scooped lasagna onto their plates and spoke deliberately. "Hey, kids, what would you say if Mom had a baby for another lady who can't have one?"

"Oh, Mom!" Julie's eyes lit up with enthusiasm. "What a great idea! You could have a pretty cute kid for her! Look look at Jeff—he's adorable."

Jeff's face shone. He gave us the most winning smile and threw back his head, laughing. His brown eyes gleamed with pride.

Laura, the quietest of the three but wise beyond her years, spoke pensively. "Mom, I think you should have a baby for Uncle Mark and Aunt Carol. Whenever she gets a baby to hold, she squeezes it so hard, like she never wants to let it go. I've seen the look on her face when we're together. Whenever someone mentions the word *baby*, she looks so sad. Could we give it to her?" Her small, sensitive features were aglow as she sought a positive answer, but Julie lashed out before I could respond.

"You dummy. Every time we went to visit them we would want to take it back. Especially when it got to be two and got cute. If Mom has a baby, we would have to give it to someone we don't know."

I spoke sternly to emphasize the importance of Julie's idea.

"Laura, you know you're still moping about that fluffy kitten we had to give away a few months ago because of Julie's allergies. How on earth could you even begin to consider giving up a baby if you had a hard time parting with a kitten?"

Laura answered without a moment's hesitation. "Mom, we don't need another baby. Maybe these people do."

I looked at her a long moment and bent to kiss the cheek of my wise and beautiful child.

The next night, still intoxicated with the understanding the children had shown, I repeated the conversation to Kent.

His only reply was a low grunt. "I feel like I'm caught in a whirlpool. Everything is moving too fast for me." He laid the newspaper across his knees and looked at me. "Ten days ago our lives were normal and routine; now I'm caught in the middle of something I don't know how to get out of. And what's worse, I don't know how I got into it." He looked completely baffled.

I smiled to myself and knew it was best to remain silent. But I remembered the remark he made a week earlier: "Because you'll do it anyway, I'll support you and help in any way I can." I knew that he had never seen me this determined about anything.

A sudden blizzard the night before we were to leave for Kentucky made me think our flight might be canceled. I spent the afternoon at work, but the snowstorm continued to build and drift, leaving the store almost deserted. Only a few customers, bundled in layers of winter clothing, strolled up and down the aisles.

I heard the rhythmic thunk of his boots before I saw him. A cowboy in a Stetson came toward me. In his arms was a very small baby in a light blue snowsuit. When the man glanced down at his son, I watched his rugged face turn tender and warm. "That's what it's all about," I said aloud.

That evening Kent met me at the front door. The porch

light cast an amber glow on the snow that had drifted against the shrubbery.

"Look at your feet," he said with a scowl. "They're soaked. Why didn't you wear your boots?"

I stamped clumps of snow off my shoes onto the carpet in the brick foyer. "Because I hate boots."

"Well, look at your feet," he chided. "They must be frozen. They're bright red."

I waved him away with one hand and kicked the soaked shoes into a corner. "Stop treating me like a child."

Kent followed me down the hallway into the kitchen. "How long did it take you to chip the ice off your windshield?"

"Fifteen minutes." I pulled plates and glasses from the cupboard.

"No wonder your shoes are soaked. Why didn't you take your boots? It was snowing when you left the house," he persisted.

I laid the forks next to the china plates.

"Kent, forget it."

Within fifteen minutes we were gathered at the table for dinner. The children bombarded me with questions about the upcoming trip.

"Where will the baby-sitter sleep?" Laura asked. She fiddled with her linen napkin, folding and unfolding it.

"Upstairs. In our bed with Jeffrey."

"Gosh, Mom, don't forget to change your pillowcases when you get back, if she's going to use your pillows."

"Don't worry," I laughed. "You'll all be fine. We'll be back in time to put you to bed on Thursday night. The fridge is full of food, and I left instructions about lunches and piano lessons. We'll only be gone two days." I patted Laura's cheek to reassure her.

"Why can't we call in sick at school to go to the airport with you?" Julie pouted.

"Because you're not missing a whole day of school to spend thirty minutes at the airport, that's why," Kent answered.

"Will you buy us a present?" Laura asked.

"If we have time," I laughed. "Now eat your dinner." The children ate hungrily and remained cheerful during the meal. Laura buried her carrots in her napkin. Because I had done the same thing at her age, I pretended not to notice. I began to push food from one side of my plate to the other.

Finally Kent asked, "Nervous?"

"A little," I lied. "I've never been to a shrink before. I don't know how I'm supposed to act."

"What's a shrink?" Laura interrupted.

Kent pushed back his chair and stood at the kitchen window. "How did we get into this mess?" he muttered. With his hands deeply buried in his pants pockets, he was lost in thought, watching the swirling snow. Then he wheeled toward me. "Hey, let's go for a ride in the snow. You only learned how to drive last spring. You're not used to driving in this stuff and it would be a good time for you to learn."

"Are you crazy?"

"No. It's a perfect night. I'll teach you how to get out of a slide."

"Please, no. I have so much packing to do, and I'm tired from working today."

"We're going," he ordered. "Put your boots on." Kent pulled me away from the plate of cold food toward the hall closet. The children raced to the living room window, squealing with delight. "Do a wheelie, Mom!" They cheered encouragement as we stepped out into the fog of white.

We drove slowly down the small hill that led to the country club parking lot across the street from our house.

"I hate this. I'm afraid." I objected to Kent's deaf ears and drove slowly until we reached the large, empty lot. "Okay," I sighed with resignation. "Show me how to do a 360."

Ten minutes later I was caught up in the amusement of sliding and fishtailing madly across the parking lot, learning to control the car without thinking about it, and before too long I was a pro. We slid back and forth, with the tires slashing crazy geometric designs on the clean snow.

"Let's not go home yet," Kent urged as I drove back up the hill with confidence. "It's too beautiful outside."

Packing, baths, laundry. All to be done in the next two hours. I held up a gloved hand. "Only ten minutes," I warned.

The winding streets in our subdivision were free of cars tonight. We drove in silence, alone with our thoughts. When we returned home, refreshed, we stood and kissed each other gently.

"Thank you." I smiled at Kent and squeezed his hand.

Many hours later I lay in our bed, with Kent snoring peacefully beside me. I knew if Kent was awakened by my restlessness, he would want to make love. On the eve of my voyage I could not share myself with anyone.

I remembered the miscarriage I had had five years earlier. The baby had not been planned, and it had taken me some time to adjust to the pregnancy. But in the last weeks before I lost the baby, I was looking forward to putting together the crib in the nursery and proudly wearing maternity clothes. Yet not a single friend or relative had seemed to share my pleasure, and I puzzled over their assurances that the two daughters we now had were enough to fill our marriage.

The miscarriage was sudden, cruel, and painful. When it was over, my physician had glibly recommended a hysterectomy and suggested we discuss it again in a few weeks. I tried to comprehend the loss, bitter and angry at everyone. Even God.

The death of that infant affected me deeply. I emerged an empty shell. I began to envy and resent every expectant mother I saw and would stare unashamedly at their round bellies, obsessed by the evidence of their fertility.

We had stood next to a pregnant woman and her toddler at a parade. The fullness of her term pregnancy spoiled the pleasure of the clowns and floats as the children continued to shout, begging me to share their delight. My eyes were riveted to her bulge while I bathed in self-pity. My Lutheran origins mocked me. I thought God was punishing me for something evil I had done or thought.

The anger continued for more than a year. My baby would have been born on Christmas Day, and each time I saw an infant anywhere near the age mine would have been, I would ask its age and yearn to hold it.

Eventually the pain had eased. The affection of my two toddlers at home filled the void. But I wondered about the women who lost children through miscarriages or stillbirths and had nothing left to fill the emptiness.

I remembered the recovery period and how devastating it was to have no one to talk to. My family had stayed away and reacted without emotion. "Well, you've got your hands full with the girls anyway. You didn't need it," they had said. Their words were little comfort.

As I drifted into sleep I remembered the title of the sermon in church the Sunday before: "If God is for you, then who will be against you?"

Chapter 4

February 6, 1980

We left nine inches of snow behind us and landed in Louisville thirty-five minutes late. Kent's irritation dissolved the moment Dr. Levin's secretary, Karen, introduced herself at the airport. She was tall and attractive, with dark eyes and thick hair brushing the shoulders of her gray wool coat. Kent smiled broadly. After our introduction, I liked her almost as much as he did.

Karen drove expertly along the congested expressways until we spotted the tall white medical building sparkling in the Kentucky sunshine. She slid to a halt, and within moments I was standing on the second floor staring at the brass plate nailed to the door: RICHARD M. LEVIN, M.D.

The small, comfortable waiting room seemed crowded, but it contained only three people. A tall, dark-haired man was engrossed in conversation with an attractive blonde whose hair swung loosely around her oval face. She perched on the edge of the striped sofa. A photograph of a snarling tiger peered over her left shoulder. The other man looked in their direction but seemed uninterested in their intense conversation.

My eyes were drawn back to the tall man with perfectly styled hair. He seemed to exude confidence. When he glanced up and noticed the three of us filling the doorway, he straightened and smiled brightly. His eyes were dark and intelligent.

"Hi," the man drawled. The voice was familiar.

I watched him intently and stood motionless. My head spun. This kid is the man with the list of credentials? The guy who's going to deliver my baby? I'm supposed to trust this boy with my body and an insemination? I glanced at his clothes. Fitted black slacks, a white shirt with sleeves casually rolled to the elbow, and a sporty necktie made him appear even younger than he was. I wanted to blurt, "I'm sorry. I've made a mistake."

Kent's breath on the back of my neck snapped me out of my paralysis. I spoke to my inner self and inhaled sharply. "All right, Mary Beth. Keep your end of the bargain. Talk and listen, but don't you dare chicken out now."

I found Dr. Levin's face and forced a smile onto my lips. He was shaking hands and talking, but I heard nothing. Suddenly the name of the blonde woman floated through the air—a reporter from *People* magazine Dr. Levin had arranged to interview us. My jaw tightened as I repeated her name under my breath. *Sarah Moore Hall.* A musical sound. Would she report everything I said? Would she write it all down? Would I have any privacy? I scanned the room quickly, looking for a tape recorder or camera. Sure enough, I next was introduced to the photographer for *People*, Dale Wittner.

Dr. Levin inspected me, from my short brown curls to my high-heeled shoes. He missed nothing. His black eyes flashed with satisfaction. When he crooked a finger, we followed him stiffly down the narrow, brightly lit hallway. The instant he closed the door to his office behind us, I felt Kent's tension fill the room.

The telephone broke the silence. Dr. Levin reached across his desk to answer and waved us into the large leather chairs that faced his desk. I sat rigidly, despite the comfort of the soft cushions.

He spoke quietly into the telephone, seemingly absorbed in the conversation but watching us both with a keen eye while we looked around the plush office.

It was expensively furnished. A massive walnut desk was littered with files, art objects, and telephone messages scribbled on notepaper. The floor next to his desk was cluttered with large camera cases. A tall pecan cabinet to the right of the desk was filled with a collection of porcelain birds. Directly opposite the desk was a striped sofa—brown, beige, and rust. A round, low-legged coffee table stood in front of the sofa, overflowing with letters from grateful parents and photographs of new babies. Tall, leafy plants grew profusely near the narrow windows that stretched from floor to ceiling.

Dr. Levin replaced the receiver and leaned forward in his chair. "Let me tell you something about myself." He talked rapidly, telling us things that I already knew; I had done some research into his record by calling the medical schools he had attended. I lapsed into thought as he continued to speak in soft, self-assured tones. Now and then he would pause long enough to laugh at a joke he had told or to smile warmly at us.

Mentally I walked toward the closed door of the large, pretentious office. I visualized myself stepping over cases of camera equipment and rushing toward an exit, making a frantic dash for the elevator, a taxi, the airport. I wanted to go home to my children and forget this whole crazy scheme of babies for other women.

As I watched his lips move and began to hear the words, the uneasiness began to fade. Little by little his magnetic personality began to win me over.

Within fifteen minutes my worries and fears were forgotten. I was totally absorbed in Dr. Levin's enthusiasm for his work. He talked about his search for the right surrogate mother. Even though he claimed to have more than forty applicants, and even though he had given me no indication where I stood, there was no doubt in my mind he would choose me.

I found myself leaning toward him eagerly, asking a multitude of questions, all the things that had kept me awake at night and had whirled through my mind during the day. I told him about all my pregnancies, including my first, the one that had ended with my giving up a baby girl for adoption. We interrupted each other constantly in our zeal to ask and answer.

Kent slouched in the leather chair next to mine and methodically chewed each fingernail while he listened and observed. It could have been my imagination, but I swear he looked visibly relieved when Dr. Levin revealed that he was thirty-four years old. He looked ten years younger. I suppressed a smile, knowing full well Kent had had the same thought I had earlier.

The office door opened, slowly and silently. A young woman had entered without bothering to knock, interrupting our conversation. I resented the intrusion and felt the tension return.

A petite blonde with porcelain features, she looked sixteen years old. Her brown tweed suit gave her a professional appearance, a dramatic contrast to her adolescent features, which had the merest dab of makeup.

The woman flopped onto the sofa under a collage of family photographs and let her boots drip melting snow onto the upholstery. The mother in me resisted the urge to tell her to put her feet on the floor or else take off her boots. I said nothing, but looked with bewilderment at Dr. Levin.

"I'd like you to meet Katie Brophy, my attorney." Dr. Levin leaned back in his chair, enjoying my stare of disbelief. He continued, "Katie has the distinction of graduating from law school at the age of twenty-one and has been in practice for three years now."

I gawked at her outstretched form. She seemed oblivious

to everything. I was immediately filled with respect and felt ashamed for judging her too quickly. Dr. Levin chattered on while I was lost in thought. "—She's been working on the legalities of this project for seven months now. She did all the legal research for me, but we worked on the contract together." He spoke of her with obvious pride. This was the woman I had written to last December.

As she squinted at me, I felt myself stiffen.

"How'd the case go?" Dr. Levin put his pipe to his lips and searched his desktop for a book of matches.

"We won," Katie replied flatly.

"Good," he smiled.

"Barely. It was a tough battle. Two hours. My client missed a prison sentence by this much." She held two dainty fingers together, then closed her brilliant blue eyes.

I threw a sidelong glance toward Kent, but he refused to meet my gaze and concentrated instead on tracing lines on the palm of his hand with an index finger.

I took a deep breath, leaned forward in my chair, and almost touched the massive desk. "Dr. Levin, there's something that's been on my mind for the past week. Before you say no, I just want you to think about it. I don't need an answer now."

He drew deeply on his pipe and looked into my face. "Okay."

"I want the parents of the baby in the delivery room when their child is born. I want them to experience the delivery and watch their child take his first breath."

The clock hummed in the stillness that followed. He searched my face.

Attorney Brophy heaved herself into a sitting position and spat angry words at me. "Now wait just a minute. The legal ramifications in this—"

Dr. Levin held up his hand, signaling her to stop.

He spoke gently as one would to a child. "I know what she's trying to say, Katie." Then he directed his attention to me. "What you just said blew my mind and that's why I hesitated. Not because I don't like the idea—"

"I know the parents of the baby have to guard their identity," I interrupted, "but if they're gowned and masked, why couldn't they be there when I go into labor?"

"They can," he bobbed his head several times. "There's no reason why they can't be." His face crinkled in a smile.

I thought of the months ahead and an exhilaration began to spread slowly through me.

Katie jumped off the sofa, scowling at her wristwatch and doing nothing to hide her irritation. "We're late for your appointment with the attorney. Karen will drive us over there and I'll introduce you, since he's a friend of mine. If you have any problems, he'll be representing you."

I rose reluctantly and followed Dr. Levin. We passed a closed door next to his office, and he smiled wryly. "The prospective parents are in there waiting to be interviewed by Sarah." I insisted on meeting them in the near future. Dr. Levin assured me it would be possible, if they were not opposed to the idea. My curiosity about the mysterious couple behind the closed door was insatiable. In my mind, I walked through the barrier and embraced them. I wanted to assure them that all would be well, that their hopes and dreams were about to become a reality.

Karen drove through the slushy streets toward the downtown area. Kent and Katie carried on a cheerful conversation while I sat in the backseat and watched them. I tried to analyze my feelings, to find a reason for my intense jealousy of the woman attorney. Did I resent her close relationship to Dr. Levin, her obviously brilliant mind, or her liberation? As the car pulled to a stop in front of a stone building and Kent hurried to help her from the car, I decided it was all three.

We spent several hours going over the preliminary contract Katie and Dr. Levin had drawn up, making only a few minor changes. Our attorney, John, was young, with cocker spaniel eyes. His wool tweed sports jacket added bulk to an already stocky frame.

We sipped steaming mugs of coffee to appease the hunger from a skipped lunch and listened to legal language I had no hopes of deciphering. Until now, Kent had been quiet; he had asked Dr. Levin nothing. But in the attorney's office he sprang to life, raking the contract word by word. I made no attempt to hide my boredom and yawned often, grateful for Kent's awareness of and interest in what to me seemed utterly trivial. The attorney was patient with Kent and methodical; he paid little attention to my restlessness as the clock on his desk neared six-thirty.

Katie waited for us and, when we finished, informed us she would be driving me back to Dr. Levin's for a physical examination and would drop Kent off at the hotel next door. "After that we're meeting the folks from *People* magazine for dinner."

My protests about needing a snack and a shower fell on deaf ears, and when Katie followed me into Dr. Levin's office, I flopped into the leather chair with weary resignation. Dr. Levin sat at his desk, signing papers that were fanned in front of him. When he finished, he neatly stacked the documents to one side and looked up at Katie, who was spread the length of the sofa with her wet boots once again crossed over the armrest.

"Katie, would you mind waiting in the outer room? We won't be long." He smiled pleasantly at her, unabashed by the glower she returned. She pushed herself off the couch and slammed the door behind her.

Dr. Levin reached for a small note near the phone, appearing to study it. "When was your last physical examination?" he asked, eyes riveted to the message he held.

I grimaced at my reply. "Four years ago."

I felt a little light-headed during the examination, but was surprised when he reinflated the blood pressure cuff to take a reading for the second time. "Is it high?" I asked.

"A little," he fibbed. I was shocked.

"There isn't any hypertension in my family. What's wrong?"

"Don't worry," he assured me. "It's probably a result of fatigue and the lack of food. You're experiencing a lot of nervous tension right now. It'll probably be normal tomorrow. We'll retake it then."

I dressed rapidly, worrying about hypertension despite his assurances. Could I be eliminated as a candidate for that reason alone? Kent had returned, and he and Katie waited patiently in the outer office while I repaired my makeup.

The long drive through the twilight to the restaurant was soothing, and I felt some of my fatigue slip away while we chatted, enjoying Dr. Levin's quick sense of humor that had emerged in the past hour.

We crossed the parking lot to the restaurant, and I touched Kent's arm. What was he thinking or feeling? We hadn't had five minutes alone since our arrival. Tiny snowflakes had begun to fall. The cold air was refreshing, and I began to feel energetic and alive again.

Raucous entertainment from the bar greeted us when we pulled open the heavy wooden doors. We were greeted by Pam, Dr. Levin's pretty blonde wife, and by Sarah and Dale from *People* magazine.

I nervously checked the table for a tape recorder or notepad. Sarah caught my eye and smiled easily. Even though she wrote nothing down, she listened closely to my conversation with Dr. Levin throughout the evening. Whenever I would become aware of her rapt attention, I would lower my voice and withdraw instinctively. But these were only momentary distractions. Dr. Levin and I talked as though we had known each other for a very long time.

Beep. Beep. I looked around, puzzled. Dr. Levin reached inside his suit jacket with his left hand. "I'm being paged." He hurried toward the lobby and rounded the corner.

Kent immediately leaned toward me. "If these people from the magazine want you to do an interview tonight, make up an excuse. Tell them anything. Our day has been too long and you know after two glasses of wine and no food, you'd tell anybody anything. You'd be a reporter's dream."

Without waiting for an answer, he sat upright and gave Sarah an angelic smile. I caught his eye and nodded slightly in consent.

A waitress carried in plates of steaming food, and when she placed a plate of luscious pink shrimp before me, my appetite sprang to life. Dr. Levin returned as I was spearing a shrimp.

"By the way, Mary Beth, I forgot to tell you. You have an appointment with Dr. Lee at ten o'clock tomorrow morning." He spread his linen napkin across his knees and began to slice through prime rib.

My mouth was filled with the sweet, tender shrimp. "Who's he?" Dr. Levin's knife moved across the beef. "He's a psychiatrist. You'll see one in the morning and the other one in the afternoon."

I felt a knot in my throat and swallowed hard. The food was no longer appealing. I picked at the salad and seafood, unable to eat, while I waited patiently for the others to finish their meals. I longed for a steaming shower and a soft mattress.

Dr. Levin pushed his chair back from the table, placing his napkin alongside his plate. "Let's go to the bar for the interview."

"No," I balked.

"Let's do it tomorrow," Kent offered.

"No," Dr. Levin replied firmly. "It won't take long. I'm not going to have time tomorrow."

A raised eyebrow and a grimace were the only signals of

defeat I was able to send to Kent. A gloom had descended over his features.

We found a small table in the dimly lit bar. Sarah and Dale sat on either side of me.

After two glasses of wine, I was relaxed and uninhibited. I began to talk about my intense advocacy of surrogate motherhood. I wished aloud there were programs such as Dr. Levin's nationwide, so that other infertile couples could take advantage of this new opportunity. Sarah smiled at my enthusiasm and listened politely. Dr. Levin watched us closely from a nearby table, looking thoughtful and amused at the same time.

Dale leaned his curly blond locks toward me, shouting above the din of the cocktail crowd. "Let's meet for lunch tomorrow."

"Nope," I laughed, "you're just going to try to talk me into pictures for your magazine."

"You already said no to me."

"I doubt if you give up that easily," I teased. "Besides, I have a full day of psychiatric examinations and you're catching a morning flight back to Chicago."

"I'll change it."

"I won't have time, Dale."

"You have to eat lunch somewhere, don't you? Now pick a spot and I'll be there." He looked like a small boy begging for something from the ice cream truck. I smiled at his persistence and agreed to meet them the next afternoon.

A king-size bed had never looked better. I dove for it, kicked my shoes across the room, and collapsed. "Gosh, what a day. How do you feel, Kent?"

Kent pulled his tie from under his shirt collar and draped it across the desk chair. "Tired."

"No. No. I mean about everything. About today."

He unbuttoned his shirt, starting from the bottom. "Pretty

good, I guess. Better. I'm not worried about a scandal anymore, if you want to call it that. Katie and that Levin guy seem to know what they're doing." He tossed the shirt onto the closet floor.

"I'll tell you one thing." I sat up and slid out of my coat. "I'll feel a lot better when those shrink sessions are over tomorrow."

"Listen, when we have lunch with Sarah and Dale, don't you dare agree to any pictures."

"I'm not going to," I snapped. "You heard me tell them, didn't you?"

"Yeah. Sure. I just want to make sure you understand what I mean."

"I'm too tired to argue with you." I slipped off my clothes, dropped everything onto a nearby chair, and turned on the hot water in the shower full force. The steaming spray poured down the back of my neck and seemed to wash the tension down the drain.

I smiled to myself, remembering the apprehension I had felt about talking to Sarah and Dale. I had been sure they would be lurking nearby for the entire time, writing down everything, and trying to photograph us without our permission. Instead they turned out to be honest, straightforward people, and I liked them both very much. They were beginning to feel like friends.

I wanted to sleep and envied Kent's even breathing. Before he punched his pillow into position he said, "You know, I really enjoyed myself tonight. I'm still not sure about this pregnancy, but I do feel better now that we're here." That reminded me of my promise to him on the plane to observe and get information only. Did he have any inkling I had made my decision hours ago?

I curled myself against him and listened to the sounds of the hotel—cars growling in the parking lot, showers running, toilets flushing through thin walls, and loud voices returning from a party. In frustration I got up and walked to the window. The light snowfall had ended and the quiet streets cut dark paths in the city below. Stars in the inky sky increased the beauty of the nighttime stillness. I tucked my feet under my legs and sat in the vinyl chair to watch the night become morning.

I knew I had to sleep or the psychiatrist would probe too deeply and find me wanting, so I reluctantly climbed under the covers again. I awoke an hour later with nausea and stomach pains. Now what? The flu, a virus? Nerves? You goose. You haven't eaten for almost twenty-four hours. I retrieved a banana from my luggage and fell back to sleep within minutes, free of discomfort. It seemed only minutes later I was awakened by the noisy invasion of a ringing telephone. The hotel operator told me it was 7:00 A.M. She sounded cheerful and alert. I resisted the temptation to ask her to talk to the psychiatrists today. Somehow she seemed more capable than I.

Kent and I sat in the hotel coffee shop. I played with the pool of yellow on my plate, destroying what was left of the eggs, and sipped coffee. Kent devoured his breakfast, took a deep gulp of coffee, and sighed with satisfaction. He wiped his mouth with a napkin, crushed it into a ball and tossed it onto his plate.

"You know, if these guys don't pass us today, if one of these shrinks says you're not stable enough to go through with it or if they think our marriage won't make it through to the end, it won't bother me in the least. I could get on that plane today with no regrets and never look back."

"It would devastate me," I murmured.

"Nope. Not me. I'd never think about it again." He pushed back his chair to stand, stretched, and reached for his billfold to pay the check.

I knew he meant every word.

• • •

The stone hospital building was imposing and gloomy even in the bright sunshine. I entered reluctantly. My heels made a snapping noise in the dark, narrow hallway, the sound bouncing off high ceilings with peeling paint. We approached the nurses' station, where an older woman wearing a starched uniform slouched over her paperwork. Her gray curls stuck out at odd angles from under her tiny white cap. She appeared to be distraught.

I cleared my throat nervously. "We have an appointment with Dr. Lee at ten o'clock."

"He's with a patient," she snapped, not looking up. "Have a seat." Kent and I exchanged glances, shrugged, and walked toward a tiny alcove occupied by four people seated on orange plastic chairs. Kent began to flip through a magazine while I paced the hall, amazed at the bleakness. I searched for a glimpse of sunshine through a window and was startled to see heavy steel bars obstructing the view. Beyond the window was a stately snow-covered tree. The February sun danced on its branches.

Several people shuffled up and down the hallway silently. Their mouths hung open; their stares were vacant. As I watched them, the skin on the back of my neck began to crawl.

Like a shot, Kent jumped off his chair and grabbed my arm, steering me down the hall. "I saw a Ping-Pong table when we passed this door. I'll play you a game," he challenged me.

We were soon laughing with a renewed sense of relaxation. I missed every shot and spent more time chasing the ball than playing. Then I hit a low ball that barely cleared the net, but Kent's paddle hung loosely in his hand. He was staring past the top of my head, and I turned to follow his gaze.

An elderly man with graying hair had been watching us. His clothes looked as though they had been slept in. The rumpled navy blue blazer and gray slacks hung over his stooped frame. His black loafers probably hadn't seen polish in all the years he had worn them. The skin on his face fell in loose folds, forming a permanent scowl. I knew this was Dr. Lee.

I haven't got a chance, I thought to myself. Where had Dr. Levin found him? Surely this man would never agree to the concept of surrogate parenting.

We introduced ourselves cautiously and politely, picked our coats off the Ping-Pong table, and headed toward the door. Dr. Lee slapped his hand on Kent's tweed sport coat. "Wait here. I want to see her alone." His tone was gruff, accentuated by a toss of his head toward the alcove and the orange plastic chairs. I was stricken with fear and followed him like a robot into a stark, tiny room with two folding chairs. A small barred window looked out onto a flat roof.

"Coffee?" Dr. Lee stood in the doorway.

"No, thank you," I answered quickly. But maybe it will make me feel better, I thought. "Yes, I think I will." No, it will only nauseate me again. "No, thank you." He turned and left the cubicle. I bolted from the room and ran after him down the hallway. "Yes, I will," I called to his back.

He stopped, turned slowly as though his back hurt, and raised one unruly eyebrow. "Cream or sugar?"

"Cream."

"Are—you—sure." It was not a question.

"Yes."

"You want one cup of coffee with cream?"

"Yes."

Now he stood motionless, watching me, and I began to laugh. "I really do." He chuckled to himself and walked slowly away, shaking his head. I returned to the tiny room to wait, choosing a chair against a wall.

He returned shortly, handed me a Styrofoam cup filled to overflowing, and asked me to sit in the chair near the window. "I'm a creature of habit."

He settled into the chair I had just vacated, placed his cup on a narrow ledge near his elbow, and stirred the liquid into a whirlpool. Then he sucked noisily at the hot fluid until the cup was empty.

He set it down in the corner, leaned forward until his large nose was only a few inches from mine, and looked directly into my eyes. "Why are you doing this?" he demanded brusquely.

One after another, the questions lasted ninety minutes. He flung them at me with machine-gun speed, urging me on when I paused a moment to think. His gray eyes were kind and gentle as he probed.

His compassionate and considerate manner made me relax. He uncovered things that I had not thought about for many, many years. By the time we finished, we'd been both light and serious. And I had grown quite fond of this magnificent gentleman.

Without warning, Dr. Lee hoisted himself from his chair and took two steps toward the door. He motioned wordlessly for me to follow. Was it over? With one hand resting on the doorknob, he watched my face for a long moment, then broke into a ragged smile. He placed one arm loosely around my shoulders while we stood in front of the closed door, and declared, "You're okay. I like you."

I grinned like a fool. I wanted to grab him in a bear hug and shout for the sheer joy of it. "Thank you," I said calmly instead, and walked through the door he had just opened for me.

Dr. Levin had seen to it that his secretary was available at all times during the two days we were in Louisville. Karen was waiting for us in her silver sports car when we stepped outside the hospital building into the sun. Kent chatted amiably with her as we wove our way through heavy traffic to meet Sarah and Dale for lunch. I remained silent and began to feel unnerved by her constant presence and by the lack of privacy for Kent and myself. There was much I wanted to share with him.

While we drove, there was no mention of what had taken

place during the psychiatric examination, and I knew even the airplane ride later that evening would not afford us the solitude we needed for an in-depth discussion. I would have to tuck away all my thoughts until we were home again.

Sarah and Dale were already seated near the back of the restaurant—an old renovated train station in downtown Louisville. We ordered wine and talked freely while Sarah made rapid notations on her pad. I didn't answer her questions about the psychiatric session with Dr. Lee.

When Dale politely repeated his request for photographs, I wavered. "If you absolutely have to have pictures to go with your story, could you photograph us from the back or in the shadows?" I avoided Kent's glare from across the table.

"No. We don't do things that way. People's backs don't sell magazines."

A small bowl of clam chowder refreshed me, and the thought of the afternoon session with another psychiatrist, Dr. Stein, did not seem quite as ominous as it had earlier in the day.

Dr. Stein's office building was on the outskirts of town, and even with Karen's expert chauffeuring, we arrived ten minutes late. The modern, one-story brick building was surrounded by rolling hills and hundreds of snow-covered trees.

Dr. Stein caught my eye when I peeked through the open door to his office, and he waved me in with a signal to close the door behind me. He was engrossed in a telephone conversation, so I crossed the large, plushly carpeted office and sat down on the edge of a small French provincial chair near his desk. The elegant room contrasted sharply with the tiny barred cubicle of this morning. Oil paintings and antique display cabinets graced the walls. A large window behind his mahogany desk revealed the beauty of yesterday's snowfall. The serenity began to ease my tension. I turned to my left and noticed a large brown leather chair, much like the one in Dr. Levin's office.

I watched it longingly, trying to resist its invitation. Should I poise ladylike, in silk blouse and high heels, on the elegant chair, or give in to the bone weariness and curl into the leather chair? Was this the first test? Did a psychiatrist note the chair a person chooses on entering the room? Yes, I imagined he did. I kicked my shoes under the leather chair, flopped like a rag doll into the softness, and felt the pressure lift.

Dr. Stein watched me with a Santa Claus face. Smile lines framed his blue eyes. He had a full head of wavy white hair. His very presence soothed me. This is going to be a piece of cake, I thought.

I fixed my gaze on Dr. Stein's silk tie as he got off the phone and planted himself before me, hands clasped behind his back.

"I am a psychiatrist for the Baptist Church," he boomed. "Before they send missionaries to remote areas of the world, I have to examine the husband and wife together and then again separately. I am required to write a twenty-five-page report about my findings on this couple. If the couple is not one hundred percent agreeable about mission projects, they will never work out, and I guarantee you, they are always back in the States within one year."

He began to pace the length of the carpet, from the door to his desk, while he looked at the floor in thought. "I will give you and your husband the same type of examination, and if at the end of that time I feel one of you is not able to follow through with this project, or if I feel it will harm your marriage in any way, I cannot give my approval."

Dr. Stein stood before me now and looked into my face somberly. "Then it will be up to Dr. Levin to decide what to do. What I'm trying to tell you," and now his eyes met mine, "is that one person in a marriage cannot intimidate another into doing something unless the other person is one hundred percent for it also. I do not feel a mate should go along with something for fear of disapproval."

Every nerve came alive. Kent was there only because I had asked (forced?) him to be. But was he convinced enough to be able to fool Dr. Stein? If in the past twenty-eight hours he had not accepted my part in the program, this would be the end.

I inhaled sharply, closed my eyes for a moment, and mentally uttered a short prayer for the strength to brave one more hour.

We talked about my past, my childhood, my brothers, sisters, parents and my relationships with them. We talked about my marriage, and I admitted the same problems and misgivings most couples experience in a period of thirteen years.

He did not cross-examine me or look at me piercingly as Dr. Lee had done, but he was much more quiet and gentle in his questioning. He moved deliberately, without the sense of urgency I had felt in the morning session. He asked one question to find an answer to another. "How often do you see your parents?" he asked. I knew he was trying to discover how I felt about them. I told him. There was no need to dig.

Abruptly he ushered me to the door. I groped for my shoes and padded in stocking feet into the waiting room. He seemed anxious for me to leave. Or was that, too, my imagination?

I had told him about Kent's fears for the endurance of our marriage if the pregnancy took place. I talked about Kent's feelings and how he kept them locked in a secret place, how he was unable to admit certain emotions, even to himself. I confessed to having talked Kent into being with me and said I had no idea how he felt about the project. I wondered if I had said too much.

When Kent entered the office, Dr. Stein turned to me soberly. "We'll only be a few minutes."

Karen and I sat in the tiny, elegantly furnished waiting room, saying little. She ground another cigarette into the already full ashtray. "What's taking so long?" Her brow furrowed with concern.

I shook my head, unable to speak. My palms were damp and I ran them down the sides of my skirt. I tried to stop the rapid movement of my swinging foot, but could not.

Karen looked at her watch again. "He said a few minutes. It's been over thirty. I wonder what they're talking about?"

I couldn't respond. If I expressed my fears, they might come true. But I just knew that Dr. Stein had decided we were not suited for the pregnancy and that he and Kent were trying to decide how best to tell me.

I watched as Karen smoked another cigarette, and I wished I hadn't quit five years before. I thought back on the past two days in Louisville—the probing examinations, the interviews, the lack of sleep and food. How, at the last minute during the final test, did one man have the right to decide I was not suitable?

Anger flooded me. If Dr. Stein's decision was negative, I would not let him ruin this for me. I would call Dr. Levin and ask him to make an appointment with another psychiatrist on a different day. And another and another and another, if necessary, until we could find two who agreed that I was emotionally stable enough to cope with any problems that might arise. I would not let him deprive me of the opportunity to give another woman a child.

The door to his office opened slightly. Dr. Stein stood in the doorway and nodded for me to enter. I shot off my chair and pushed through the door. Kent sat in the soft leather chair. Dr. Stein walked back and stood in front of the picture window, hands tightly clasped behind him. He gazed at the pale, cloudless sky.

I sat guardedly on the edge of the hard antique chair, my hands gripping the edges, my palms aching. I glanced at Kent.

He looked somber. The room was still for several minutes. We seemed to be frozen in place. The silence became intolerable.

I concentrated on keeping my voice light and casual. "You fellas must have had a lot to talk about. You were in here a long time." I clutched the chair for the inevitable blow.

Kent's face exploded with the pleasure of a shared secret. "Yeah, we did. Dr. Stein and I have lots in common. He knows some of the same people I went to college with in Iowa. We spent most of the time comparing backgrounds and going over old times."

Dr. Stein turned and looked at me for the first time since I had entered the room. "I'm sorry, Mary Beth. I have a patient I am very concerned about. I was thinking over the best way to manage his case."

I leaned back against the carved wood and let my muscles go limp.

Dr. Stein smiled wisely, talking to both of us. "Don't make any quick decisions about the publicity and what to tell people about the pregnancy, and I think everything will work out just fine."

And that was what I had been waiting to hear all afternoon. He held the door for us and put his hand on my arm. "If at any time, during or after the pregnancy, either one of you needs anything, please let me know."

"You mean," I asked, "if we have any difficulties that we don't know how to handle, we can just call you and ask your advice?"

He looked at me with the greatest kindness. "I am speaking to you as a parent. I will not abandon you."

Many times throughout the pregnancy I remembered those words. I never did return to him for advice, but knowing he was there often gave me the comfort I needed.

The weariness that had invaded my every muscle and bone

disappeared. I stood in the snowy parking lot, watching the late afternoon sun glitter and feeling that I was free.

"Thank God, it's over, Kent," I cried. "It's finally over."

He looked over my head to the snow-covered hills. "Maybe it's just beginning."

Chapter 5

At home the next morning I sat at the breakfast table and looked at the grapefruit halves that had been squeezed of their juices during the children's breakfast. A jar of peanut butter sat next to some opened strawberry preserves. The lunches had been packed and sent off with the children on the school bus.

"Well, what's next?" Kent asked, spreading butter on a toasted English muffin. "I mean with your Louisville thing."

"I don't know." I held a mug of coffee in my hands, warming them. "Dr. Levin said he had it narrowed down to another surrogate and myself and that he'd let me know in a day or two. Although—"

"What?"

"Nothing."

"What? Say it."

"Well, after meeting me, I don't know why he'd want to choose anyone else."

Kent drew his knife through the butter and slid a pat onto the other muffin half. "The other girl's about fifteen years younger."

"I saw her picture. I have more class," I smiled, teasing.

Kent looked at me wryly while he sipped orange juice. "So what's next?"

"Well, if I get chosen, the insemination. I had an argument with Dr. Levin before we left. He would want me to fly down there for three days to be inseminated, and I keep insisting one insemination will be enough. I know my body better than he does. He finally agreed, but insisted if it doesn't take, next time I'd have to do it his way. There wouldn't be a next time."

"What if there is?"

"Then I wouldn't go back until May. If I get pregnant in April instead of on March second, that would make the baby due on December twenty-third. I'd never give up Christmas with the children."

Kent pushed his dirty dishes aside and picked up the newspaper. "One thing I gotta say about Levin, he's a real salesman."

"Now what the heck is that supposed to mean?"

"Just what I said. He's really smooth."

"Don't you trust him?"

"Oh, sure. It's just that I'm still skeptical about this whole thing. I don't like the idea of publicity. He could turn this whole thing into a circus and end up pretty famous."

"I don't know what you're so worried about. Sarah and Dale promised us they would sit on the story until I conceived."

"I know."

"Well, then, what is it?"

"I just don't like it. I don't mind you having the baby if you feel you have to, but I don't want my picture in any magazines."

I stood up and began clearing the table, with a clatter of china and silverware. "How can they put your picture in a magazine if they haven't even taken one yet? What on earth are you talking about, Kent?"

"You just wait. Someone will talk you into it."

"No, they won't. I promised you. No pictures. Besides,

we don't even know anybody who reads *People*. Who would recognize us? Now quit stewing."

"I just don't want to do anything to jeopardize my job. Remember your promise." He bent to kiss me and drew back. "You feel awfully warm. Take your temperature before you get dressed."

He was right. A temperature of 103 degrees gave me good reason for having felt so tired in Louisville. But despite the virus, the exhilaration stayed with me all day and I attacked mounds of laundry, sorted through toys and puzzle pieces scattered in the family room, and started planning a dinner menu.

Hours later the sound of the doorbell drifted to the laundry room. I dumped soap into the washing machine and bounded up the stairs three at a time, still carrying the bottle of bleach.

Cold air blasted into the foyer when I opened the door. "Caryl! What a surprise!" I said. My friend bounced through the door.

"Tell me about your trip. The suspense is killing me," she bubbled.

I bumped past her in the narrow hallway and walked into the kitchen to avoid her gaze. "I told you. I flew down there with Kent on business."

"Baloney. Look at me. Now how was your trip?"

"Fine."

"What did you really go down there for?" she persisted. "Do you have any fresh coffee?" She peered into the cold pot. "Let me make some. Boy, you look terrible."

"I need makeup."

"You need more than that. You look sick."

"I am."

"Go to bed."

"I don't want to. God, I wish I had your energy. Don't you ever get tired?"

She stopped scooping coffee into the pot and looked at

me with her impish green eyes. "Only at eleven o'clock at night when my husband wants to make love," she laughed wickedly. "Now tell me. *Why did you go to Louisville?*"

"I can't."

"Why not?"

"Because I promised I wouldn't tell anyone."

"I'm ready to burst. Can you tell me anything?" Caryl pleaded. The aroma of freshly perked coffee soon filled the kitchen. Caryl loaded the dishwasher with the rest of the breakfast dishes and wiped off the table before she pulled out a chair and sat beside me.

"I can only tell you it's a type of medical research project. And you are right about one thing. I didn't go with Kent. He went with me."

"Is he in on it, too?" Her face was aglow with a rush of questions.

"Sort of. It's still experimental." The excitement of the day before returned and heated me beyond the fever.

"Caryl, until we finalize everything, I'm not at liberty to say any more," I continued. "But I wish you could see the doctor we're working with."

She leaned across the table and grinned seductively. "Is he gorgeous?"

"Ummm, sort of. It's hard to describe him. He's a marvelous dresser and so dynamic. I've never met anyone like him in my life."

"What's his name?"

"I can't tell you. Caryl, in another few weeks you'll know all the details. Believe me, you'll be the first to know," I promised her.

After she left to walk the few short blocks home, I pondered our friendship. Caryl did not offend easily, was broadminded and not judgmental, and always took the time to listen. She was worth more to me than fifty casual acquaintances. I knew she'd be as delighted as I was about this pregnancy. She would love it.

Kent came home from work early that afternoon, tucked me into bed, gave me two aspirin and a large glass of orange juice, and took over the care of the children.

Long after they were asleep, I heard him clean up the kitchen and tiptoe into our bedroom. A book was propped on my knees and the television was on as a matter of habit. I had no idea what was on.

"Here." Kent laid a small box on the bed next to the mound of my legs.

"What is it?" I asked.

"Just something I picked up for you today. I thought you might be able to use it."

Kent rarely brought me presents—"What on earth?" I opened the box and lifted a thick book with a smooth green cover the color of grass.

"It's a diary," he beamed. "There's so much going on lately, I thought you might like to write down some of your feelings."

"How did you know I needed this?" The clean white pages snapped with newness.

"I saw you writing on the kids' school paper last night. You can't do that for the next nine months if this thing goes through."

That one small gesture meant more to me than the words I had longed for him to say.

In spite of the new support, every now and then, when I least expected it, Kent would comment about how the pregnancy might affect my mental and physical health. The questions just popped out of his mouth late at night when he knew I was almost asleep and too tired to argue.

"What if you have trouble with the delivery and need a

cesarean section? That's surgery. At your age it would mean six weeks of recovery and a big scar on your belly."

"It wouldn't be a big scar. They make a bikini cut nowadays."

"What about high blood pressure or toxemia? My brother-in-law's niece was in the hospital for four weeks with her last kid for toxemia."

"She was fat. I'm not."

"You know, even though it's 1980, women still do die in childbirth."

"Kent, really."

"Well, where would that leave me and the kids?"

"I am not going to die in childbirth. Jeez."

"What if you flip out? What if you can't handle it when it's time to give the baby away? If you're in a mental hospital for six months, I don't think any of this will be worth it."

"Give me a little credit, Kent. Maybe you were born with a silver spoon in your mouth, but I wasn't. This wouldn't be the first crisis I've been through in my life. I always land on my feet. I gave up a baby for adoption fifteen years ago, remember? Besides, if I have problems, I'll see a shrink."

"You wouldn't. You're too proud," he eyed me warily.

"Yes, I would. If I start to go a little crazy and it's affecting you and the kids, I promise I'll talk to Dr. Stein again."

"Promise?"

"Promise. Girl Scouts' Honor."

"It's a deal," he smiled.

Some of the fears were real and I knew it. Yet it was easier for me to make fun of Kent for digging them up than it was for me to deal with them. The dark thoughts were pushed to the back of my mind, the part I had reserved for taboos.

The one thing Kent and I agreed on was the fact that now there seemed to be a certain closeness in our marriage that hadn't been there for years. A bond.

One night he told me he had admitted to Dr. Stein that when I first mentioned the pregnancy, he had thought of leaving me until it was over. I was shocked. It had never occurred to me he would think of leaving me or the children. Sure, Kent can be unemotional and it's often hard for me to know what he's thinking, but I do know he's the type who makes commitments. To me, to the kids, to his job.

We talked about the possibility of his looking at me one day, swollen with the child of another man, and finding the sight impossible to bear. And then maybe, just maybe, he would have to leave. But I never for a moment thought he really would. He might have wished he could leave us, but I knew he loved all of us too much. He would not desert us when we needed him most.

Each day passed slowly. I lunged for the phone each time it rang, and it was always for the girls.

"Call Dr. Levin after lunch," Kent suggested on the morning of February thirteenth, as he sat on the edge of the bed and pulled on his socks. "He said he'd let you know in a few days and it's been a week. I don't think he'll mind."

I pushed the curtains aside, pulled up the window shades to see the heavily clouded skies, and sighed, "At least I'll know where I stand."

Clutching the telephone tightly, I dialed Dr. Levin's number.

"Dr. Levin's office." A nasal voice.

"May I speak to him, please?"

"I'm sorry," the voice said detachedly, "Dr. Levin is not in his office on Wednesday afternoons."

"This is Mary Beth calling and I—"

"Oh, hold the line please." The voice came alive.

I waited several minutes and listened to the clock ticking like a meter in a taxi, aware of the many long-distance charges that could equal our mortgage payment this month.

"Hi!" My fingers trembled when I recognized Dr. Levin's drawl.

"I thought I'd call to see what was happening down there," I said, with what I hoped was a casual tone.

"Well," he began, "I'm waiting for the written reports from the psychiatrists to show to the prospective parents. After they've seen the reports, they'll sign the contracts."

Contracts? I tried to think quickly. He had asked us to read documents, but never asked us to sign anything. Contracts meant he had chosen the other woman.

Anger began to fill my breast, and I swelled with indignation, ready to defend myself.

"Then you've made your decision, Dr. Levin," I stated flatly.

"Of course I have."

"And?" A note of sarcasm hung over that one small word.

"I've chosen you, of course."

Laura sat on the edge of the bed and read aloud the valentine that had been taped to the outside of the red paper. Jeff played with the ribbon while Kent watched me, beaming.

"Open it, Mommy," Julie urged.

"Me! Me!" Jeffrey whined.

"It's not your present. Hurry up, Mommy," Laura chimed in.

I tore into the paper eagerly, pulled the cover away, and lifted out a beautiful nightgown in a dusty rose. The satin fabric slid through my fingers. "It's beautiful," I whispered.

"Try it on," Kent urged.

I took my jeans and sweatshirt off quickly, slipped the gown over my head, and wriggled until it fell over my ankles. Kent whistled, long and low.

His eyes traveled the length of the gown and back up, pausing at the slit on my upper thigh. His cheeks lifted in a smile. "I hope that fits you when the weather gets warm enough for you to wear it. If you get pregnant right away, you might be too big to wear it this spring." He beamed with admiration.

My Valentine's Day was complete. Here was the man who just three weeks before had said "No, never" when I asked him about having the baby. Now he seemed comfortable with the idea. The insemination was set for March second.

As I pulled a sweatshirt over my head and stepped into a pair of jeans, I remembered our conversation from that morning. We had lingered over breakfast while the children watched Saturday morning cartoons in the family room.

I sipped coffee and cut a sweet roll in half, reaching across the table and handing the smaller piece to Kent. "I'm getting nervous," I confided. "The closer we get to the insemination date, the closer I am to getting pregnant. I think about that every morning. The minute I wake up."

He sank his teeth into the sweet roll and looked at me over the rim of his glasses. "Really? That's funny. I'm getting more and more relaxed about it."

I watched him finish his breakfast and thought, that's what I need to hear, Kent. I need to know your support is real and not a facade to avoid hurting my feelings. I'm going to lean on you a lot in the next months. Stay strong, Kent. Stay strong for me.

Soon my excitement about the impending insemination spilled into my working hours, and my coworkers began to wonder openly about "my secret." I was elated and had to tell someone. Even though I had promised Sarah and Dale and Dr. Levin not to mention even one word about the surrogate baby, I decided to tell Caryl.

She answered the phone on the second ring with her cheery hello and promised to be over in ten minutes. She sensed I needed to talk and canceled her plans for the morning.

We settled her little son Matt in the family room with Jeff's toys, then went into the kitchen. Caryl waited quietly for me to begin. She knew better than to urge me to talk. I studied her face. Her mouth, always active with laughter or chatter, was still. I placed a cup of coffee and a plate of fresh peanut butter cookies in front of her and sat down opposite her.

"Caryl," I hesitated, and she grinned encouragement. "Caryl, I'm going to be inseminated in ten days with the sperm of a man whose wife can't have children." The smile on her face froze.

"Isn't it wonderful? I'm going to have a baby for them."

She was still. For a full minute she said nothing. Without warning she dropped her face into her hands and rested her head on the table.

"Caryl, say something."

"I'm thinking," the muffled reply came through her hands.

When she finally raised her head to look at me, the questions gushed from her.

"What about the medical bills? What if something happens to you, for god's sake? Who will take care of the kids? You're thirty-eight years old!"

"Thirty-seven."

"Why would you want to have a baby at your age? Do you remember what it feels like to be pregnant? The backaches, the throwing up, always being tired? And the labor! My god, have you forgotten what the labor feels like?" She shouted at me as though I had lost my senses. "What if this couple changes their mind and you're stuck with the baby? Are you gonna ask Kent to raise it?

"What if your insurance company finds out it's not Kent's baby and you have to pay the bills?

"How can Kent let you do this?

"What have you told the kids? How are you going to explain it to them?"

The questions went on and on for twenty minutes until I couldn't stand it any longer. "Stop it, Caryl!" I shouted back at her. "I have a lawyer who's taking care of everything. I'm not going to get hurt or cheated or anything."

"I'm worried about you. I'm not so sure this is a good idea. You're going to get the short end of the stick. I can feel it." She looked into my face, leaned closer, and frowned. "Why do you want to do this for two people you don't even know?" Without waiting for my answer she leaned back in her chair, balancing on its back legs while she continued her lecture. "You're never going to see that baby again. Why don't you do it for a friend? Or your brother? How can you do this to yourself?"

"I couldn't do it for anyone I know, Caryl. I'd want to take part in raising the baby. Don't you see? They won't have to share this child with anyone. That's the beautiful part of the arrangement. They'll have a child they're genetically related to with no strings attached."

It was a long time before she spoke again. "Do you know what the people in this town are going to say? Especially this neighborhood?" she sneered.

"We'll probably get egged," I laughed, referring to the house.

"What about the children?"

"What about them?"

"Aren't you afraid some kook in this town will threaten them or wait outside the school yard for them? I remember that kid that disappeared a few years ago in the middle of the day. They never did find his body."

"Come on, Caryl. Now you're getting dramatic." I was becoming irritated with her.

She pushed her chair away from the table and rushed through the kitchen to stand at the top of the stairs that led to the family room.

"Matthew, we're leaving. Now!" Matt bounded up the stairs on short, four-year-old legs. She took his arm, grabbed their jackets off the chair, and headed out the front door. I sat helplessly and listened to the squeal of rubber in the driveway.

The morning blended into afternoon while a nagging doubt began to creep through me. I had been so sure of a positive reaction from Caryl. But if I couldn't get through to my closest friend, how could I expect other people to understand why a happily married woman with three children of her own would want to carry another man's child?

I had been agitated several days earlier when Dr. Levin told me he had arranged for Sarah and Dale to be present at the insemination. They were in a hurry to finish their story for *People* by the first week of April. Now, with the sting of Caryl's reaction so fresh, I began to think that perhaps publicity *was* the answer. Perhaps the public did need educating; publicity could well be an opportunity to express my strong feelings about giving infertile women the same chance for parenthood that infertile men had had for years through artificial insemination by a donor.

I didn't see Caryl again until the weekend. I went to her house to ask her advice about a television interview Dr. Levin had asked me to do, as I had serious qualms about appearing on a program that would dissect my family's personal lives.

She advised me against it, much to my relief. Then we stared at each other, sensing the awkwardness.

"How do you feel now, Caryl? I mean about the insemination, the publicity, everything. It's been four days since I told you."

She smiled weakly. "Some of the shock waves are beginning to wear off."

"I knew they would."

"I'm still not convinced you're doing the right thing."

"Now you sound like Kent." I turned and left without closing the door behind me.

Chapter 6

March 1980

The next several days seemed to flow into one while I prepared for the insemination. The plan was simple. I would fly to Louisville on the morning of March second, be inseminated in the early afternoon by a member of Dr. Levin's staff—Dr. Levin would be at a medical conference in Aruba—have a quiet meal with Sarah and Dale, and fly home in the evening in time to put the children to bed. Kent would stay home with the children.

For weeks, every time I looked at the calendar, the date stood out in a magical way: *March second.* I don't know why. It just seemed to have a special look to it. I knew, even weeks before, that I would conceive on March second.

The room was still heavy with the predawn darkness of a winter morning. I slid the thermometer from my lips, afraid the mercury would fall if I jiggled it. The impossibility of that happening didn't matter this morning. With my back to Kent, who slept deeply, I snapped on the flashlight, squinted at the mercury, and remembered Dr. Levin's words before we left Louisville: "On the day of ovulation your temperature will take a sharp rise to 98.0. It doesn't sound like much, but on your temperature chart you'll really see it shoot up." My normal body temperature is 97.6.

The silver streak had stopped at 98.0. That day I would

get pregnant. The next morning I would wake up in the same bed, and miraculous changes would be rapidly taking place inside my body.

Kent's back moved in the rhythmic pattern of sleep. I touched his shoulder gently to wake him, then stopped. No, I thought, if he doesn't share my joy, it will dissolve. I will just lie here quietly until . . .

"Breakfast," Kent called cheerfully, pushing into the bedroom with a steaming mug of coffee. He was followed by Julie, Laura, and Jeffrey, still clad in pajamas and robes, carrying a tray of French toast, orange juice, sausages, milk, and more coffee.

"It was their idea," Kent beamed.

I had told the children I was flying to Louisville for a secret project. Kent and I knew the weeks of waiting for the pregnancy to occur would seem endless to them. If by a slim chance I would need to be inseminated several months in a row, their impatience would overcome them, and the news would spread through the neighborhood before we were ready to answer questions. Yet today they seemed to sense the excitement. Their faces were gleaming with pleasure at the breakfast they had prepared for me.

"Eat it all, Mom, or you won't grow," Laura teased, using the words I always said to her. She watched closely while I sliced the French toast into cubes. Julie joined in the laughter until the girls grabbed Jeff and hurried back to the kitchen.

"What does the kitchen look like?" I asked, concentrating on cutting into a juicy sausage.

"Let's put it this way," he grinned. "It's a good thing you're not wearing a pacemaker. The sight of it would stop your heart."

"I'll stay in bed."

"By the way, Katie Brophy called while you were sleeping." Kent lifted the glass of orange juice from the tray and took a swallow.

"What did she want?"

"She told me I have to go with you today."

"For what?"

"I haven't signed any of the contracts yet either. We can't go through with the insemination until you and I both sign."

I nodded my understanding and let him continue while I ate.

"She'll meet us at the airport and drive us to the attorney's office so we can sign the papers before you go in for the insemination."

I watched his face closely and spoke cautiously. "Do you mind?"

He answered without hesitation. "No, I think it will be fun to fly down there. I'll enjoy seeing everyone again." I knew he was referring to Karen.

I grabbed the breakfast tray, set it aside, and jumped from bed to flop into his arms. "Oh, Kent, I'm so glad. I dreaded going down there alone. I love you so much. Thank you. Thank you." I kissed him.

I dressed slowly and carefully, glancing only once in the mirror at my still firm stomach, nicely flat in well-fitting black slacks. Tomorrow I'll be pregnant, I thought, and ran my hand over my abdomen.

I tried to imagine the day ahead of us. My reservations about the publicity had not eased, and the thought of Sarah and Dale being present for the insemination made me nervous. But Dr. Levin had finally convinced me how important it was for this story to be available for other couples who were infertile. I was so eager for other women like myself to volunteer to become surrogate mothers that I had agreed, with trepidation, to be photographed. Kent muttered for days about my sanity.

"I'm not crazy about the idea either," I defended myself, "but Dale promised he would photograph me only from the back during the insemination for the sake of privacy. He said it's the focal point of the whole story."

"Your mother will be thrilled when she picks up a copy of *People* at her local supermarket and sees a picture of her daughter on the cover."

"For God's sake, I'm not going to be on the cover. And my mother never reads *People* magazine. She'll never have to know a thing about the pregnancy." When I turned back to the mirror, I saw the deep lines on my forehead.

Before he left the room, Kent looked at me like he always does when he knows he's right and I'm wrong.

Within minutes he had reentered the room. I dug through shoe boxes on the closet floor, searching for black heels. Kent watched me fish out the heels and examine them for scuff marks.

"Are you sure you want to do this?"

"Yes."

"It's not too late to back out."

I turned toward him. "I know that. I don't owe anybody anything. But I do want to follow through with this. More than anything in the world." I watched him a moment, his hands shoved deeply into his pockets, his shoulders hunched as if he were a much older man.

"Kent, this is one of the most exciting days of my life. Please don't do anything to spoil it for me," I pleaded.

He studied my face a moment, crossed the room, and disappeared in silence. I sighed into the oppressive stillness. Damn the lousy communication in my marriage, I thought. Is that his answer to everything? To always leave a room in silence and never, *never once* finish a conversation?

At the Louisville airport we caught sight immediately of Katie and Sarah, waving their arms like flags of surrender. We hurried toward them eagerly.

"Hello. How are you?" Katie asked. "Adam and Margo want to talk to you on the telephone."

"Who are they? More reporters?" We walked down the concourse, four abreast.

"The parents of the baby."

I stopped and stared at her. Richard Levin had always been careful not to mention their names. *Adam and Margo. Adam and Margo.* I clung to the names, saying them over and over to myself. The sound was delicious. At last, the parents of this child-to-be had identities.

My feet remained glued to the tile floor. "Richard told me I would meet them today," I protested, looking at Kent for confirmation. "He promised I could."

"Leave me out of it," Kent muttered to the floor. "I don't want to know what this guy looks like."

Sarah watched him carefully, her reporter's mind logging every detail. Katie cast a wary glance from Kent to Sarah to me. "I don't want you to meet them," she said.

"Dr. Levin said I could. I've been counting on it."

"He did not," she shot back through clenched teeth. "He said he would arrange it if he could."

"Well?"

"I just don't think it's a good idea at this time." She scuffed the floor with the toe of her shoe and studied it.

I could feel the beginning of a deception and began to shake with rage. "Why not, Katie? Richard promised I would meet them today." Tears increased my frustration.

"Because I'm representing them and Margo told me she doesn't want to meet you." She turned away and strode down the concourse, her voice firm. "If you want to talk to them on the telephone, fine. But there will be no meeting."

We parked the car at Dr. Levin's office building. I was too irritated with Katie to ask her why we hadn't gone to our attorney's office as planned.

My question was soon answered. The lawyer, John, stood near the elevator, briefcase in hand. He nodded hello with a quick jerk of the head before he followed us to the second floor. Kent opened the door to the waiting room, and I was transported back in time three weeks to when we had been there "just to talk."

Richard's assistant, Venisa, entered the waiting room, professional and pretty in crisp whites. "Shhh," she put a finger to her lips and waved at us to follow. She pointed to the wall that divided an examining room from Dr. Levin's office. "The parents are in there trying to get a specimen."

"Oh." I nodded my understanding and smiled. It had never occurred to me I might have to go home because of a lack of semen. Good Lord, I thought, of all the things that could go wrong, that's the last thing I would have imagined.

"Ask them if they'll talk to me before they leave. Just for a minute. Please?" Venisa nodded her assent and closed the door behind her.

John joined us, opened his briefcase, and spread the contracts we had read in February on top of the baby pictures and letters scattered around the small tabletop. Kent pored over the revisions we had made. I looked with disinterest across the room and strained to hear the voices of the parents.

"You'd better sit down," John addressed me, "and look over the changes in this contract."

"Let Kent look at them." I waved my hand, and walked to the leather chair that held my tote bag. I took out the small bottle of wine I had brought for Kent, found a coffee mug on Richard's desk, and poured a few inches of the clear liquid.

Like a caged tigress, I paced the office, the mug in hand. As I passed the sofa, John put his hand on my arm. I glared at him.

"Look these changes over and give them your approval," he spoke gently.

I pulled away. "I don't care what they say. I'm too nervous to care."

His eyes narrowed to slits. His jaw bulged above a thick neck. "You'd better care."

"I'm sorry," I mumbled, suddenly aware of my rudeness.

I quickly initialed each change above Kent's initials already scrawled here and there among the eight pages. "Looks fine to me." I pushed the last page away and resumed my pacing. "What on earth is taking so long?" I wheeled toward the door impatiently.

Venisa opened the door. "No specimen yet."

I remembered previous childbirth training and began to breathe deeply, counting to ten.

Why is everyone so unorganized? I wondered. We're creating a new life. Can't we be quiet and dignified for a perfect and memorable day? And why did the parents have to be trying for a specimen in the next room? I hated the closeness, the personal touch it added to the insemination, which I had always thought of as a strictly medical procedure. Couldn't they have done that this morning, before I arrived?

A tall, boyish-looking young man interrupted and Katie introduced him. "This is Steve. He has an insurance policy he wants to write."

Steve stood awkwardly, arms dangling, and held a briefcase loosely in one hand. He looked like a first grader on the first day of school, waiting for the teacher to tell him where to sit. Now what is *he* doing here? I thought.

Katie stepped into Richard's private bathroom while Steve settled next to John and Kent on the sofa. I could see Katie's profile from where I sat at the desk. She stroked her blonde hair and studied her image in the mirror.

"By the way, Mary Beth, did you see the last page I added to the contract?"

John interrupted her abruptly, visibly irritated. "I was just getting to that. We haven't discussed it yet."

I straightened in Dr. Levin's chair, mildly curious. "What does it say?"

He read in a monotone: "Page nine, item twenty-one. 'The surrogate agrees not to smoke cigarettes, drink any alcoholic beverages, use any illegal drugs, non-prescription medication or prescribed medications without written consent of Richard M. Levin, M.D.' "

I peered into the coffee mug half-full of wine that sat before me on the desk.

"Hey, look. I quit smoking five years ago and I never take anything that would come close to a drug. I rarely take even an aspirin." I looked from John to Katie.

"You don't have to sign this contract," John advised. "It's negotiable."

Now Katie turned fiercely toward us, hairbrush in hand. She held it like a weapon. "No, it is not negotiable." Her brow furrowed as she stared us down. "That's the way it stands."

I leaned forward on the desk. "Katie, do you mean to tell me if I drink a glass of wine, I'm breaking the contract?"

She turned back to the mirror. "Mary Beth, what you do is between you and your conscience. I'm only telling you what it says."

I pounded my fist lightly on the desk. "This is absurd. Nobody ever mentioned this to me before today. Katie, go into that room and talk to the parents. It's unreasonable." My agitation increased. "I can't believe I have to sign a legal contract stating I won't drink a drop of alcohol for the next nine months."

"I can't talk to them."

"Yes, you can. They're in the next room."

She turned back to the mirror to concentrate on her grooming and began to brush her hair until it snapped with electricity. "They've already left."

I scanned the room and saw John, Kent, Sarah with her notepad, Dale with his camera, Venisa in the doorway, Karen, Steve with his insurance papers, and, of course, Katie. Was my only contact with the couple to be a sterile jar filled with semen? Kent met my gaze, but there was no message for me.

I had no alternative. I had ovulated that morning. The next move was mine.

I exhaled loudly. If only Richard Levin were here, I thought. He would take charge, and everything would fall into place.

The semen was getting cold. I picked up the pen and pulled my lips into a smile while Dale took twenty pictures of me for an April issue of *People* magazine. I felt wooden and manipulated as I scratched my name on the straight black line.

Steve approached me, shoving insurance papers before me and smiling weakly. "An insurance policy in case you should die as a result of this pregnancy. Your children will be named as beneficiaries."

I recalled the three typewritten pages in our contract marked "Exhibit A" that John had read to me. The papers were filled with morbid information on maternal mortality and the complications of pregnancy, childbirth, and the postpartum period. "Only when you are satisfied that the risks of the pregnancy are small enough for you should you then sign this contract," it had stated at the bottom.

I signed Steve's papers automatically. Dale's camera clicked nonstop. I was constantly aware of the camera's eye and my discomfort in its presence.

Venisa leaned jauntily against the door frame. She caught my eye and raised her head slightly, bringing it down again in a barely perceptible nod. "We can't wait any longer. You'll have to finish the papers later."

"Where's the specimen?" I asked. Her hands were empty.

She pointed to the cleavage of her uniform and grinned wickedly. I giggled with relief. At last.

Kent rose, crossed the room to our tote bag, and pulled the bottle of white wine out of the first compartment. I wanted to reach out to him, to comfort him in some way. But the room was filled with strangers who didn't belong. Especially the reporters. There was no privacy for a short message of love or encouragement. I stood in front of him for a moment, ever aware of Dale and his camera. Kent had sunk into the massive leather chair, pretending he didn't know it was time for the insemination. He took a long, slow drink from the glass of wine, avoiding my eyes and fooling no one.

I sighed, feeling every eye in the room. With a straight back I walked through the door, away from my husband, to conceive another man's child.

The examining room was empty, and I lay on the table covered with a sheet of paper. I waited ten minutes for the insemination to take. A chill of anticipation enveloped me while I waited quietly. Please let it take, I prayed. For the sake of the parents, Dear God, let it take the first time.

I dressed rapidly, suppressing the desire to rush from the room and shout for joy. Instead, I composed myself, assuming what I hoped was a dignified manner, and reentered Dr. Levin's office. The entire cast were in their same positions, like enormous ice sculptures. I wanted them all to melt away, so my husband and I could go home.

I leaned over Kent, still slouched in the leather chair, and kissed him on the forehead. "Congratulate me. I'm pregnant." He looked up at me with glazed eyes and a crooked smile.

"Let's get the insurance forms and medical history finished," Steve suggested. While Dale reloaded his camera, I picked the forms off the desk, attempting to scan them before signing the last few papers, but Katie signaled to me frantically. The telephone receiver was balanced over her shoulder.

"There's a lady from CBS who wants to talk to you," she whispered.

"About what?"

"She wants to interview you now and get your viewpoint on the insemination. She just wants to know how you feel about the whole thing." Katie blinked her long lashes rapidly and innocently.

The insemination had taken place less than fifteen minutes before. Did this woman really have the gall to think I wanted to tell her how I felt during the procedure?

"Katie, I don't want to talk to her," I said, my exasperation underscoring each word.

"Maybe you'll change your mind later."

"No, I won't. I told you and I told Dr. Levin. This is Sarah's story. If there even is a story in this pregnancy, Sarah will be doing it. Not CBS. I'm only talking to *People* about this, no one else!"

"What will I tell her?"

I clenched my fists and felt the stab of my long fingernails. "I don't care what you tell her or anybody else. That's your problem. No more publicity. Period!" I turned sharply and ground my heels into the carpet. I dropped onto the sofa and filled out the last form. The production had ended. No encores of the performance, thank God!

March 3, 1980

The pale winter sun cast shadows on our living room carpet. I looked up from the legs of the antique walnut table I had just dusted and shuddered involuntarily, glancing around the room again. Knowing I was alone in the house, I still could not shake the scary feeling that there was someone or something intangible hidden in the room with me.

Gloom settled over me like a gray cloud. I had been naive enough to think I would board the plane the night before and actually feel pregnant. And I was disappointed at not having met the parents.

I was restless, confused, and agitated.

The trees were bare against the March skies. Branches

nodded to the heavens in a brisk wind and a fragile sparrow sat on the edge of a lower branch, enjoying the ride. A neighbor drove past in her station wagon, children piled in the backseat wrestling against a sack of groceries. Nothing had changed outside.

I hugged myself for reassurance and turned toward the large mirror in our hallway. The image stunned me. I noticed my right hand placed instinctively over my lower abdomen. I stood motionless and watched the reflection. The familiar, protective stance of a pregnant woman.

Adam's child. I could feel the strong presence of a stranger I had never met. I knew that at that very moment, his child was growing within my body. I yearned to share this moment with Adam and Margo. Wouldn't they feel the same elation at the beginning of their child's life?

The moment of joy was suddenly replaced by fear. I had spent hours thinking about what it would mean to carry the child of another man, but it had not occurred to me I would feel the father's presence during the pregnancy. I was determined to remain detached from this child. But the strange power over me was overwhelming and frightening.

I wondered how it would affect my sexual relationship with Kent. To what extent would my pregnancy become a barrier between us?

I did not mention the strangeness of my afternoon to Kent. How could I begin to explain? The evening hours wound routinely into bathtime, homework, piano practice, and bedtime snacks and stories before the children were willing to give up another day.

Finally it was our turn and we lay in bed, bundled against the cool air. Kent rolled off his side, hit the OFF button on the television, and hopped back under the quilts, shivering. He grabbed me and held me tightly to warm himself.

His touch soon became a caress, but after only a moment

of fondling he sat upright and turned on the bed lamp. He stared down at me, bewildered. He opened his mouth to speak, but did not.

"Do you feel it, too?" I asked cautiously.

He nodded slightly and scowled as if he were just beginning to realize what "it" was. "We're definitely not alone," he confirmed.

Guilt crept through me at the sacrifices he was going to have to make.

"Will you be all right?"

"Yeah, I will. Just so I don't have to meet this guy. I don't even want to see his picture. I'll be fine." Then he beamed. "I told them you'd get pregnant the first time." He smiled smugly and reached up to turn out the light.

So it was not my imagination after all. I drifted to sleep with one hand over my abdomen, wondering if Kent would learn to accept this third party in our bed.

Chapter 7

Nine days later I stared blankly out the kitchen window, trying to comprehend the words Kent had just spoken to me over the telephone. Outside, bare branches nodded against the cold gray skies that hung low.

"Well?"

"I can't believe you mean it," I said softly.

"You don't have a choice, do you? You might have to get an abortion."

The word cut like a serrated knife. *Abortion. Abortion. Abortion.*

"The father wants the baby. I know he does."

"Fine. Who is he? What's his last name?" Kent's words were sarcastic.

"Adam something. I don't know."

"Didn't your Dr. Levin tell you anything about him?"

"No, he wouldn't. But I didn't ask him much, either."

"You don't know a thing about this Levin guy when you think about it. We only met him for a few hours. Who is he? Except for the fact that he has a fancy office in Louisville, we don't know anything about him." Kent's tone began to frighten me.

"He's a doctor. You know that. I checked his school records."

"Did he graduate? Listen, Mary Beth, don't be so naïve.

Anybody can rent office space, hang a couple of degrees on the wall, and open a business. For Christ's sake, they do it in California every day."

My voice was husky. "I don't want to believe that."

"I don't either. But face facts. If that's what happened, if you were just an experiment or someone's idea of a practical joke, all you can do is get an abortion. Just chalk the whole thing up to experience and kiss the two grand we've already spent good-bye. You'll never see that money Levin owes you."

"Kent, even if I wanted to get an abortion, which I don't, we wouldn't have enough money for one now."

"Guess what else we don't have?" his singsong voice mocked me. "A copy of the legal contract."

I gripped the phone and sank into a chair. The reality of his words was beginning to hit hard. "Do you know," he continued, "that we can't prove any of this actually took place? Those people in Louisville could deny any of this happened. They could deny even knowing you—we couldn't prove a thing," he snickered bitterly.

"Sarah and Dale were there from *People*. They're on our side."

"Were they from *People*? Did you see credentials? Or were they friends of Levin's with a camera?"

I feared the worst. Tears glazed my eyes. "Kent, I'm so sorry." The words choked from me. "My intentions were so good. Now we're two thousand dollars in debt, we can't pay our bills because of our 'friends' in Louisville, our credit rating is ruined for at least three months, and worst of all, we don't want any more children—your vasectomy after Jeff was born guaranteed we never would—and I'm pregnant with a baby that isn't yours." I stood at the window again. "God, how I wish we could get in touch with the father of this baby. He has no idea any of this is even happening. He is as much a victim as we are because he already put eleven thousand dollars into Levin's account."

"Jeez, who would believe this soap opera?" Kent sighed. "Even the boys in Hollywood couldn't come up with something like this."

I was so filled with despair, there were no tears.

The familiar squeal of the brakes on the mail truck sent me racing to the front door. My hand plunged deeply into the metal box for the check I had been waiting for with a Louisville return address. I shuffled through the few things in my hand: bills, *Young Miss* for the girls, and a packet of food coupons. The door slammed behind me. I tossed the mail onto a chair and dialed Caryl's number. She had begun to accept my surrogacy, and in spite of some trepidation on her part, our friendship was regaining its closeness. Within minutes of hearing her voice the story of our financial crisis was pouring from me, so complicated and twisted I didn't know if Caryl would be able to follow it.

I started at the beginning, in early February, when we flew down for our initial interviews and psychiatric testing. Dr. Levin had promised to pay all of our expenses. Flights, hotels, baby-sitter fees, and meals. I was to send him the receipts and an expense report. We had charged everything on our VISA card. I sent him the bills within a few days and waited. And waited.

We owed $1,500 for two round trip flights to Louisville, plus Kent had written our lawyer, John, a check for $500 the day I was inseminated. John knew it was rubber but promised to hang onto it until Karen mailed us a check the next day. Well, it seems he forgot his promise and cashed the check on the way home without telling us. He was very insistent on being paid that day. Now I know why. Our bank had called and we had checks bouncing all over town. Our credit rating was shot.

"Do you know, Caryl, we have never owed anyone a cent except for a little on our mortgage? Now, thanks to Levin, I can't cash a check to buy groceries."

"Why don't you call Dr. Levin and just ask him to send you the money?"

"Because he's soaking up the sun in some godforsaken place, and Karen doesn't have the authorization to sign any checks. I'm pregnant with a baby I don't know what to do with, I don't know the father, and I'm two thousand dollars in debt."

"Whew!" was the only comment she could make.

We soon received the vital reimbursement check after Dr. Levin returned from his trip to Aruba. He also mailed us a copy of the legal contract and, after hearing our side of the story, admitted he had "possibly taken a vacation at the wrong time."

"*That* is a gross understatement," Kent snorted.

"It won't break my heart if I don't see Louisville again until I deliver," I added, and meant every word.

One afternoon that following week I dragged the stepladder, drop cloths, and paint up to Laura's bedroom. Bent over the paintbrush box, I searched for a brush that wasn't brittle with age or caked with old paint.

"What do you think you're doing?" Kent stopped me abruptly.

"Repainting Laura's room. She reads with her feet on the wall. It's a mess."

"You painted her room less than a year ago. You don't have to do it again."

"Yes I do. Look at it." He followed the wave of my arm toward the smudged wall, stripped bare of paint.

He reached for the scruffy brush and dropped it back into the box. "Not today," he said firmly. Then he carried the ladder, drop cloths, and paint can back down to the basement.

I followed with the brush box, protesting weakly.

Kent stood firm. "I want you to wait until you have an official pregnancy test. Then you can ask your doctor what he thinks about painting before the fourth month. But right now, I don't think those fumes are good for you or the baby. Just take it easy today."

I kissed his cheek and smiled. We're making progress, baby, I thought. He's protective of you already.

Kent's acceptance of the baby gave me a serene feeling that Sunday afternoon.

The next two weeks were kaleidoscopic. I had a blood test at Pekin Memorial Hospital to confirm my pregnancy and register the hormone level of my blood. I had been spotting lightly but tried to believe the reassuring words of Dr. Levin, who insisted it was only implantation bleeding. Yet my emotions careened wildly from one day to the next.

One afternoon I shoveled away a light snowfall from the front walk. Within a few hours the cramps I felt were not in my imagination.

Kent took my fears in stride. He reassured me that I was not going to miscarry and scolded me harshly for being foolish enough to shovel snow. "There is no such thing as light snow. Don't do it again. If I'm out of town, it can wait until I get back. Or let the girls do it," he ordered.

But I worried about the pink spotting and wondered if the baby would develop properly. The words of a close friend with a mentally handicapped daughter began to haunt me during the dark nights: "I threw up and spotted constantly during the whole pregnancy. Cynthia should have been a miscarriage."

Her words shocked me at the time, she spoke so frankly. But now I understood and prayed feverishly for a miscarriage rather than have a handicapped child for this young, hopeful couple.

Several weeks after it started, the spotting and cramping ended. My breasts were already aching, the first sign of a conception. I began to make frequent trips to the library and took out every book I could find on pregnancy—especially in older mothers—and postpartum depression. I pored over the sections on nutrition, continued to swallow the monstrous prenatal vitamins I had been taking since four weeks before the conception, and added more fresh fruits and vegetables to the grocery list. And ice cream. In huge amounts. Kent would often tease me about a twenty-five-percent increase in the grocery bills. I felt as though I were training for the Olympics.

One dreary afternoon I curled up on the sofa with a stack of library books. I casually flipped pages of the book on my lap until they fell open to a section of black-and-white photographs that startled me. "My God, how repulsive," I said aloud. A photograph of a woman in her ninth month of pregnancy stunned me. Her naked body bulged grotesquely below sagging breasts. Surely she must be carrying twins. Had I ever looked that terrible, or had I forgotten?

And then I remembered. In flashback, it all came back to me, and almost overwhelmed me. I remembered the shortness of breath, the nausea and fatigue, my rapidly expanding waistline, piercing back pains, not being able to tie my shoes near the end or shave my legs or paint my toenails a pretty pink for the delivery room. I inhaled sharply, remembering the hours of discomfort in the labor room, the terrible thirst, the incredible crushing pain, and the consuming weariness. And then, days and days of soreness and healing. But the sweetness of a beautiful new baby soon made it all a fleeting memory.

Then I thought of another scene: my new baby's mother slender and lovely after the birth while I remained flabby and sore for weeks. I thought of her in her beautiful home, attractive and serene with the baby cradled in her arms.

I quickly turned to another section of the book. A large photo of a woman breast-feeding her newborn, both of them calm and peaceful. My breasts began to ache with imaginary fullness. I had many pleasant memories of early morning hours spent nourishing Jeffrey. The unexpected, primitive urge to suckle a child was still there. Was I strong enough to remain detached and objective until this pregnancy was over? My maternal instincts were still strong. Would that mean trouble when it was time to give the baby away? Was the whole idea of being a surrogate mother a terrible mistake? I pushed these distressing thoughts deep into the back of my mind. I'd deal with them another time.

Several days later I crept out of bed at six-thirty in the morning, quivering with anticipation. Within an hour my home pregnancy test revealed the brown doughnut-shaped circle that signified a positive test. Just like the ad! I raced down the stairs and yelled with joy, demanding that Kent listen to the details while he filled the coffeepot with hot water. I jumped up and down, the words bouncing from me. Kent stood in his bathrobe at the kitchen sink and counted out scoops of coffee. "*Two—three—and a half.* There. I told you a long time ago you were pregnant. You didn't have to spend ten bucks on a test," he teased. I was relieved at his obvious pleasure, but didn't fail to notice that he looked more pleased than he had when I told him the news about being pregnant with Jeffrey. Was that because the pregnancy would mean no additional responsibility for him for the next twenty-two years? Oh, who cares? I was glad he was glad.

As soon as the girls awoke, I reminded them of our conversation the month before, and told them of the pregnancy. They raced down the hall to the bathroom, squealing with delight at the test tube. I was too thrilled to wonder why Laura then so quietly slipped back to her bedroom to dress for school.

The next day I awoke early and tiptoed to the window.

A new-fallen snow reflected the pale morning sky. A streak of pink framed the horizon. I watched until the golden eye of the sun rose and peered down through the trees.

Back in bed I wriggled with satisfaction, in awe of the child that grew inside me. This pregnancy had changed my relationship with my husband. In the past weeks we seemed to be much more tolerant of each other. I loved our new marriage. It seemed we could talk and love each other more freely than before. Like newlyweds. How many years had it been since we had had a conversation without criticizing each other, either aloud or in silent thought?

I chuckled out loud, waking Kent. He yawned and stretched, then reached toward me. "What's so funny?"

"I was just thinking about last night."

"Oh, yeah? Want to try it again?" His hand slid to my breast.

"No!" I slapped him away playfully. "That's not what I meant. Afterward. When we went down to the kitchen because you said you were hungry."

"Yeah. And I asked you to come along to keep me company."

"Well, we managed to polish off two tuna sandwiches, dill pickles, and a quart of milk. By candlelight yet. Wasn't it romantic?" I rubbed his back as I talked.

"We can do it again tonight," he grinned.

"Why do I get the feeling you're not talking about the tuna sandwiches?" I pulled the blankets off his legs and smacked his bottom. "Get going or you'll be late for work, you dreamer." I ducked just in time to avoid his grasp.

While he dressed, I pulled the blankets up around my chin and watched.

"You know, Kent, I feel sorry for poor Adam."

He dug through his middle dresser drawer, searching for a pair of gray socks. "For Adam? Why?"

"Because he must want to shout it from the rooftops that he's going to be a father. But every day he has to go to the office and act as though nothing unusual has happened in his life. I'll bet he's on cloud nine. It's too bad he can't tell anyone."

Kent bent over to tie his shoe. His voice was barely audible. "Neither can I."

Why did I always think this baby was something that involved only Adam, Margo, and myself? I kept forgetting Kent was involved as much as we were. I had begun to take his tolerance for granted, yet weeks before, the idea of a surrogate pregnancy had been outrageous to him.

He picked his gray suit coat off the end of the bed. "Want me to bring you some coffee?"

"I'm sorry."

"For what?"

"For hurting your feelings."

"You didn't. You just seem to forget that I'm facing a lot of new things, too. Sometimes it isn't easy."

"I know. Are you angry?"

"Naw. Do you want some coffee or not?"

"No, I'm still queasy. Maybe later."

Jeffrey pushed through the bedroom door. He slid between Kent's retreating legs with four books clutched against his chest. "Read me," he pleaded. I grabbed him, kissed his cheek, and hugged the top half of his little body.

"Good morning, sweetie. Come on. Hop up." I patted the edge of the bed. He threw himself across my chest for leverage while he boosted himself up. I screeched in pain and swung out in one reflexive motion, sending the books sprawling to the floor.

Jeff howled in indignation and tears streamed down his round pink cheeks.

"I'm so sorry, baby." I pulled him to me and kissed away

the wetness. "Mommy has an 'owie.' Next time jump on the end of the bed, not my chest. Okay?"

I rocked him until the sniffling subsided and didn't even try to make the little three-year-old understand how sore a woman's breasts are in the early months.

"Are you ready to read now, Jeff?" I asked. He nodded, his lower lip stuck in a pout. I reached for *The Pokey Little Puppy*, then laid my cheek on top of his corn-silk hair, smelling the sweetness of him before I pressed my lips to his temple. Forgive me, little darling, for hurting you so soon, I thought, and began to recite, almost from memory, "Five little puppies dug a hole under the fence. . . ."

Soon Jeffrey tugged at the sleeve of my bathrobe. "Mommy, me want a puppy." I looked into his dark, eager eyes and thought of the puddles, the midnight howls, the antique furniture being gnawed, and endless walks on a leash. Even in the rain. "I think that would be a very good idea. For all of us. We'll look for one this weekend."

Several days later a small collie with downy beige fur joined our family. Jeffrey had the honor of naming him Bubble Gum, or B.G., for short. We gleefully shopped for a leash, a dog dish, doggie treats, and Purina Puppy Chow, and we made an appointment with the veterinarian that cost more than the pup. B.G. was a joy to us all from the moment we brought him home. The family baby.

Chapter 8

April 1, 1980

"Is this the day Dale's coming down from Chicago to take pictures for *People*?" Kent stirred the frozen orange juice and dumped in another can of water.

I nodded and wrapped sandwiches.

"Well, I'm not going to be here, and he'd better be gone by the time I get home from work," he snapped. "We're not using our real names, are we?"

"No, Richard insisted we remain anonymous. I promised Dale we would have a name picked out by the time he got here."

"Well, I don't have time for that right now. I'll be late for work."

"Don't be such a grouch. We can do it while you eat your eggs." I pulled the telephone book from the cupboard and perched on a tall stool next to the phone.

"Pick something easy. You know I can't spell." Kent stabbed the yolk of his poached egg, and yellow seeped across his plate.

"How about five letters?" I smiled.

"Fine."

We chose the name Keyes from the phone book. I decided on Elizabeth, which was my middle name, and Kent chose David, after his favorite nephew. Later the editor of *People* magazine changed the last name to Kane, after *Citizen Kane*, a film about an impoverished family who could not raise their small son and gave him instead to a wealthy family involved in the publishing business . . .

The blue carpeting in Laura's bedroom was under a rainbow of crumpled clothing by mid-morning, until finally I reminded her that Dale had asked that she look natural and dress the way she would every day. She settled cheerfully on a pair of blue jeans and a polo shirt. I thought of the beautiful dresses and pert jumpers that hung in her closet, but when she promenaded before me, I smiled approval.

With the appeal of a Saint Bernard, Dale quickly won the hearts of the children. Their anxieties about being photographed soon vanished, and before long they seemed to forget he was in the room with us. He shot roll after roll of film. Jeff and I played with B.G. in a hammock in the family room, Julie played the piano, and all of us baked chocolate chip cookies.

Laura carried a tray of cookies, it began to slip, and before she could right it, every cookie was on the floor. Dale's camera clicked rapidly while she self-consciously cleaned up, trying to avoid the lens. B.G. found the stray crumbs, and the mishap disappeared within minutes.

Jeffrey stood on a chair in blue-striped overalls, grabbing mounds of soft dough and stuffing them into his mouth with lightning speed. I asked him several times, in my "we have company" voice, to stop eating the dough. But his child's sixth sense told him I wouldn't enforce the request with Dale behind the camera. Jeffrey's chubby fist closed over yet another mound.

I hissed at him softly. "Don't you dare. You'll spoil your dinner." He held on tightly, his little fist squeezing hard. White dough squished between each knuckle.

"Let—go—right—now!" Each word leaked slowly between my clenched teeth. Dale danced around us, snapping furiously. Jeff broke my grip, crammed a gooey palm into his mouth, then rolled the dough on the tip of his tongue while he savored the taste. His eyes met mine in triumph.

When Kent arrived home, he did his best to be polite, but irritation at seeing Dale seeped into his voice. He flatly refused Dale's request for a photograph.

"How about one from the back?" Dale persisted. "I'd really like to get a shot of your family together. Come on, Dad." He clapped Kent on the back for persuasion.

Kent put on his jacket against the cool April winds, and we walked near the low white fence that divided neighboring yards from the eighteenth green of the nearby golf course. Dale photographed us there.

When I look at those pictures today, it seems as though the children and I were walking together or touching each other in some way. Kent was removed from us. He was walking with his head bent, nearby but clearly apart from the family. My heart wrenches every time I see these photos, because I now know he felt much more left out than I realized.

In the first few days of April I quit my job. I had enjoyed selling cosmetics at the fashionable department store, and I spent the extra money on clothes for the children, Christmas gifts, and things we needed for the home. But I never seemed to have enough time for the children. There was never enough time to listen to them or to love them or to simply sit still long enough to marvel at their growth and intelligence. I knew the girls would be grown and on their own in ten years. But what memories would they have of home besides Mother walking out the front door to tend to the wants of strangers?

I watched the clock nervously and finished making supper, knowing within a few minutes I would have to explain my rather abrupt decision to Kent.

"But you have to work to make ends meet," he protested.

"Those ends aren't meeting. They're tying me in knots." I stirred the cheese sauce, keeping a careful eye on the texture. "I'm doing poorly at two jobs. I can't be a mother to three children and sell makeup to women who think a new shade of lipstick will change their lives."

"What made you decide? I don't understand what happened. You said you would work until school was out in June."

"Laura was kept after school again. For not doing thirty-five math problems last night. I wasn't here and you were reading the paper. You didn't even bother to ask her if she needed help. She said you didn't."

"I thought she was finished by the time I got home from work."

"Don't you see? My job is here. I don't like coming home at night and cleaning up a kitchen full of cold, greasy plates. I fall into bed every night too tired to watch the news."

"Why don't you ask me to help?" Kent plucked a swizzle stick from the cupboard and began stirring a manhattan.

"I shouldn't have to. If you can't see what needs to be done around here, I'm not going to beg. You live in another world anyway. A world of insurance and figures and stacks of paper. Sometimes I think the children and I just share the house with you. You don't know anything about us. When I work, it's even worse. I'm too tired to talk to you when I get home and the last thing I want is to make love."

"I've noticed."

"Good. Then maybe you'll agree that my job is here with you and the children. Those so-called luxuries I'm working for aren't worth a tinker's damn if my children are becoming strangers to me."

"I guess you're right. But we'll have to tighten our purse strings a little more." He took me securely into his arms and kissed my cheek.

"Let me tell you something you may already know." I pulled away from him. "The girls need me here every day a lot more than they need designer jeans or ballet lessons. The jeans will be gone in less than a year, but the memories of the cookies I bake will last forever."

The following weekend Laura brightened at the suggestion of a shopping trip and lunch. She dressed and scurried through her chores more quickly than I thought possible.

We planned to look for an Easter dress and for spring clothes for school. A four-inch growth spurt during her tenth year had ruled out the possibility of wearing anything from last year's wardrobe. Once at the store, she dodged in and out of the merchandise and disappeared.

"Laura, Laura," I called softly. I scanned the girls' department for her familiar blonde head, but my search ended in the adjoining baby department.

"Look at this, Mom," she called as I approached her. She held a pink ruffled dress with minute puffed sleeves. Her slender fingers lovingly touched the delicate lace on the petticoat. "Isn't it beautiful?" She seemed oblivious to my obvious impatience. "Can we buy it?" Her delicate features seemed to sparkle.

"Laura," I sighed, "you know very well we came here to look for a dress for you. There's no reason to waste our time on baby clothes. Stop that nonsense and get over here right now."

Her head hung sheepishly. "I know, but I like baby clothes."

"Well, so do I, but we don't know anyone with a baby small enough to fit into any of those things. What's the matter with you?" I scolded, dragging her back through racks of little sailor suits and Carter's sleepers into the girls' department. The dresses I had chosen for her waited in the dressing room.

She tried them on quietly, unsmiling. We soon gave up and drove home in silence without making a single purchase. Neither the baby dresses nor our failed lunch date was ever mentioned again.

Sometime during the middle of that night I awoke, jolted

by the reality of the scene as it was replayed in my memory.

She wanted to buy things for our baby. I sat up in shock, understanding why she had seemed to turn inward these past weeks. Her inability to confide in me, the long hours spent alone in her room, her lethargy at the supper table. How could I not see? Why was I so harsh with her? She was still a little girl.

Several hours later, in the early morning shadows, Laura climbed into bed next to me. She cupped her body against mine for warmth and sighed with pleasure at the closeness.

"Mom?" she whispered.

"Hmmm?" I mumbled sleepily, eyes still closed.

"It doesn't seem possible that we can spend nine months watching your baby grow and feel it kick inside of your tummy and then just give it away. I'll never get to see it."

"That's right. You won't."

"I wish we could bring it home and raise it ourselves," she sighed wistfully.

I placed my hand on her cheek while she searched my face. This sensitive child was going to be hurt the most. I'd known that I would have to contend with that sooner or later, but it was happening already.

Would Laura hurt more than I on the day I handed the baby to his new mother? I know now that she will keep the pain tucked away in her memory forever.

How could I prepare her if I was not yet prepared myself? How could I help her understand something I didn't know how to explain? Her pain was inevitable, and I ached because there were no answers at six o'clock that Sunday morning.

The producer of "The Phil Donahue Show" called from Chicago on the morning of April 7. She wanted me to appear as a guest. The next week.

"Donahue!" My hand rested lightly on the telephone in

our bedroom. I sat on the edge of the bed and stared at the faded areas on the knees of my jeans, then laughed at the irony of the situation. Years ago I had tried to get tickets to the show, but they were sold out. The disappointment clung to me for days.

I crossed the room to my dresser and stood in front of the mirror studying my blue jeans and the sweatshirt with the I'D RATHER BE FLYING logo over a soaring biplane. What would I wear? My waistline had begun to swell already. And what would I say? How on earth should I act? I can't do it, I thought. I won't. I've never traveled alone.

The children were waiting for me in the car, eager to get to the zoo. I backed out of the driveway and a new wave of fear engulfed me. What would I tell my mother?

I hit Kent with the news before he had a chance to set his briefcase on the library table in the foyer.

"Who's Phil Donahue?" He tossed his hat onto a chair.

"Good grief, he's one of the biggest talk show hosts on television today. A daytime Johnny Carson with an audience of upper middle-class women." I held out my hand for his overcoat before he could drape it across the chair.

"What did you tell them?"

"That I'd call them back. They have to know by tomorrow."

"What about your mother? Does she watch his program?" I followed Kent into the kitchen while he talked. He reached into the refrigerator, picked up a carrot stick, and snapped it in half with his front teeth.

"I'm sure she does. If she doesn't, someone else in that small town of hers would recognize me. Most of our relatives live there yet. She'd get a phone call from somebody." I threw chunks of lettuce into a dented metal colander.

"I thought you weren't going to tell her about the pregnancy."

"Don't remind me," I groaned. "It would be much easier to call back and say 'no dice.' But Phil Donahue! It's just starting to sink in, Kent."

I rested on our bed while Kent watched the evening news on television.

"What am I going to tell Mother?" I interrupted Kent.

He turned toward me. "Just call her and tell her. It's that simple."

"Are you crazy?" I sat upright, irritated by his advice. "That's not something I can drop on her over the phone."

"What would you suggest, Mary Beth?" Kent sounded impatient. "Be realistic. She's going to find out sooner or later. You might as well tell her now. You can't get through the entire pregnancy without her knowing."

"You know," I sighed, "we've spent two months trying to figure out what to tell my relatives. We've not come up with a satisfactory answer. Now I need one in the next few days."

"Would you like a glass of wine?"

"No. I feel like throwing up. Your supper's in the oven. Eat when you're hungry." I lay back on the pillow and closed my eyes while Kent listened to the twenty-four-hour collection of world woes coming from the small screen.

"Write her a letter." Kent continued to watch the screen while he made the suggestion.

"Now how on earth would I say something like that in a letter? I wouldn't know where to start."

"I'll help you this weekend. We'll send one to all our relatives and try to explain what's going on in our lives."

I puffed out my cheeks, exhaling. "Okay," I agreed. Then I sat bolt upright and clapped my hands together like cymbals. "Donahue! Donahue! Gosh damn, can you believe it?"

The next morning I decided to watch the Donahue show. I wanted to observe with a critical eye how his guests acted and how he treated them. Maybe, I thought, if I watched every day that week, I would know how to handle his quick tongue when my turn came.

I pushed aside a mountain of clean laundry, turned the wash basket upside down, and watched another load of clothes tumble onto the sofa and carpet in the family room. I switched on the television set and sat on the sofa in the small space I had cleared. The show had already started; a dark-haired woman sat on the stage. Phil Donahue strutted in front of her with his microphone and introduced her. She squirmed nervously, tugging at her skirt, and tried to assume a graceful pose on the low, carpeted cube that left her legs sprawling unattractively. I needed a new dress, and I made a mental note to shop for something with a full skirt.

My curiosity was piqued when Donahue held up a book, *The Baby Brokers* by Lynn McTaggart. The next hour was a revelation to me. McTaggart's extensive research revealed the desperate plight of infertile couples and the means they would go to in order to obtain a child. She talked of couples who pay an attorney $10,000 to find them a baby. She spoke of the risks, that the child's parents might be involved in drug or alcohol abuse, or be a product of poor nutrition and unknown hereditary factors, but the adoptive parents would never know a thing about it or what they were paying for.

She talked about abortion clinics that lied to young girls about their pregnancies being far more advanced than they actually were, making an abortion "impossible." The clinic would "find" them an attorney who in turn would collect $10,000 from an adoptive couple for the promise of a child in a few months. The unmarried mother would receive nothing, while the clinic would receive $3,000 to $4,000, and the attorney the remainder.

McTaggart told of infertile couples who were unable to adopt through a licensed agency because they were overweight, over a certain age limit, the "wrong" religion, or because they themselves were adopted and could not provide a family medical history. Some couples were turned away simply because they could not prove their infertility. I was outraged. I snapped bath towels, folding them rapidly and throwing them onto a growing pile. I rolled the socks into balls and tossed them forcefully into the wash basket.

While the show was on the air, a woman called to tell McTaggart that her teenage daughter had had a child recently and that an attorney had stood outside the high school, watching for pregnant girls. She also talked about the lack of financial aid available to pregnant teenagers who could not afford the cost of prenatal care or hospitalization. The agencies wanted the babies, but refused financial assistance to the girls who were carrying them to term. The woman said her daughter was referred to an attorney by her obstetrician. They found out later the attorney and the doctor were brothers. Now she wondered aloud if they had split the $10,000.

The program ended with McTaggart telling of a man from the East Coast who flew to Florida just before the Christmas holidays. He walked into an attorney's office, tossed $10,000 in cash onto the desk, and held out his arms for the baby the attorney was holding. There were no questions asked. When the man left with the newborn in his arms, he said, "This is a Christmas present for my wife." I had a sudden vision of a cocker spaniel puppy with a red ribbon around its neck.

My God, I thought, if this type of thing goes on daily, how could anyone object to what we were doing? How could anyone object to a man's having his own biological child?

After two weeks of mild temperatures and the sights and smells of an early spring, it was hard for me to share the children's delight at the snowstorm that surprised us when we awoke on the morning of April 14. Giant snowflakes continued to drift from the skies when we left for the airport late that afternoon. We drove slowly, and the fifteen miles to the airport seemed to take hours. Jeffrey squirmed in my lap. I held him tightly, wishing I didn't have to leave him on his birthday.

"Did you call the airport to see if they canceled your flight?" Kent squinted through the windshield into the blinding white that stretched over the narrow roads, farm fields, and ditches, smoothing everything into infinity.

"No, why should I?" I puzzled. "Don't they call you if they cancel a flight?"

"Are you kidding?" Kent took his eyes off the road for a brief moment and looked at me as though I had gone mad. "No!" he shouted. "Jeez, Mary Beth." He shook his head from side to side. "Sometimes."

"Well, how was I supposed to know?" The car hummed over the snow-packed road, filling the heavy silence.

Finally I said, "Kent, listen. I have to ask you something. After I get to the airport—"

"Yeah?" He leaned over the steering wheel. A passing car threw a white screen of snow in front of us.

"The one in Chicago—"

"Yeah? Yeah?"

"How do I get to the hotel?"

"Isn't somebody from the Donahue show going to be there to meet you?"

"I don't think so. Nobody said anything about it."

"Well, then, just follow the signs inside the airport. Around the area where you get your baggage, there usually are phones for all the hotels. Just call the Hyatt and they'll send a van or something to pick you up."

"What if they don't?"

"For God's sake! Then call a cab."

"How?"

"Oh, Mary Beth," he sighed. "Just ask one of the porters,

or one of those guys in uniforms. They're always standing around the baggage area. Just ask anyone. Don't worry about it. There's always a line of cabs at O'Hare."

We rode in silence for the next five miles while I clutched Jeffrey against my chest. I was ashamed to admit to Kent how terrified I was to travel alone or to stay in a hotel room by myself. I longed to stay in the security of my own home on that cold wintry night.

I did not want to take those first independent steps. Who would be there to catch me if I fell?

Kent was right. The Hyatt Hotel did have a telephone at the airport. A bus magically appeared and dropped me off at the door. I stood in the lobby gawking like a tourist at the glass elevators, lush plants, and lavish furnishings. I cataloged every detail to recite for the children the next day.

Richard and his wife Pam, as well as Katie and Karen, would be arriving much later—we had planned to meet for breakfast in the morning. I was shown to a large, plush room with a king-size bed. I switched on the television for company and double-bolted the door against intruders.

I awoke at dawn with an excruciating pain tearing through the left side of my face. The sinus infection that had started the day before had worsened during the night, and the thought of enduring the hammering while facing Donahue and a television camera set off a new alarm.

The fine print in the legal contract I had signed on March 2 swam before me: "No non-prescription medication or prescribed medications without the written consent of Richard M. Levin, M.D."

I dialed Richard's room. "He's in the shower," Pam offered kindly, and suggested Tylenol from the gift shop. "We'll meet you for breakfast in an hour."

At the appointed time I went to Richard and Pam's room. Richard opened the door.

"You look wonderful, you old pregnant lady." I hadn't seen him since February sixth, during the initial interviews, but it seemed like only a week.

"I might be old and pregnant but I feel rotten."

"Did you get your Tylenol?"

"Naw. I'll survive. I hate to take anything at this stage of the pregnancy."

"Will you be all right?" An eyebrow rose in concern.

"Yes. But hurry up or we'll miss breakfast. I'm famished."

Richard hurried to the mirror. "There's a darling couple here from the West Coast. Pam's already down with them. I want you to meet them before the show." He slipped into a dark suit-coat, picked a hairbrush off the dresser, and examined his perfectly groomed dark hair. "They should be having breakfast with us."

"Not if you don't stop primping, for heaven's sake. I haven't seen you for months but you sure haven't changed," I teased. "Come on." I grabbed his arm and pulled him toward the door. He leaned back to catch one last glimpse of himself.

We sat in the crowded dining room at a large rectangular table cluttered with food. The infertile couple, Jane and Scott, sat across from me and talked openly about their infertility. Jane nibbled a sweet roll and asked me one question after another about surrogate motherhood and my pregnancy.

Scott watched me while we talked, eager with anticipation at their new adventure into parenthood. They spilled over with hopes and dreams for a baby of their own and expressed gratitude at my selflessness in this pregnancy. Their admiration for my motives made me warm with embarrassment, but I soon forgot to feel uncomfortable and felt a kinship for them I could not explain. Their eyes gleamed with new hope at finally finding the answer to years of prayer and seemingly futile searching for a way to become parents. Surrogate motherhood seemed to be their last chance.

An hour later we stood in a small conference room in a

television studio on the outskirts of Chicago. A short, heavyset woman with a severe, unbecoming hairstyle asked us to sign release forms, which would give the Donahue show permission to rerun the program as often as they wanted. She left and returned with a large tray of snacks and beverages.

The tiny conference room was packed as we waited anxiously for eleven o'clock. I whispered to Jane, "Come on. I'd better go to the bathroom again."

Katie Brophy stood at the mirror in the ladies' room applying another layer of mascara to her long lashes. We had spoken only briefly at breakfast. The friction between us remained and was evident in each word.

"Listen, E.K." Katie spoke first.

"Listen *what?*"

"E.K.," she said matter-of-factly, "short for Elizabeth Kane."

"Katie," I laughed good-naturedly, "I am *not* Elizabeth Kane."

"You are today and don't you forget it. You'll have to remember to answer to that name all day." She scowled a warning in the mirror.

My only answer to her was the silent application of my lip gloss.

"Listen," she continued, "if anything comes up about your being paid to do this, don't tell anyone how much you're getting."

I turned toward her with visible annoyance and snapped, "Why not? What am I supposed to do? Lie?"

"No, of course not. It's just nobody's business."

"Katie, have you forgotten that *People* magazine hit the newsstands last week and Sarah printed the figure for all the world to see? She had promised us she wouldn't mention the money, but it seemed to be the most important part of her story." I snarled my disillusionment with reporters.

"Yeah, I know."

"Well, then, what's to hide?"

"Don't argue with me, Mary Beth. Just remember what I told you." She tucked her hairbrush into her purse, which she zipped with finality. When she wheeled past me toward the door, I spoke to her back. "It probably won't even come up. Don't worry about it."

Richard slouched in a straight-backed chair in the conference room, his legs stretched in front of him. He was admiring his new cowboy boots recently purchased at a fertility conference in Houston.

"When did you have that last blood test done for the pregnancy?" Richard was looking at me, chewing thoughtfully on his pipe.

"The one at the hospital? April first. Why?"

"It's just unusually high for such an early stage of pregnancy."

"What does that mean?"

"Nothing, yet. It's just that sometimes when the hormone level is that high, there's a possibility of twins. I'll want you to repeat it again in a few weeks."

"Twins, Richard?" I asked flatly, not believing him. "Ha-ha. You're funny."

"Wouldn't that be nice?" He grinned wickedly, emphasizing each word.

I shot him a long, glaring look. "For whom?"

The door to the conference room burst open with a rush of cooler air, and Phil Donahue stood in the doorway, a gray suit jacket draped casually over his right shoulder.

"How many of you are here for the show today as guests?" he asked. We raised our hands like obedient second graders.

"I would like everyone here who is not going to be a guest on the show to leave the conference room. There's a lady outside who will show you where to sit in the audience. We have some special seats reserved for you in the front row." He smoothly ushered Pam, Karen, and Katie's boyfriend, Charlie, to the door.

My tongue felt thick and foreign. How many times had I seen Donahue host his show? Interrogating guests, cutting them to shreds when he disagreed, smiling warmly when he seemed to take their side. But he was always cunning and clever, every second of every minute of the entire hour. Here he was standing five feet from me, talking and looking exactly the same as he did when I watched his show from my family room.

Jane leaned toward me, looking pale. "I don't think I can go through with this." She squeezed my hand.

"Just tell them everything you told me at breakfast and the audience will love you."

"I hope so," she smiled nervously.

"Now." Donahue slipped into his coat-suit, buttoned it, and stood before us as a stern professor before his class. "I want to remind you all of one thing. You are not the show."

He ignored our startled glances and continued. "There are two hundred thirty people in the audience today. *They* are the show. They can react any way they want to. They can say anything they want to. Without them we wouldn't have a 'Phil Donahue Show.' Some of the people out there have been waiting for over two years to get tickets to my show, so let's give them a good one.

"Now let's get your names straight. I understand some of you have stage names to protect your identity, am I right?" We nodded in unison. "I will remind the audience you have the right to remain anonymous and will ask them to respect those wishes and not ask anything that would reveal your identities."

He continued, "We have just about two minutes, but I want to remind all of you that you will be nervous for the first segment and then the rest of the hour will fly by."

A groan floated through the room and Jane squeezed my hand again.

"Don't forget," Donahue added, "with all the commercials and breaks, the airtime is actually very short."

A producer opened the door slightly, stuck her head through the opening, and warned, "Phil, the yellow light is on."

"Let's go," he shot tersely over his shoulder. We followed him along a maze of hallways until he slid through some double doors with a flashing red light above them. I glanced up at the ON THE AIR sign and gasped. We stood just inside the door at the back of the studio and could hear Donahue warming up the audience with jokes and light conversation. He motioned for us to stay where we were. I craned my neck and saw row after row of spotlights mounted on the ceiling. The studio looked much smaller than it had on my television screen at home. I recognized the backdrop of tropical plants and carpeted cubes on the stage and felt a catch in my throat. The cubes we would be sitting on were only three feet from the audience.

I'm not ready for this, I thought. Why am I here? What will I say? My mind reeled dizzily while I tried to comprehend the reality of appearing on a national talk show. Suddenly Kent's teasing me on the ride to the airport about baptism under fire took on a new meaning.

"Let's give our guests a big hand as they come up front." Donahue's voice sounded far away. I saw him motion to us. Did he mean me? I remained planted and felt Richard's hand press against my lower back. The sound of applause filled my head and I felt myself move woodenly toward the stage. Someone came out of the haze and told me to sit in the center. Obediently I bent my body and sank awkwardly onto the cushion.

"Thirty seconds," a voice echoed off the studio walls. Richard sucked casually on his pipe, watching the audience watch us. I leaned toward him and whispered, "I'm going to throw up."

He smiled sweetly at the audience, never taking his eyes from them and hissed at me, pipe still clenched in his teeth, "Don't you dare." When he turned toward me, he gazed deeply into my eyes. I inhaled slowly, fighting the nausea.

"Fifteen seconds."

Donahue stood in the audience with a microphone held loosely in his left hand. "I have to go potty," he whined and began to shuffle cross-legged down the aisle. The audience responded with a roar of laughter, and the tension lifted like a curtain.

He took his place inches from me, grinning slyly. The boyish face didn't quite belong with the wiry gray hair and beautifully tailored three-piece suit. *King of the Talk Shows. Donahue the Great.* He leaned toward me, seconds before the red light went on and the cameras came to life. His icy blue eyes sliced through my fear as he introduced me to the audience, and before long, in a voice like my grandmother's chocolate fudge, he was asking, "I understand that you're being paid ten thousand dollars to have this baby, Mrs. Kane. Is that true?"

I sat stiffly, responding with one or two words to the continued probing. I wanted to sound intelligent and articulate. I wanted the audience to approve of my pregnancy. I was on trial and they were the jury. It was important they approved of my actions. But my monosyllabic answers continued, and Donahue supplied the audience with basic information I should have been able to give. "Yes." "Nope." "Right, right," and a quick jerk of my head to acknowledge the accuracy of his statements was the most I was capable of at the moment. When he groped for further details, I was unable to tell him what the audience wanted to know. Thousands of words lay on my tongue, and I could not shake them loose.

Eventually he surrendered to my diffidence and turned to Doctor Levin and Attorney Brophy for answers to the mystery surrounding this new concept in parenting.

Somehow I had convinced myself, foolishly perhaps, that Donahue would understand immediately the altruism involved in the surrogate arrangement. Instead he seemed to be settling on his prey like a vulture.

In a slow, soothing drawl, Richard explained how the fee was a compensation rather than a payment. He said that the surrogate was involving herself mentally and physically for almost a year and sometimes longer while the inseminations, pregnancy, and healing process were taking place. He explained his objective of reimbursing each surrogate for her time and to balance the fact that she would relinquish the child. "If she's doing it for nothing, there might not be a reason for her to sign the termination papers when the time comes," he said. He leaned back and sucked on his unlit pipe, looking pleased with himself as the audience murmured their understanding. I glanced at the sea of faces and did not see the rejection I had expected, but intelligent attentiveness to a possible breakthrough for infertile couples. They were trying to learn and understand.

"Is Kentucky the only state that allows this kind of legal freedom?" Donahue asked, and we all turned our attention to Katie, who sat next to me on my left.

Her drawl was even more pronounced than Richard's, and even though her voice was soft, her tone was strong and confident. I envied her poise. "Yes, it is. As far as I know, but I have not had reason to research all fifty states. I know it is illegal in Alabama, Michigan, New York, California."

"But however ironclad your contract, you have to leave the door open for that human emotional factor," Donahue warned.

"I realize that," Katie answered sweetly. "That is why we

have chosen a surrogate who would not change her mind."

"So you think Elizabeth Kane is an unusually attractive candidate for this kind of thing, isn't she?"

"That's right," Katie beamed as she turned toward me. Wedged between Katie and Richard, knowing how important the success of this project was to them, I felt momentarily like the prize heifer at the county fair. When the audience tittered, I had no idea if it was nervous laughter or if they thought the entire concept sounded insane.

Donahue turned his attention to Scott and Jane, the couple I had met at breakfast, and began a steady dissection of their infertility problems. When he disclosed that Jane had developed an infection while wearing an intrauterine device, and that they'd received an out-of-court settlement of $125,000 from the manufacturer, I tensed. But when Donahue admitted this was none of his business, the audience roared. Did they find this digging into such private affairs amusing?

Jane revealed she had conceived and lost a baby through a miscarriage the previous summer, and Donahue clucked with sympathy at her loss. "So you flirted with success and now you've got all your baby meters running again," he said callously. That last comment blew away any notion I might have had that he understood. Only for a fraction of a moment—or less—had he seemed human. I was still terrified of what was in store for me.

She continued, "It's been fascinating for me to meet Elizabeth. I was really nervous about meeting her this morning and had no idea what to expect. But she's quelled my fears with her warmth and dedication. I'm impressed. And I'm confident that by agreeing not to abuse herself with alcohol or drugs or cigarettes, she's doing her share to have a healthy child."

The sinus infection invaded the left side of my face, and without thinking I blurted, "Yeah, I can't even take an aspirin for a headache."

The sympathetic laughter from the audience rippled toward the stage and boosted my confidence. My words finally began to unravel in an articulate, fluid stream. I explained my side of the story. How I had seen the news articles about Attorney Brophy's looking for a surrogate, how I had written to her the same day and waited an endless six weeks until Dr. Levin called to ask if I was still interested. I revealed my failure to inform Kent during that six-week period. There was a chuckle from the audience in appreciation of my reticence.

Donahue propped one foot jauntily on the stage and leaned toward me, smiling. I looked at him wide-eyed. "Well, how do you tell your husband you want to have another man's baby?"

He shrugged with exaggerated motion and mimicked a dumbfounded expression. "I don't know. I have no idea," he said, and shook his head slowly.

I was no longer aware of the monstrous eye of the camera fixed on my face, and I looked into Donahue's eyes as though we were the only two people in the studio. "Do you know what?" I quipped. "I didn't either." I matched his muddled expression and the audience roared.

I had known from the very beginning, even before I had my first interviews with Dr. Levin, that I would be swimming in an uncharted ocean of emotional and legal turmoil. What I could not have known, when I revealed my feelings and motives to the American public for the first time over live television, was whether the audience I faced would be bloodthirsty or receptive. I was glad to find the latter.

The remainder of the show passed as quickly as Donahue said it would. The audience waved their hands, and the telephone lines buzzed continuously with questions about the legalities, the morality of it all, my feelings about the unborn child. They asked about paternity testing, genetic counseling, and so on. The questions were well thought out, intelligent, and logical. There was no undertone of hostility or anger, no accusation of "selling babies" that I would hear from audiences later in the pregnancy.

Suddenly the familiar "Donahue" theme song began to bounce off the studio walls, signaling that the hour had passed. The audience surrounded me, continuing to ask the questions they hadn't had time to ask during the program. Donahue disappeared after thanking me warmly, and a member of his staff grabbed my arm and pulled me backstage through an open doorway toward a waiting taxi. A reporter from the *Chicago Tribune* followed me through the studio into the cool spring air, jotting rapidly on a small notepad while I talked to the women from the audience waiting outside. As I ducked into the taxi, a well-groomed, attractive woman in her early forties asked if I would be taking a Lamaze course to prepare for the birth. The taxi was ready to leave and I answered quickly, "I don't see any reason to. I have babies so easily, they just pop right out."

Imagine my chagrin when I read that quote in the *Tribune* the next morning. And for weeks and months to follow, any paper or magazine that picked up the story of Elizabeth Kane seemed to headline: SURROGATE MOTHER'S BABIES POP RIGHT OUT. The one time I should have remained tongue-tied, I did not.

Phil Donahue had been wrong about one thing. I did not receive $10,000. I received $11,500 plus $500 reimbursement for our attorney's fees.

When I originally volunteered to become a surrogate mother, I was unaware that any fee was involved. The money itself was never important to me. In fact, if the parents had experienced financial difficulties, I would have forfeited the fee willingly. I had mentioned this to Richard on several occasions, but each time he would reassure me that the couple was financially stable.

I was not paid for any magazine or newspaper interviews nor was I paid for appearing on any television programs during the pregnancy. In fact, a large percentage of the time I paid all my own expenses for airfare, hotel accommodations, and meals, only to be reimbursed by the television station after submitting receipts and expense reports. This often would take eight to twelve weeks. At one time we had almost $2,000 due us from various networks, with bills of our own long overdue.

I had a moderately extensive maternity wardrobe purchased mostly for the traveling and publicity I was doing. My telephone bills were enormous each month because of the calls to Louisville, and Uncle Sam relieved me of forty percent of my earnings in 1981. There was little left to put aside for the children's college fund.

I had planned to fly directly home after the taping of the Donahue show. Against my better judgment and despite the sinus infection, I stayed in Chicago for an interview with "ABC World News Tonight."

"We'll do it early and you can be in bed by eight-thirty tonight," Richard had pleaded. His brown eyes melted my resistance and I agreed. "Tell Kent to pick you up at the airport tomorrow. It's just one more night."

The interview was postponed several hours, but we finally finished taping at ten o'clock that night. The evening ended in the elegant dining room at the Hyatt Hotel, where I was surrounded by more delectable food than I had ever seen at one time. Tuxedoed waiters bobbed back and forth with cocktails and trays of hors d'oeuvres for our party of nine. Bottle after bottle of exorbitantly priced wine was consumed, and it was all paid for by ABC.

I dipped my spoon into the onion soup I had ordered and played with the blanket of cheese on top. Without warning, the normal clatter and conversation in the large, crowded restaurant became an unbearable roar in my ears, an incessant pounding.

I stood abruptly, laid my linen napkin next to the full bowl of soup, and reached for my leather clutch bag.

"Rich, I have to go to bed." The din at our table ceased instantly.

"What about dinner? You've got lobster coming!"

I waved the question away with my hand. "Cancel it. I'm too tired to eat."

"You old bag," Richard teased, smiling at me.

"I know," I grinned at the pet name. "I'm sorry. But if I weren't pregnant, I wouldn't be so tired. Good night, Rich." I bent to kiss his cheek and hurried toward the elevator, overcome with relief at the blessed silence in the hallway.

My eyes traveled around my richly decorated hotel room, and I lay there thinking about the last thing I had said to Richard: "If I weren't pregnant, I wouldn't be so tired."

Silly girl, I thought. If you weren't pregnant, you wouldn't be here in this elegant room. You wouldn't have put in a fifteen-hour day. Or done interviews for two newspapers. Or been on "The Phil Donahue Show" or "ABC World News Tonight." You'd be home in bed where you belong, taking medication for your sinus infection. Just a normal person like you were two months ago.

I lay on the soft mattress feeling every aching muscle and racked nerve. My hand slid absentmindedly over my lower abdomen to ease away the queasiness. My fingertips pushed into the soft skin over the smooth, round bulge: a uterus that even a doctor shouldn't have been able to feel for another four weeks in a normal pregnancy—with a single fetus!

Gently I probed the outside of my lower abdomen, again and again, to convince myself that a multiple birth was impossible. There weren't any twins in my family. But what about Adam's? I didn't know. I just didn't know anything about the father of this child.

The following morning Kent met me at the airport, anxiously waiting for me to tell him every detail. Silently I handed him the *Chicago Tribune* with a large article on the second page. A picture of me in my new dress smiled back at him with the name "Elizabeth Kane" printed underneath.

It was too outlandish to warrant much of my attention. Too glamorous for a housewife whose immediate concerns were three children, a new puppy that left a trail of puddles, and a kitchen floor that wouldn't stay clean.

Chapter 9

The morning after my return from Chicago I sat at the cluttered kitchen table, pulled my woolly bathrobe tight around me, and slouched further into the hard wooden chair.

"I would give anything for two aspirin right now," I said to the box of cereal in front of me.

Laura rounded the corner. "Mom, can I borrow your new beige sweater?"

"No, it's much too big for you."

"But I love it. It looks so good with my blonde hair."

Her smile won me over. "All right. For heaven's sake, look at that clock. I don't care what you wear, but hurry up."

"Thanks." She bent to brush my cheek with her lips and pounded up the stairs toward my bedroom.

The next ten minutes were a mad scramble to help the girls find money for their lunch milk. When the front door slammed behind them, Jeffrey awoke and began to cry loudly. I cursed silently at not having had the wisdom to take a steaming shower while he slept. As I bounded up the stairs, the telephone began to ring. I bent to kiss Jeff's forehead while I reached for the phone. He was burning with fever.

I recognized Karen's drawl immediately. "Hi. Can y'all come to Louisville today to do an interview for CBS?"

"I hope you're kidding, Karen." I held Jeffrey in my arms, stroking his hair.

"Dr. Levin said he'd like you to be here today."

"Karen, I can't! I'm still in my bathrobe, Jeff's sick, and the house is still a mess from the two days I spent in Chicago. Besides, there's nothing left in my closet that would possibly fit me. And how on earth could I get to the airport on time when the plane leaves ninety minutes from now? I don't want to. I can't," I insisted.

Richard's voice broke in from another line. "We need you, E.K. The press loves you!" I heard him chuckle. "Come on down and do it for us." I visualized his engaging, crooked smile.

"What on earth do they want?" I snapped, worried about Jeff's crying.

"They want to do a spot for their nightly news program. It's a national thing. Come on," he pleaded, "it'll be fun."

"I'll call you back," I sighed, hoping Kent would say no.

I quickly dialed Kent at the office, and he encouraged me to go ahead. Then I called Caryl, asking frantically for help getting ready and a ride to the airport twenty-five minutes away. "I'll call in sick at work. See you in ten minutes," she promised, calming my fears about missing the flight.

Our sitter agreed to take Jeff to the doctor, and while I rapidly gave her instructions over the phone, Caryl's van roared to a stop in the driveway. She came through the front door without knocking, tossed her coat onto a chair, and set Matthew on another, while she bent to tie his shoe. "Where do you want me to start?"

"Tell me what you told your boss."

"I told him I was sick to my stomach. Betcha he thinks I'm pregnant again." Her hearty laugh rolled through the living room and I joined her, forgetting the clock for a moment. She vacuumed the house, canceled B.G.'s appointment with the vet, made an appointment for Jeff with the doctor, and drove to the store for groceries.

The scrambled eggs she had made were propped on the edge of the bathroom sink, and I shoveled them into my mouth while I curled my hair. I scratched a note to the pharmacist to fill Jeff's prescription, gave it to the sitter as she walked in, scooped up a pair of black heels, and headed for the front door. I bent to kiss Jeffrey's warm, wet cheek. "Bye, precious. I'll be home in time to put you to bed tonight." He clung to me, trying to smile through his tears. I kissed him again. "I promise I'll tuck you in tonight. Be a good boy for the doctor." I ran on tiptoe in stocking feet to the van and waved goodbye to Jeff while his lower lip quivered bravely.

Caryl sped us down the street while I slouched in my seat. What was I doing flying to Louisville when I should be home with my sick child? Why should I be more concerned about doing publicity for Richard Levin? What was the matter with me? Someday I'd have to learn to say no to that man whether he likes it or not.

Caryl watched me out of the corner of her eye as she sped down the freeway. "What's the matter?"

"Nothing."

"Tell me."

I sighed. "I just feel lousy about leaving Jeff when he's sick."

"Then why did you? You could have told Dr. Levin you'd come another day."

"No, I couldn't. CBS wanted to do it today. They're worried about their deadline. Good grief. Do you know we were scheduled to appear on "Good Morning America" yesterday, and when they found out we were doing "Donahue" first, they canceled our interview? I'm telling you, Caryl, those people are competitive." I peeled a banana and bit off the end. "Besides, I can't say no to him. He's so persuasive."

Caryl threw me a sidelong glance and grinned impishly. "And good-looking."

"I guess," I shrugged.

"You guess?"

"All right. You win. He *is* good-looking. But you have to admit, it is flattering. How many midwestern housewives do you know who are flying somewhere today to appear on national television?"

"Only one." She smiled knowingly as I jumped from the van to hurry to the airport ticket counter.

Richard was right. It was fun. I didn't even mind gulping cold hamburgers and two cartons of warm milk between interviews he had arranged for me. It was flattering to know a reporter was waiting to scribble my every word on his pad while I explored my feelings aloud about this new venture. A day later my innermost thoughts would be printed in major newspapers or quoted on radio stations. Was the issue so important that the media should be in such a mad rush to get my story? My naïveté was stunning.

Later that night, after I had returned home, I tucked the children into bed and kissed them good night. Jeff had already started taking an antibiotic, and I was relieved, knowing he would be better in the morning. Kent lay in bed watching the news and looked up when I pushed the bedroom door open. "Got the kids tucked in?"

"Finally. The girls had so many things to tell me about school. I was so tired I hardly listened to them."

"Did you fix yourself something to eat?" He watched me unbutton my new maternity top. I had worn it reluctantly, but seeing me in the maternity clothes had seemed to delight Richard when I arrived in Louisville.

"No, I'm too tired to eat. All I want to do is go to bed."

"Jump right in," Kent patted the blanket next to him, leering at my bare chest.

"Whatever you've got on your mind, mister, change it!"

Even though my tone was teasing, he knew I meant it.

"Heck, it was worth a try," he shot back good-naturedly, then wolf-whistled when my nightgown slipped over my head and slid to my ankles.

"Do you ever think of anything else? Now do you want to hear about my trip or not?" I slid under the blankets, stretched out my legs, and let the softness surround me while I took delight in the sheer comfort of being able to lie down.

Kent propped himself up on one elbow to talk to me. "Who interviewed you? Anyone I'd recognize?" he asked eagerly.

"I don't even remember his name, but we've seen him on the news. He was really considerate, Kent. I've always imagined people who work for the press to be only half human, since they're exposed to so much in a given week. I was really expecting them to object to my pregnancy and give me hell on the air, but everyone so far has been encouraging and objective rather than critical."

"Ah, those guys have seen everything, Mary Beth. They have to be open-minded. I don't think you'll ever have any trouble with the press." He took an oatmeal cookie from the plate beside him, shoved it into his mouth, and washed it down with a noisy gulp of milk.

"The thing that simply astounds me is that in the past few days, I'll bet at least a dozen cameramen, crew members, and news commentators have taken me aside to talk about their own infertility problems."

"Really?" Kent gave me an incredulous look.

"Yeah, they have. You know, infertility isn't exactly cocktail party talk, but as soon as anyone finds out the details of my pregnancy, they feel free to tell me the most intimate and sometimes embarrassing details of their lives."

I reached for a cookie and Kent kidded me about getting crumbs on the sheets. "I'll brush them over to your side," I promised and began to spray the air with cookie crumbs from my lap. Then I sobered and continued. "I wish you could have been there, Kent. The man who interviewed me took me aside later and told me how badly he and his wife want a child and what they've been through trying to have one. You should have seen the pain in his eyes. Here's a man with a good job, making more money than we'll ever have. But the one thing he wants the most can't be bought. His wife can't get pregnant, they're both in their thirties already, and he's worried sick. It was obvious he's been to hell and back. He actually seemed relieved to be able to talk to me about his problems. You know, it makes me realize even more how important it is for me to publicize surrogate motherhood. Wouldn't it be wonderful if more women decided to do this after seeing me talk about it on the news and on 'Donahue'?"

Kent shook his head. "Somehow I can't see more than a handful of husbands agreeing to it."

"Maybe not today, Kent. But I'll bet if Richard and I keep talking about it, surrogate parenting will be a household word in a few years."

Kent brushed crumbs from his side of the blanket onto the floor. "I doubt there'll be much more publicity. You've done all the major networks plus 'Donahue.' "

"Hartman! You forgot we haven't done David Hartman. I adore that man. He's gorgeous!"

Kent laughed. "Maybe you'll get your big chance someday and 'Good Morning America' will call you again."

"I hope so. But I agree, I think the publicity is over until the baby is born. Then there will be a flurry for a few days and that'll be it. Now I'm going to sleep. In the past three days I've had four flights, four television shows, one radio show, and three newspaper interviews. It was fun, but I'm beat." I slid down under the blankets.

Kent reached up to turn out the light. "With all the

publicity you've been doing, you should be hearing from your mother soon."

I groaned in reply and pulled the blankets over my head to shut out the thought.

The warming rays of a spring sun coaxed tiny green tulip spears from the earth. Jeffrey and I walked through the neighborhood each afternoon watching every day bring more and more growth and deeper tones of green, then color and soft blossoms.

My body was changing, too. A tiny human being was miraculously being formed—for another woman. She was still slim and physically active, while I grew heavy with her child. There were times I resented her.

Days were full of ups and downs. Just the sight and smell of food was so unappealing to me that fixing meals for the kids became an ordeal. I hated and loved my symptoms, yet the conflicting feelings confused me. Was it normal to hate the pain and illness but love what it represented? Did other pregnant women alternately love and hate their bodies within fifteen minutes?

Then I would think of the faceless parents waiting for this child, and be filled with awe and wonderment at the gift of life I was able to give them. I would glance in the mirror, suddenly proud of my growing silhouette.

Within several days of the "Donahue" taping, both of the newspapers in our area had reprinted the article from the *Chicago Tribune*. I waited for repercussions and wondered about the nature of the phone calls I would receive when my photograph was recognized. But there were no calls.

The day after the photograph appeared, Kent came home from work grinning like a kid who had just hit his first home run. He had run into a fellow worker who had been transferred to another part of the large insurance building.

Jim was a young bachelor, a blond, attractive athlete who

was eternally optimistic. I remembered him the moment Kent mentioned his name.

Kent leaned against the refrigerator while I checked the beef roast and made gravy, and he proceeded to recount his conversation with Jim that afternoon.

Jim had been excited about seeing me in the newspaper, though Kent denied it was my photograph. He claimed he hadn't seen that paper because we didn't subscribe to it. He lied.

Jim insisted it was my picture with the name "Elizabeth Kane" underneath, and he maintained that, if it wasn't me, it was a woman who could be my twin. Kent grinned as he told how he had to suppress a chuckle while refuting that claim. Finally Jim had become embarrassed and begun to mutter that he might have been mistaken. When Kent changed the subject, the newspaper article was not mentioned again.

"Did he ever get right to the point and just ask you if I was a surrogate mother?" I asked. I counted potatoes and dumped them into the sink to scrub their skins.

"Nope. And I never offered any information. You know, I wondered how long it would take before somebody at work said something."

I looked steadily at him. I didn't comment; I just dug through the kitchen drawer and searched for a potato peeler.

"You know, I think I'm making progress," Kent confided. "I've gotten to the point where I don't worry anymore about what people think about your pregnancy. I figure if they don't like it, it's too bad. The thought of discussing it with people doesn't bother me anymore."

Baloney! If he really felt that way, he wouldn't have gone to such great lengths to avoid the subject with his coworker. Jim was a friend of his and would have understood. I wondered how the publicity would affect Kent after the Donahue show aired in our area the next week.

April 23, 1980

I waited expectantly in the stark, tiny office, anxious for my pregnancy to be checked by a physician. I had been waiting impatiently for several weeks for my first prenatal examination.

The door swung open and a stooped, middle-aged man entered the room. His graying hair gave him a tired, sad appearance. Dr. Kasten held my chart in his hand for a moment, studying the medical information recorded by his nurse.

He looked up with a smile. "Well, this is one baby that obviously was not planned for." I felt he was referring to my age.

I suddenly had a flashback to the careful calculations involved in the conception—the daily temperature taking, the circus of the insemination day—and I bit the inside of my cheek to stifle a snicker.

"On the contrary, Doctor. We planned very carefully for this baby."

Dr. Kasten cleared his throat hoarsely and looked at the floor. "Well, then, I guess you're very happy about it."

He sat on a small swivel stool next to a tiny desk attached to the wall and became engrossed in recording a history of my previous pregnancies. Richard's voice rang in my ears: "Don't say anything about being a surrogate until the fifth or sixth month when it's time for you to decide on a hospital, breast-feeding, things like that," he had advised.

"Pardon me?" I snapped back to the present.

"How do your children feel about having a new brother or sister?"

"Ummm, they're pretty happy about it, I guess." Had he noticed my hesitation?

"Do you plan to use Lamaze?"

"I don't know; should I? I mean, I never did before with my other babies when they were born in Wisconsin. I just sort of have them."

A corner of his mouth turned up. "I think it would be a good idea to be prepared. You're not as young as you used to be, you know."

"I'm not that old." I straightened defensively and the paper gown crinkled under me.

"I know. It's just that at your age, your muscles don't have the strength they had even five years ago. It would be a good idea to take classes. They offer them at Pekin Memorial Hospital near your home."

I felt his gaze and met it. "You *are* going to have your baby at Pekin Memorial Hospital, aren't you?" Dr. Kasten asked politely. "I mean, I no longer practice at Saint Francis. Were you aware of that?"

"Ummm, yeah. Yeah, I was. I'm sorry. I was thinking about something else. Sure, that'll be fine."

"Are you all right?" He craned forward and peered at me over his glasses.

"I'm fine." I sighed heavily. "Just nervous, I guess. I hate pelvic exams."

He watched me, waiting. I shifted my weight from one side to another and the paper crinkled loudly under my legs. The scratchy music that hummed through the intercom did little to break the awkwardness that had seeped into our conversation.

Dr. Kasten examined me in silence. I slid out of the metal stirrups and resumed a sitting position on the vinyl examining table.

"Well?" I asked finally.

"Everything looks good. You should deliver about—when did you say you had your last period?"

"February seventeenth. I conceived on March second."

He half smiled. "Are you sure of that?"

"Absolutely."

"Well, then, it looks like it will be about—"

"November twenty-sixth!" I shouted. "A Thanksgiving baby!"

He chuckled and washed his hands while we talked loudly above the noise of sloshing water.

"How does your husband feel about this baby?" He ripped a paper towel from the holder, patted his hands dry, and tossed the crumpled paper into a silver can near the sink.

"Fine. He's not surprised." I squirmed and tried to rewrap the paper gown around my bare back.

"Hmmm. Okay." Dr. Kasten peered at me closely. "I understand you breast-fed your other three children?"

"That's right. In fact, Jeffrey until he was two years old."

He raised an eyebrow and I rushed to explain. "It wasn't my idea. I just couldn't get him weaned. He loved nursing. But after reading *A Tree Grows in Brooklyn*, I decided to use the old Tabasco sauce trick. I'm no artist, so I put one drop on each nipple and it did the job. Weaned in a night." I slapped my thigh in triumph.

"That was a dirty trick," he grinned broadly. "But then it's safe to assume you're going to nurse this baby, too." He began to scribble a notation.

"No, no," I blurted without thinking. "I can't."

His brows almost overlapped. "If you nursed your other three children, I don't see any reason why you can't nurse this child. That is—if you want to."

I rubbed my palms up and down the paper gown and inhaled deeply. He watched and waited.

"Look, Dr. Kasten. Ummm—this isn't my baby."

His eyes bulged until he looked like the frog Julie had found in our garden days before.

"I mean," I continued, "it *is* my baby. But it isn't really. I'm having it for someone else."

His lower lip dropped and I continued to explain. "Have you read *People* magazine or seen the Donahue show this week? Or some of the evening news programs?"

"I've never seen the Donahue show. I'm at the hospital in the mornings," he stated dryly.

"Oh. Well, you see, there's this couple in Kentucky who can't have children, so I decided to have one for them." I smiled expectantly. "Actually, this isn't my husband's baby either."

The frog eyes widened.

"Well, I mean—I didn't have an affair or anything like that. It was artificial insemination. Have you ever heard of Dr. Richard Levin from Louisville?" I asked eagerly.

The shake of his head was barely perceptible.

"Oh. Well, he's a fertility specialist with a large private practice. One of his patients has been infertile for years, and she asked him to find a surrogate mother for her because she and her husband would have to wait years to adopt a baby. And by then their age would disqualify them. I was inseminated on March second, got pregnant, and the parents of the baby are so excited, they're already filling the nursery. Isn't it wonderful?" The entire story had come out in one long breath.

Dr. Kasten's complexion had turned ashen. He leaned forward in his chair, scrutinizing me. When he inhaled sharply, my enthusiasm began to dissolve. Suddenly I felt naked and exposed in the thin paper gown. I wriggled again, and the paper crackled with a vengeance.

"Are you shocked?" I finally asked him.

He opened his mouth as if to speak, but there was no sound. He cleared his throat harshly, then replied in a thin, dry voice, "Yes. You have to admit, what you're doing is a bit unusual."

I smiled slightly at the understatement. "I know. But please don't tell anyone. I just don't want the press to find out who I am and bombard me."

I felt rather than saw him bristle. His lips tightened. "If anything leaks, you can be sure it won't be from anyone in this office." His brow furrowed. "I know how to keep my mouth shut. But to tell you the truth, with all the publicity you've had thus far, I don't know how you plan to keep it a secret for very long."

He left the room abruptly and spat instructions over his right shoulder as he reached the hallway. "We'll see you in four weeks."

I drove home over the narrow country roads under a blue sky filled with cotton-candy clouds. A dull apprehension picked at me. Would this be the beginning of a chain of negative reactions?

Despite the doctor's all-too-apparent disapproval, just the thought of the child within me renewed my sense of well-being. By the time I reached home I was an optimist again. Nothing could spoil this day for me, I thought.

Several hours later I waited for Jeff to finish his lunch. We had plans to visit a friend of mine, whom I had not seen for several months. Her son Peter was Jeff's age, and Jeff was eager to play with him again.

Jeff smacked his empty glass on the kitchen table like a tavern patron. "Fill'rup," he demanded.

"Hurry, Jeff," I urged, refilling the glass with milk. "You haven't played with Peter all winter and he's waiting for you."

We walked leisurely toward their house, enjoying the warm April sunshine. The buds on the lilac bushes swelled blue with life.

Sharon answered the door almost immediately. I followed her into the kitchen through the patio, with Jeff trotting eagerly behind me. Four-year-old Peter was already in his sandbox at the end of their spacious yard. He jumped to his feet and waved a small yellow plastic shovel at Jeff while they greeted each other with gleeful shouts.

Sharon's quiet behavior began to puzzle me. She brought lawn chairs from the garage and set them near the sandbox, facing the sun. We basked in the warmth for a few minutes and watched the boys in silence. Finally she began to speak in a tight, unnatural voice about frivolous neighborhood news. When I glanced toward her, she was studying the yellow blades of new grass by her feet. The pitch of her voice was disconcerting.

"Sharon, is something wrong?"

She traced a design in the grass with her bare foot and didn't answer. The lines on her brow deepened and her mouth puckered slightly. Short, straight hair and no makeup made her look older than she was. She shifted in her chair and smoothed her sundress over her slender thighs.

"Sharon," I persisted, "have you heard about what I'm doing?"

When she looked at me for the first time, her face was hard and cold. "Yes, I have. I don't know how you could be that cheap." The last word was like a smack across the face.

"What do you mean, 'cheap'?"

"What you do is entirely up to you, but I could never sell my body." She fired the words at me, and I noticed she held both hands firmly in her lap to stop the shaking.

A stillness followed. Was this the friend I thought I knew? How could she think those things, let alone say them to my face? There had to be some sort of misunderstanding.

"Sharon." I spoke patiently and put my hand on her arm. She pulled away as though she had been burned. I went on, "I don't think you understand. I'm not selling my body. There's a woman who will never hold her husband's baby in her arms if someone doesn't help her. You have baby Paul asleep in his crib upstairs. You know how much he means to you. Could you deny another woman the chance to experience that? She's had surgery seven times, Sharon. They have no other alternative. Why shouldn't I share myself if I can?" I pleaded for a glimmer of comprehension.

She studied a small pile of sand Peter had dumped on the

grass and appeared to be measuring her thoughts. "That's the way you see it, but nothing you can say will change my mind. I see you as little more than a prostitute." Her voice shook with indignation, then she clamped her lips tightly together and stared stonily ahead. I realized then that her mind was closed as tightly as her mouth.

I pulled Jeff from the wooden sandbox, scooped up his shoes from the lawn, and despite his protestations, dragged him away from his friend. Sand clung to his little feet.

Peter was shrieking, "Where's Jeffie going, Mama?"

We crossed Sharon's lawn and hurried away from the friends I had once known so well.

Hours later, while I swept the kitchen floor of the flour and sugar Jeffrey had spilled when we baked sugar cookies, the tears began to roll. I had told myself it didn't matter what others thought. I had buried everything negative as Jeff and I baked and giggled, not minding the mess. The tears that had been there all along, waiting to be let out, came quickly.

I thought of Sharon's voice as she said the word *prostitute.* Would the opinion of a special education teacher be shared by others in our neighborhood? I had always thought of Sharon as a refined, open-minded person. I began to cry harder, sorry for myself, but saw that Jeff had started whimpering, too. I pushed all the fears aside and composed myself.

Sharon's accusations haunted me for days, like a tape recording that played over and over. There seemed to be no escape from the anger in her voice and eyes. The joy of the pregnancy faded and her fury followed me everywhere, even into my dreams.

Several days later I was undressing for bed in front of our full-length mirror. I noted the soft roundness of my torso, the slight swelling of early pregnancy that steals the waistline and smooths the skin like ivory.

Then, without warning, I imagined a large green dollar

sign prominently displayed on my belly. It stretched like a tattoo from my rib cage to a few inches below my navel. I watched in fascination as the illusory dollar sign seemed to dominate my form. The words *selling your body* popped into my mind, and I began to shriek with laughter at the thought of having to wear a dollar sign on my stomach for the rest of my life. I would never be able to wear a bikini again.

For several days afterward, I laughed every time I thought of the dollar sign and narrow-minded people. I vowed that never again would a stupid remark by a thoughtless person put me into such a state of defeat.

Many weeks later I related the story to a close friend, who remarked, "The people in central Illinois think this is still 1953 and Eisenhower is president. Don't let it bother you."

I had many occasions to remember those words in the months that followed.

Chapter 10

With the weather warming considerably each week, I knew it was time to shop for a maternity swimsuit before the selection dwindled.

The girls ran into the store ahead of me, eager to help. We finally chose one in a sunny green terry cloth and celebrated by stopping for chocolate chip ice cream cones before we drove home.

We pulled into the driveway and hurried upstairs, where we could hear Kent giving Jeffrey a bath. I rolled my eyes at the mopping job I knew was in store for me.

"Don't show Dad yet," Julie begged. "Just try it on and surprise him."

The girls sat Indian-style on my bed while I undressed and stepped into the suit.

"Do you think you'll be much bigger than that when summer comes?" Laura asked.

"Heavens, yes. Hey, do you girls want to see what I'll really look like this summer?"

"Yeah!" they yelled in one voice.

I half skipped down the hallway to Jeff's room and pulled a small semi-inflated beach ball from his overflowing toy box. I shoved it into the bikini panty of the suit and carefully arranged the soft green folds of material over the ball, then patted the new bulge in satisfaction.

The girls howled, rolling over the bed in hilarity at my

new profile. "Okay, you guys. Quiet. I want to show Dad."

I pushed open the bathroom door, put both hands on the small of my back as though in the early stages of labor, thrust out my belly, and penguin-walked toward Kent. "It's time, Kent," I groaned in mock pain.

Kent's mouth hung open while he tried to comprehend the all-too-realistic scene of a wife about to deliver. The shock wore away quickly, and he began to laugh with the girls, who hung on the door frame for support.

"Oh, Mom," Julie gasped through her tears, "that's really terrible. You're not going to get *that* big, are you?"

"Julie, if I'm carrying twins like Dr. Levin thinks I am, then this is small compared to how I'll really look this summer."

Laura's dainty features seemed to freeze. "Mom, are you gonna come to the pool this summer? I mean, where everyone can see you?"

"Of course I am. That's why I bought this suit. I want to take Jeff so he can learn to swim. Do you think I'm the only pregnant woman who ever belonged to the club? Good grief, Laura. Pregnancy's not something to be ashamed of."

"Laura, you brat," Julie scolded her. "Now you've hurt Mom's feelings."

"No, she didn't, honey," I lied.

I looked at Laura's downcast eyes. "Laura, I'm not going to wake up tomorrow morning looking this huge. It will be so gradual none of us will even notice. It's just a shock now because I'm wearing this beach ball. See?" I reached down and removed the ball, immediately returning to my tiny bulge. I did not miss the flicker of relief on Laura's face before she smiled again.

I managed to cover the stab of hurt I felt. Would she be ashamed of me when my figure changed? Or was she already ashamed and just hiding her feelings?

I dressed in a warm bathrobe and made a mental note to

drive to the library the next day. There had to be a book or two about children's reactions to their mothers' pregnancies. Perhaps it was normal for a girl Laura's age to be ashamed of distended waistlines.

Then the irony of it all hit me. "The library?" I said aloud to myself. How could I be foolish enough to think that a surrogate pregnancy could even begin to be compared with pregnancies described in self-help books?

What was really bothering Laura? I wondered. The growing of a baby that would result in my ungainly appearance, or the actual giving away of a sibling? There weren't any books in the world on that subject. I would have to figure it out for myself.

May 1980

I began having nightmares. Always the same one. I dreamed that I would emerge from a long, long labor exhausted and weak, drenched in sweat from the exertion of pushing the baby out of my body. At the moment of triumph, after the final barbaric cry from my throat and the first lusty one from my child, I held out eager arms, anxious to hold the warm, naked little body and put it to my breast.

But in the dream there were other arms reaching for the child. Two nameless, faceless people waited while Dr. Levin delivered the baby. When I was done, the three of them would celebrate his birth and toast his health while I lay on the delivery table, legs still in metal stirrups. I was alone and lonely and my arms were empty.

I always fought to wake up, and shivering and damp with perspiration, I would huddle under the quilts and ponder the foolish vision that might not be too far from reality.

I thought back to the interviews with the psychiatrists in February. What if I crash? What about postpartum depression?

I would ask. "Oh, you'll be fine," the doctors would respond. "You'll bounce right back. You're very stable." Then they would chuckle, as though these were questions a child might ask, and quickly change the subject.

But what could any man know about childbirth or the emotions of a woman during and after a pregnancy? In nine long months the thoughts and feelings pile into a mountain of emotion. But doctors were unable to help. It was easier for them to intimidate me with their aura of wisdom than to hold my hand and say, "I don't know. What you're doing is so new, we don't know what to expect."

I remembered innocently asking a friend several years before what it was like in Vietnam. Our closeness dissolved as he recalled the senselessness of the war. He became distant. "I won't talk about it. Ever. No one could begin to understand unless they were on the front lines. It wasn't pretty, Mary Beth."

I felt like telling my friend: childbirth and labor weren't pretty either. And there wasn't a male psychiatrist in the world who could begin to understand the emotions of a woman carrying a child as a gift.

After one particularly difficult night, I awoke, drained and confused. Kent sat on the edge of the bed, listening to me complain about not being able to meet Adam and Margo, despite the fact that Richard had promised me often I would meet them "soon."

"I thought Katie told you Margo didn't want to meet you," Kent said.

"She didn't say that," I snapped. "She just said Margo didn't want to meet me *yet.* God knows what that means."

"Maybe they just need time to get used to the idea." Kent sipped from his mug of coffee and peered at me over the rim.

I sat up and raised my voice. "They've had time, for heaven's sake. If I'm going to carry their child for nine months,

I have to know what kind of people they are. When I ask Richard about them, all he ever says is, 'You'd like them. Trust me.' Bull. He makes me feel like a pregnant teenager having a child out of wedlock. If I hear Richard or Katie refer to 'poor Margo' one more time, I'll scream. What about *my* feelings? *I'm* the one who's pregnant!"

Kent stood and opened the bedroom door. "All I can tell you is, you paid your nickel and got on the train. Now it's a long ride. You can't get off this one until the end of the line."

I knew he didn't mean to be unsympathetic, but the cruelty of that remark stayed with me for a long time.

By May Caryl had returned to work full-time, giving us little opportunity to nurture our friendship. Her weekends and evenings were full of errands, household chores, and a demanding husband. I missed her companionship and ever-ready laughter.

Many times during those days of her return to work, I would dial her number to share something funny or sad and then would remember, halfway through the call, that her house was empty. I would just hang up and sit next to the phone for several minutes, trying to think of someone else I could call. There was no one. The few neighbors I had been friendly with before the pregnancy sent clear signals for me to keep my distance.

The early months of the pregnancy, full of nausea and fatigue, seemed endless. Kent was studying diligently for his insurance exams in mid-May, and he retreated to the public library each evening for peace and quiet, something that was not to be found within the walls of our home. So I was left to cope with the constant demands of the children—presiding over bathtimes, enforcing television curfews, and settling battles over unfinished homework.

I would fall into bed each night as soon as the children

were asleep and only mumble in a sleepy stupor when Kent tiptoed into the bedroom around nine-fifteen. There was little communication between us as his exams drew closer.

Kent came home from work early one night during the first week of May. He told me to put dinner in the freezer and call a sitter. I knew from the tone of his voice not to ask any questions.

Within an hour we were sitting in a dimly lit restaurant, our favorite place to get away when we wanted a quiet, private dinner. Kent's brow furrowed as he explained, looking all the while into the clear rosy liquid in his wineglass. I tried to grasp as quickly as I could what he was saying, knowing he would tell me only what he wanted me to hear. Further information would come only as a result of my determined interrogation—a normal pattern in our marital relationship.

"But probation is for people who are doing a bad job or who have been warned over and over about sloppy performance. In all the years you've worked there, Kent, the only person I remember being put on probation was Steve, the alcoholic."

Kent agreed, then assured me he had always, in his nine years with the company, received outstanding reviews for his work.

I eyed him over the table. "Do you think this probation Morgan put you on has anything to do with the Donahue show that aired here last week?" I asked, already knowing the answer.

"Naw, Morgan doesn't even know what you look like. Don't worry about it." He dismissed the suggestion. "That's one of the reasons you used the name Kane. So no one from the company would realize you were my wife."

"But Jim did," I protested.

"He never figured it out, Mary Beth." Kent stabbed at his

salad. "I bluffed until he thought he made a mistake."

Kent, Jim *did* figure it out, I thought. And Betty and Sally and Audrey and how many other people in your office? They're all your friends, but you're still their boss, and anything you do is news. How much gossip was repeated to the home office? I watched Kent push the wooden salad bowl aside and begin to slice through his pink meat. The realization hit me with a thud and settled in the pit of my stomach. He's going to lose his job. He's actually going to be fired because of me. Six months from having his pension vested!

Kent's face blurred when I looked up. I blinked rapidly, aware he had been speaking to me.

"I asked you, are your contacts bothering you?"

"Yeah. Yeah, they are," I lied.

He went on to describe the conditions he would have to meet to be removed from the probation list. Morgan had given him two months to meet requirements that seemed unreasonable and almost physically impossible to complete within that time period.

Kent remained undaunted. He reminded me again that his work and production records were better than anyone else's in his territory.

"I'm not worried," he soothed me. "These days a company can't fire a guy over forty without one heck of a good reason."

The festive mood that had filled me earlier faded away during the conversation. Dining out tonight had been no treat. I ate automatically and said little during the rest of the meal. Deep down I hoped against hope that this was just another game being played with a loyal employee to keep him on edge and ever-fearful.

Within thirty days of that night at the restaurant, Morgan stormed into Kent's office, ranting and raving at Kent about an affair one of the men in the office was having, as though

Kent were personally responsible. He barely glanced at the papers Kent showed him to prove he had almost fulfilled the demanded requirements.

"If I were you," Morgan gruffed, his Irish features growing dark, "I would start looking for another job." Before Kent could react to his words, Morgan turned sharply and slammed out of the office.

"I'm going to bust my ass and fulfill every stupid demand he listed on that paper," Kent confided to me later that evening. "They don't have a reason. They *can't* fire me." With all my heart, I wanted to believe him.

I returned from the grocery store one Saturday afternoon with the backseat of the car lined with bulging brown bags—a week's supply of food. The driveway was still wet from the car washing Kent had just finished, and Jeffrey drove his Big Wheel back and forth, knees like little pistons. B.G. ran alongside, yapping excitedly at the spinning wheels. Jeff would turn his neck while he raced and watch dark, wet streaks grow on the dry concrete until they thinned and faded. Then he would race back toward another small puddle, calling gleefully for me to watch him before I carried the bags into the house. The sun had already bleached his hair the color of corn silk. I wondered if the new baby would have hair that silky white.

I turned toward the house, half dropped the heavy bags on the kitchen counter, and headed for the small bathroom off the kitchen, where I heard the blow-dryer whining loudly. Many times during the past few months I had wondered if the beautician the girls and I had gone to for several years would be able to remain objective when she cut our hair, if for some reason surrogate motherhood was offensive to her. That day my worst fears became a reality. Julie's hair looked about the same way it had when she cut it herself with pinking shears at the age of three.

"What did Joan say about 'Donahue'?" I asked, watching Julie try to style the varied lengths.

"I don't remember much, but she talked about the money a lot." Julie reached for the hairbrush and looked at me without animosity. "She sounded mad, Mom."

I stroked the chopped mess on her head, as though my touch could restore some style to her blonde hair. "Honey, I'll call someone else and see if we can get that mess fixed up."

"Do me a favor?" An impish grin played on her mouth.

"Sure. What?"

"You go first to make sure they like surrogate mothers. Then send me." I chuckled at her spirit, but my resentment at the incident stayed with me all day. I was sorely tempted to buy a maternity T-shirt and have the words SURROGATE MOTHER emblazoned on the front, with an enormous green dollar sign across the back.

Even though I thought my expectations about the reactions of others were realistic, there was always another surprise waiting for me. I was reminded of Jeffrey's jack-in-the-box. The handle turns and turns, with the listener totally absorbed in the musical notes. Even though the jolt is anticipated, the moment the doll jumps out at you, the effect is startling. Almost daily, the fact that so many people, including the media, seemed to focus on the fee puzzled and annoyed me.

The following week Caryl called, inviting Jeffrey and me to have lunch with her and Matt. It was a warm, sunny day bursting with spring sounds; we decided to walk to her house. Jeffrey proudly led B.G. on the leash, eager to show off his new pet to Matt.

Caryl and I talked nonstop, catching up on old news. We were both relieved all the earlier strains had passed, leaving today's mood festive. The boys played on the lawn with B.G. while we set the table for lunch.

Matthew burst into the house seconds before we were prepared to call the boys in to wash up. "Mama, B.G.'s hurt," he shouted, his little face full of alarm.

We rushed to the screen door to follow Matthew pointing to the driveway of a neighbor across the street. Only a mound of fur lying on the cement was visible from where I stood.

My stomach rose to my throat and I clutched my abdomen. Caryl took one look at my face and ordered, "Stay here. You're in no condition to cope with this."

I held onto the boys, and we watched in silence while Caryl carried the small puppy toward us. Our frantic calls to two veterinarians' offices informed us that the doctors would be back from lunch in an hour. B.G. didn't wait for their return. We dug his grave in the field behind Caryl's house.

We all stood next to the shallow gash in the earth. Tall grass waved a salute in the gentle spring breezes. At our feet lay a small cardboard box.

"Can't we give him some medicine to make him wake up?" Jeffrey looked down and his lower lip began to quiver.

"No. He's dead."

"Forever?" His tiny voice pleaded with me.

"Forever." I answered flatly.

Jeffrey stooped down and tenderly patted the cool, lifeless body. His small hand nearly disappeared in the soft, thick fur.

"Bye-bye, B.G., I love you." Jeffrey's chin puckered. He pulled the towel around the puppy's face. When he stood, he looked up at me.

"Mommy, if Jeffie would run into the street and get hit by a car like B.G., would you cry?"

I knelt down on the damp earth and looked deep into his eyes. He waited for my answer, and I was overwhelmed by his trust and by my love for him.

"Yes, Jeffrey, Mommy would cry. I think—" I pulled him to me, clinging to him. "I would absolutely die."

We held each other then. When we knelt at the side of

our B.G.'s grave, our tears fell together onto the freshly turned ground.

One afternoon, shortly after B.G. was run over, Julie came home from school later than usual. She often stopped at the street corner to talk to her longtime friend, Sheila, where they lost track of time. That day, when she trudged into the house, my ears pricked in warning.

"What happened, Jul?"

Julie plopped down onto the tall kitchen stool near the phone and swung one leg back and forth.

"Sheila and I had a fight," she pouted. "She said some bad things."

"About me?"

She waited a long time before she answered. "Sort of."

"What did she say?"

"She said her mom said you're not a Christian."

I looked at her, puzzled. "Why would she say a thing like that?"

" 'Cause you're giving away your baby."

"It's not my baby. It's Adam's. And I'm not giving him away. This baby belongs to his father, and he has since the day he was conceived. Just because I'm growing the baby for him doesn't mean the baby's mine to keep."

"I know that and Sheila knows that. You've told me about a hundred times. But her mom keeps saying all this stuff to everyone." She paused. "Mom?"

"Yes?"

"Is Sheila's mom—what's the word? We talk about it in school when we talk about black people."

"Prejudiced?"

"Yeah, that's it." Her face shone. "That's the word. Is she?"

"I don't know, honey. I can't tell you what's in her heart.

You see, Julie, being a Christian has very little to do with how often a person goes to church. It has more to do with how you treat other people and the things you say about them when you're not in church. Being nice to someone or helping other people is more important than never missing a church service or skipping Sunday school once in a while."

"Sheila's mom never skips church, even if she's been to a party and had too much wine. Sometimes you do."

I laughed at her honesty. "That's right. But I still consider myself a Christian. I know what's in my heart and how I feel about having this baby for Margo and Adam. So if I know the truth, and God knows the truth, it doesn't matter what other people say about me."

"But why does Sheila's mom talk about you so much? I hate it," Julie said in despair. "Whenever I go over to her house to play, her mom looks at me like she doesn't like me. She never talks nicely to me."

"Maybe she doesn't like you, but don't worry about it so much. Pretty soon someone else in town will do something she doesn't approve of and she'll forget all about our family."

"Do you think so?" She drew tight little circles on a pad of paper while she listened.

"Sure, Julie. You'll see. That's one of the most important things you have to learn when you grow up. For the rest of your life, there will always be someone who doesn't approve of what you're doing. But if you like yourself more than anyone else does, and if you know in your heart that you're doing the right thing, then it really won't matter to you what other people think. Sheila's mom spends a lot of time running around like a chicken doing silly things so other people will approve of her. So I'm not mad at her if she gossips about us. I just feel sorry for her. Do you understand?"

"I think so." Julie squinted past me at the tulips that climbed the yellow wallpaper. Her face suddenly brightened.

"You mean, like, if I invite a new friend over here to spend the night. I know Sheila will get real mad and then she'll say mean things about me at school when she finds out she wasn't invited. But I'm going to have so much fun with my new friend that it won't bother me if she's jealous. Right?"

"You got it! Go ahead and do what you want, and quit worrying about what other kids say about you. The important thing is what *you* think about the things you do."

"I get it!" she shouted and hopped off her stool. "I'm gonna call Chris. Thanks, Mom." She ran down the hall toward the upstairs phone and I laughed after her, marveling at the resilience of youth. If only Laura were as open as Julie.

My younger daughter remained pensive and rarely talked about the half-brother or sister I carried.

Chapter 11

From the very beginning, even before the insemination, I had foretold the reaction of my parents to my pregnancy. "My dad won't have much of a problem with it, but my mom—I don't think she'll ever accept it," Kent heard me say more than once.

True to my prediction, Dad called to say he was proud of me and that I had his support. "Your mother's been crying a lot," he said. "Be patient with her."

We were well into the month of May, and I still waited for a letter from her in reply to the letter I had written the first week of April, explaining the pregnancy and my motives for having the child. I began to stand guard at the mailbox and would do meaningless household tasks for an hour while I waited for the familiar sound of the mail truck. Even Kent began to comment about her lack of communication.

One Saturday afternoon I tried to pretend indifference while I shuffled rapidly through bills and junk mail. Kent followed me through the house to continue the conversation he had started. I replied curtly, barely listening.

He looked puzzled. "You don't have to get angry."

"I'm not. It's just that the silence is so maddening. I just wish she'd write to me. I don't even care anymore what she has to say. If only she'd write *something*."

Kent reminded me of our previous conversations, of my

prediction, but at the time I had spoken the words I felt braver than I did now.

It was easy to be tough and say "I don't care what she thinks" when I wasn't pregnant. But I felt different now that I was. I wanted her to be happy for me. More than anything, I wanted her to understand. My God, two of her own children were having problems with infertility. How could she not understand why I had to help Adam and Margo?

"It's her grandchild, Mary Beth. She'll never be able to hold him," Kent reminded me.

"I know that. But she already has seven grandchildren to love. There's a lady in Louisville who's never been a grandmother and because of this baby, she'll have that chance. Doesn't Mom realize that it's someone else's turn?"

Unfortunately my mother never quite saw it that way. As much as I love her, we have never been able to communicate well. Her response to an unpleasant subject is to tighten her lips into a straight line, fix her eyes on a distant object, and say, "Now let's talk about something nice." Feelings were not discussed when I was a child, a teenager, or a young bride. What made me think I could wish away thirty-five years of aloofness and begin a forthright exchange of our beliefs?

Because I had never received the hoped-for letter from my mother, I found it impossible to call her the next day, Mother's Day, for a casual, friendly chat.

Our family spent the day attending church services and had dinner at a pleasant restaurant in a small village near town. We played with the children in the warm spring sunshine and planted flowers in front of the house. Later that evening we relaxed in the family room watching the news, and Jeffrey sorted through pieces of a wooden puzzle, putting them back into place. When he cried in frustration, I dropped to my knees to help him put the hangar and runway together on the airport puzzle.

Kent automatically reached for the ringing telephone next

LEFT: Known to my family and friends as Mary Beth, I became "Elizabeth Kane" shortly after being selected to be America's first legal surrogate mother. (Photo by Nicolas Tikhomiroff)

BELOW: In Dr. Levin's office on March 2, 1980, reviewing the contract. Left to right: Karen, Dr. Levin's secretary; Katie Marie Brophy, his attorney; me; and the insurance agent. (Photo by Dale Wittner)

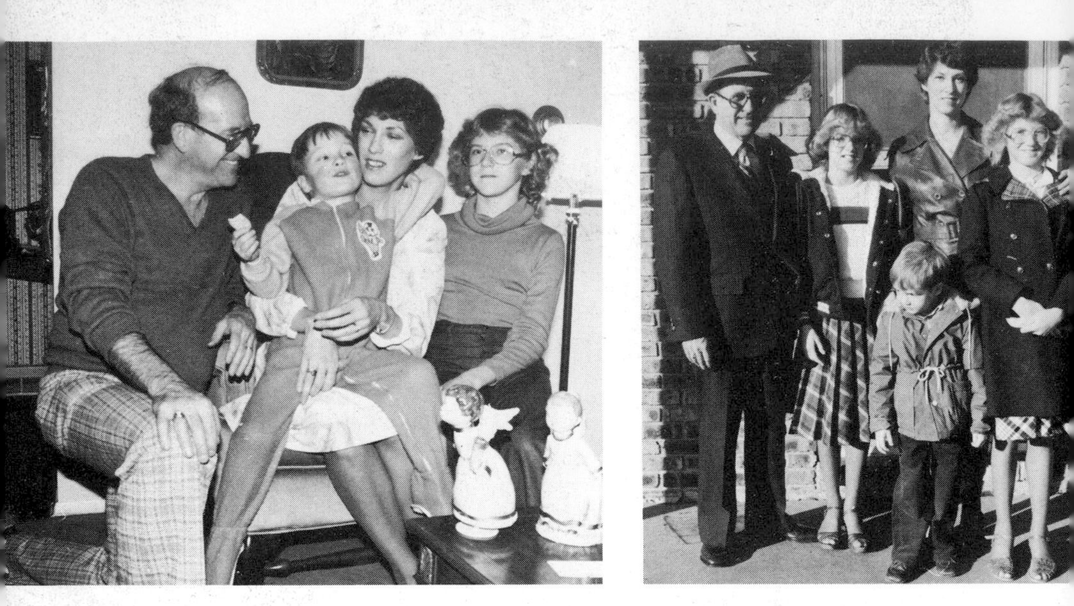

LEFT: Kent, Jeff, me, and Laura in our living room shortly after the birth. (Photo by Hiromichi Yokoyama, courtesy of Mainichi Newspapers, Tokyo, Japan)

RIGHT: We're on our way to church. Julie, the oldest, is standing between Kent and me in this family picture taken in front of our Pekin, Illinois, home. (Photo by Hiromichi Yokoyama, courtesy of Mainichi Newspapers, Tokyo, Japan)

Reading to Jeff: his favorite pastime. (Photo by Dale Wittner)

The family photo that appeared in *People* weeks after the insemination. The girls and I are baking cookies. Jeff has already eaten one too many. (Photo by Dale Wittner)

Walking together on the golf course behind our home in Pekin. Shot from the back so Dale could get a photo of us together without revealing Kent's identity. (Photo by Dale Wittner)

LEFT: Almost full term. I am standing near a small collection of the many Hummel figurines and plates we collected. I later chose a larger figure as our gift for the baby.

RIGHT: Four months pregnant. I am holding Ginger, Laura's birthday present.

Carrying pillows and a birthing kit onto the chartered plane that rushed Kent and me to Louisville for the birth.

Dozing between contractions during the long flight.

Dr. Richard Levin holding a lemon lollipop in his right hand and monitoring the fetal heartbeat at Audubon Hospital in Louisville.

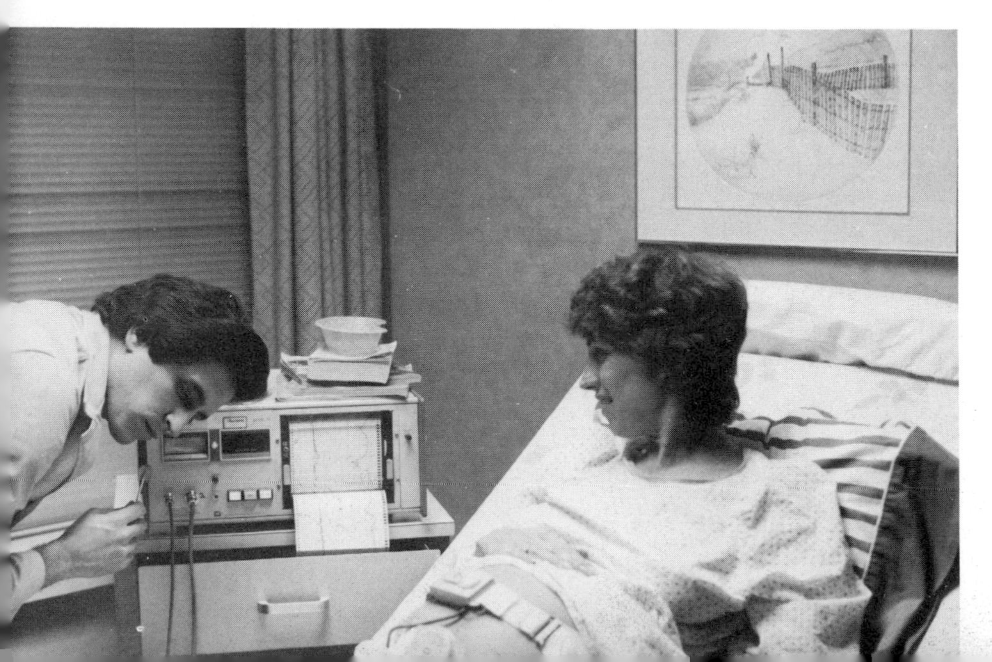

Just after the delivery on Sunday morning, November 9, 1980. Margo and I are admiring Justin's huskiness and broad shoulders.

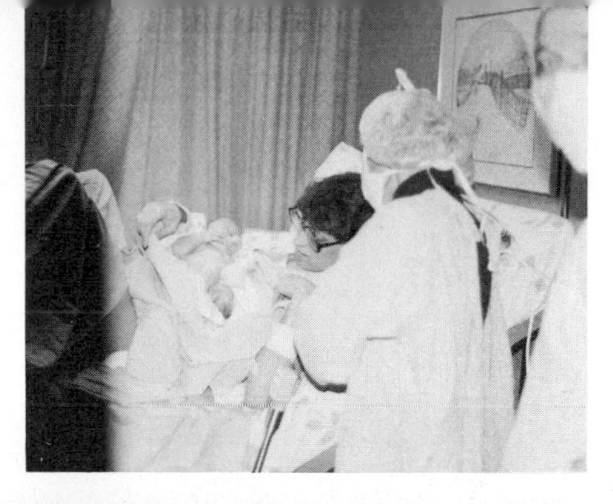

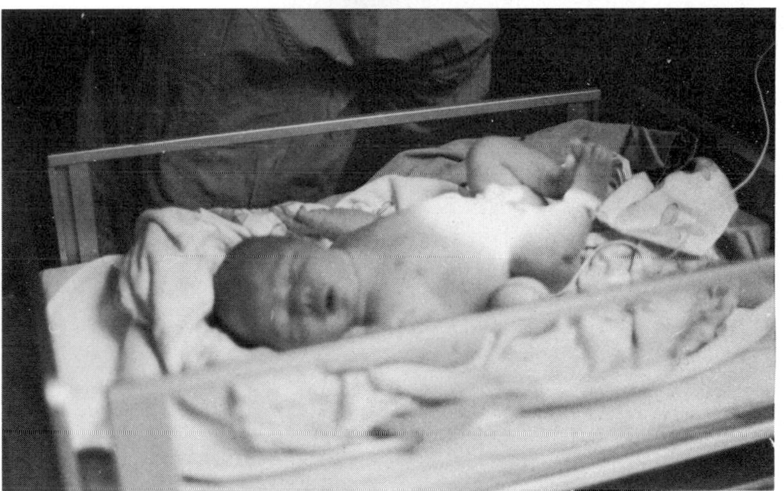

Justin in the first hour of his life.

I held Justin for a few brief moments and whispered, "Happy Birth Day, Baby Boy."

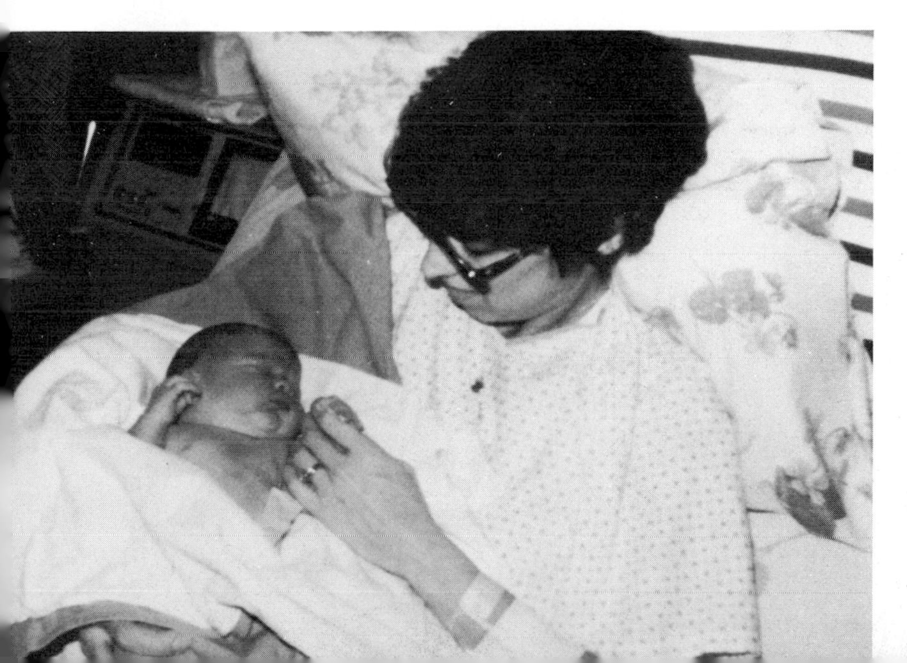

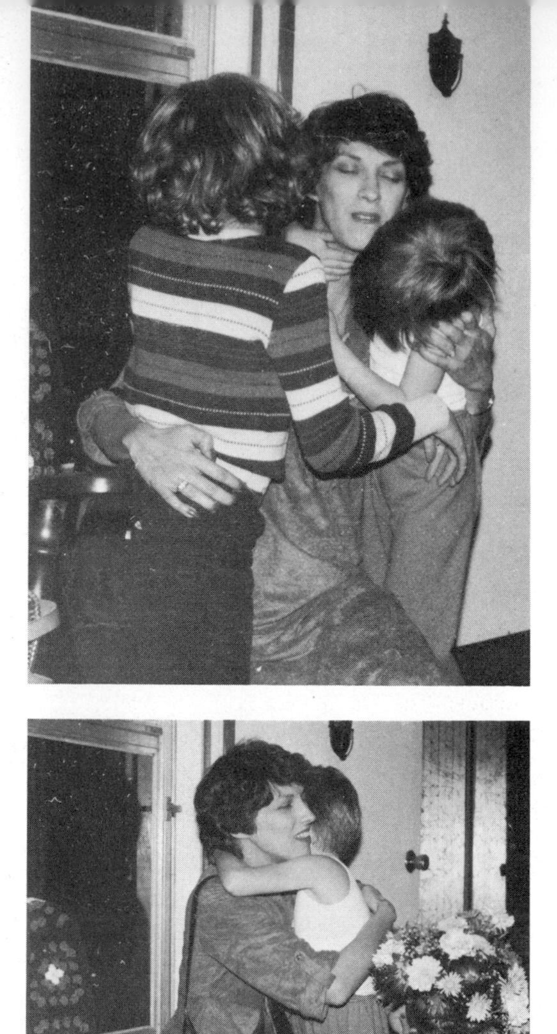

Home at last. After a seven-hour drive it was already late in the evening and past Jeff's bedtime, but . . .

. . . he couldn't stop holding and hugging me after a week's absence.

The next morning Jeffrey asked, "Did it hurt Mommy?" and continued patting my stomach saying, "Oh. Baby's all gone."

ABOVE: With Dr. Levin and Phil Donahue after taping my second "Donahue" show. December 1980.

RIGHT: I am with Kent, David Hartman, and Dr. Levin shortly after taping for "Good Morning America," a few weeks after the birth.

BELOW: Even with the joys of Christmas, I could not forget that there would not be any gifts for Justin under our tree.

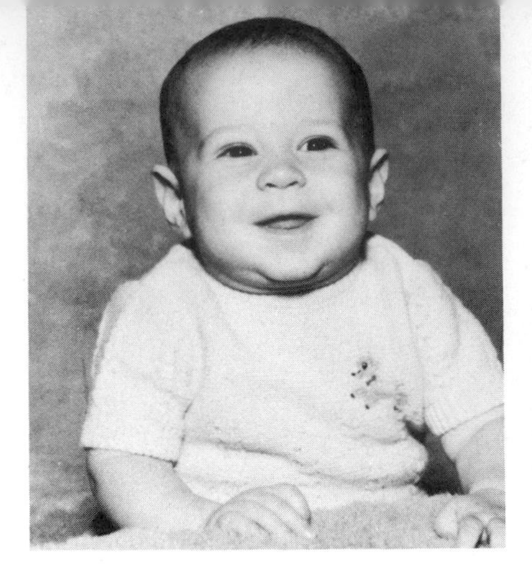

LEFT: Justin at six months, May 1981. (Photo courtesy of Margo and Adam)

BELOW: Writing and remembering. (Photo courtesy of Larry Brooks, *Peoria Journal Star*)

to him and listened, his face filled with amusement. "What? Are you sure? On the news?" He began to chuckle.

"What are you talking about?" I demanded.

"Mommy, help." Jeffrey tugged my sleeve.

"Shush. Kent, tell me!"

He cupped his palm over the phone and grinned. "Well, Mary Beth, it looks like twenty million people know you have two in the hopper. They had it on 'CBS Evening News' that 'Elizabeth Kane, surrogate mother, is suspected of having a multiple birth.' And they showed your pictures."

"What pictures? I haven't done anything for weeks."

"The ones CBS did in Louisville in April. They used clips from that interview," he said and returned to his conversation with his mother.

I kicked Jeff's soccer ball across the family room, where it bounced with a thunk against the glass patio doors. Damn that Richard and his big mouth, I thought. What gave him the right to do that?

Kent replaced the receiver and, though I was happy his mother had signaled her tacit approval, I sighed with frustration. "This whole pregnancy is getting out of hand, Kent. I don't like all this press coverage. Oh, why won't everyone just leave me alone? I hate it."

Kent stood, helped Jeff off the carpet, and said, "Let's go for a walk. It's too nice to sit in the house."

"No," I protested.

"Why not?" He lifted Jeffrey and formed a seat for the toddler with his left arm.

"Because then everyone will know about the pregnancy. I've never worn maternity clothes in the neighborhood before. I feel funny."

He looked at me strangely. "Mary Beth, everyone already knows. Twenty million people know. Your pregnancy has been announced on television half a dozen times on every channel in the last four weeks."

When the truth of Kent's words struck me, I began to laugh with him. "Come on, Jeff." I patted his little backside. "Let's take your bike and go for a long walk. It's Mother's Day."

When I called Richard the next afternoon to demand an explanation for the announcement, he pleaded innocence while admitting he had told a reporter from the *Chicago Tribune* that I was carrying twins. "But I told her it was unconfirmed."

"And I suppose you also happened to mention that I was in my third month and looked like I was in my fifth or sixth?"

"As a matter of fact, I did mention that. Plus the fact that those blood tests you had done on April 1st might indicate twins. But I told her it was unconfirmed. The next thing I knew, CBS had hold of it. I really didn't think she'd use the information."

"How could you be so stupid, Richard? You know as well as I do how hungry those newspeople are for a scoop. Give them a hint of a rumor and it's all over the wires in two hours. I wonder what they paid her for the information?" I muttered. "Richard, do you know the editor of *People* magazine had Sarah Moore Hall call me this morning to do a story on the twins?"

Richard crowed, "Are you going to?"

"No, of course not. Just to get her off my back, I told her I would be in Louisville next week for a sonogram and would call her first if there were twins. Oh, Richard," I wailed. "You should see how big I'm getting. You could just stand in front of me and watch me grow."

"Oh, I love it, I love it."

"Maybe you love it, but I feel like a fool. This whole twin issue has been blown out of proportion. There's too much publicity about this pregnancy."

Richard's tone grew serious. "Evidently there isn't enough."

"What are you talking about?"

"A couple came to me from another state last week, but it seems they had to pay to get my name."

"Pay? Pay whom?"

"Some lawyer. It seems they had heard about my surrogate program but they didn't have my name. Their lawyer was happy to provide the information to them for five thousand dollars."

"Five—thousand—dollars?" I stammered. "That's outrageous."

"I couldn't agree with you more. That's why we have to keep publicizing this program. So shyster lawyers can't take advantage of any more desperate people."

"That's illegal, Richard. It's morally wrong!" I shouted in indignation.

"It might be morally wrong but it certainly isn't illegal. He's taking advantage of misery and making a good buck out of it. It's guys like that who give all lawyers a bad name. Which reminds me." I heard him inhale sharply. "How about flying to Detroit with me on Memorial Day weekend? There's a one-hour talk show up there I want to do and I'd like you there."

"We're camping with the kids that weekend. I can't."

"But I need you there."

"No. We've been planning this trip for weeks."

"Come on," Richard pleaded. "You can go another weekend. Think of how many couples in Michigan will hear about my program if we do this show. Do you want another couple to pay this guy five grand?"

"No, of course not. Okay," I sighed softly. "I'll go."

"Good. I'll have the producer of the show call you this afternoon, and I'll see you next week when you're here for the interview with Japanese television. Then we'll do a sonogram and find out how many are in there."

"How many!" I shrieked.

"Just kidding," he chuckled.

May 20, 1980

The next week I lay on the examining table in Richard's office in Louisville. His eyes widened as he pressed carefully on the outer edges of my abdomen.

"Oh, my gosh, you either have one giant kid in there or you have two. Your uterus feels more like a sixteen-week pregnancy than twelve. Let's get you downstairs right now."

I followed him to the X-ray department several floors below his office. The sonogram revealed one fetus consistent with a twelve-week pregnancy. My disappointment caught me off guard.

"These sonograms aren't trustworthy," Richard confided to me when the radiologist was out of hearing range. "You could still be carrying twins. If one were lying under another, it wouldn't show up on the monitor."

I dressed quietly and tiptoed into the cubicle to stand behind Richard while he reviewed the sonogram. A radiologist was seated in front of the small lighted screen and tapped shaded areas with a pencil. "Looks like the placenta is in a *previa* position," he stated matter-of-factly.

I backed out of the room and waited. I grabbed Richard's arm when he walked out of the radiology room and relayed my fears. He brushed them aside with a quick answer as we walked toward the elevator.

"Don't worry about it. All placentas start out that way."

I stretched my memory for a shred of medical knowledge. "Placenta previa: The placenta implants itself at the lower end of the uterus rather than the upper end." I also remembered that with labor and dilatation of the cervix, the edge of the placenta could separate from the wall of the uterus and hemorrhage. If a cesarean section was not performed quickly, the baby died. I knew that placenta previa was always a life-threatening situation and that often, even if the baby could be saved, a lack of oxygen could result in brain damage.

Oh, dear God! I thought. "What will happen to my baby? Their baby?"

I was able to deny my feelings for the child publicly when the host of a talk show would lean toward me and ask what he thought was a unique question: "Do you ever feel you are carrying *your* baby?"

I would look him in the eye and tell him the child belonged to another woman. I had no possessive feelings. I honestly believed that. At the time. But the truth remained. My maternal instincts were as swollen as my belly, and I felt the same as when I carried the children Kent fathered. The same fierce protective instincts were already there.

Yet what on earth made me think I could carry this tiny child for a stranger and rejoice constantly in "their" child while I denied any part of him was mine?

My fourth month of pregnancy brought high spirits, more energy, and less nausea. And each prenatal visit seemed a milestone.

"Watch your weight," Dr. Kasten warned. "Your blood pressure's okay, but six pounds in four weeks is way too much. You won't get your figure back this time like you did with the other pregnancies."

"Oh, phooey," I scoffed. "I've always been skinny."

"Are you counting calories?" He frowned at my chart.

"Yup. Four thousand a day." I laughed at his crooked eyebrow. "I'm always starving."

"Then eat more carrots and drink more water. I'm not joking."

Dr. Kasten lectured me about getting more rest and slowing down. "I'm not as worried about the foot you hurt while playing baseball with your children last night as I am about all this publicity. Whoever is doing your promoting better cut way back or there won't be a baby to worry about." He crossed the room and rested now on his little wheeled stool. "I don't understand how Dr. Levin can insist you take care of yourself by not drinking, smoking, or taking any medication, and then have you flying all over the country. That schedule is too taxing for any pregnant woman."

"Then it wouldn't be unreasonable if I called the producer of the show in Detroit and told her I have to fly there and back in the same day instead of making it a three-day trip?"

"If it were up to me, you'd cancel the whole thing. If you want to leave for that show in New York the day after Detroit, you won't have any time to rest in between."

"I can't cancel it. It's already in *TV Guide* and Richard is counting on me," I protested.

"Then charter a plane and do it in one day. And in the future, I don't want him scheduling anything this heavy."

I smiled with gratitude at his advice. His initial feelings against the surrogacy had been set aside, and his concern for me as a patient had taken over. Maybe he realized it took me three days to catch up on the housework, cooking, and laundry after being gone for two days. Bless his heart.

I often asked myself why I felt compelled to continue the publicity and travel. There were many reasons, and so, with feelings of ambivalence, I went through pregnancy and continued for eight months after the birth before I finally called a halt to any further inquiries from the media.

Despite my protestations, one reason had to be the glamour. It was flattering to be asked to appear on a talk show. I enjoyed air travel, the limousine rides to the hotel, and satisfying my voracious appetite at the expense of television stations. Fresh strawberries out of season? Of course! I justified the extravagance by reminding myself I wasn't being paid to appear on the show, so the least I could do was feed "us" well. And I did.

But little did I realize when I began publicizing the pregnancy through *People* magazine and the Donahue show, that we would be bombarded with telephone calls and requests to do radio shows, telephone interviews, and newspaper features. I finally understood why Richard insisted I remain anonymous during the pregnancy. His secretary, Karen, screened all calls, and only after talking to Richard would she call me to decide together if and when I would do the interview. I remember doing many interviews over the phone for an hour or two while I refereed arguments between the children, untangled a pup from my ankles, or wiped a quart of orange juice off the kitchen floor.

I would have to be deranged not to enjoy the attention and pampering that went with being a "celebrity" for a short while, but there were plenty of thorns among the roses. The children never failed to show their misery while I packed. Though I was never gone longer than three days, they would ask me over and over if I "had to go away again." I missed them terribly even before the plane left the ground, and I would call home every evening. The nights I talked with Jeffrey before his bedtime, our conversations would always end with his heart-wrenching sobs, and I would hang up quickly only to sit alone in the hotel room for the rest of the evening, feeling depressed because I wouldn't be able to hold him for another two days. During those moments I always felt guilty for leaving the children with a sitter. Many times Kent would be on the road, and the children would have to be left with a sitter for several days. The days following my return would be spent sifting through piles of toys and laundry, and playing catch-up with the housework. I would lumber through the house and mutter under my breath, "Never again."

I would complain when Richard called to ask me to do "one more" publicity show for him. I wasn't receiving any financial benefit, while he seemed to be. His telephone would ring for days after I had done a show in another large city. The publicity generated more surrogates and drew more infertile couples to his doorstep, eager to open their checkbooks to him. Sometimes I would resent his growing bank account while Kent and I struggled with our bills. I would not get paid until after the baby was born. Even then it would be several weeks before Richard finally mailed me that check. As for the publicity, I never received one cent—nor did I want to—for all the traveling and speaking I did on behalf of surrogacy.

It took very little for these negative reactions to dissolve because often in my travels I would talk to women of all ages who had been infertile all their lives. I saw the painful acceptance in their faces. I would suffer with them as they recounted stories of emptiness in their marriages. I knew that if I could spare one woman that pain by publicizing surrogate parenting, if one more woman could be called "Mother" because of it, the trips and the inconveniences that went with them would be worth it. And it was happening. I was told repeatedly by Richard of the plight of infertile couples who were coming to him from all over the world—from Spain, Italy, Mexico, England—after reading about my pregnancy or seeing a photograph in their community newspapers.

There were times I felt hopeless, tiny, and ineffective. My one baby would not make a dent in the vicious sea of infertility. But by doing the publicity, I at least could hope that I had helped the world sympathize with barren women who craved motherhood. For fifteen months I wanted to encourage other women like myself to take up the crusade.

June 1980

The first weekend in the month our family took a long, often-postponed camping trip to the southern part of the state. We had spent the day before packing the camper. The children scurried back and forth from their bedrooms to the camper like little pack rats, taking everything they felt sure they couldn't live without for three days.

I cooked, froze, and labeled more food than we would ever eat. On Friday afternoon we pulled the camper over narrow, bumpy roads for four hours in stifling heat, until the campground greeted us at dusk with an amber glow from camp fires dotted nearby.

Kent started the fire while I poured cool drinks for the children.

Julie paled. "I don't feel well, Mom," her voice whined weakly.

"Honey, we're all hot and sticky. You and Laura go down to the lake and swim until it's time for dinner. You'll feel better if you cool off."

The girls grabbed suits and towels from their duffel bags and quickly disappeared into the bushes that led to a dirt path to the lake.

Jeff clung to my thighs while I prepared a picnic lunch. "I wanna go, too," he screeched.

My patience had ended an hour before during the hot, monotonous car ride, but I spoke slowly and softly. "Jeffrey, I promise I'll take you after we eat. The girls can't watch you now."

He sat at the picnic table and squashed ants with his little fist while he pouted. The girls were back within thirty minutes. We could hear Laura shouting indignantly from two campsites away.

"Mom, that lake is terrible. It's full of yucky bugs. Look at Julie." She stood with her hands on narrow hips, staring me down as though it were my fault. "They bit her all over her body," Laura accused.

I held Julie by her shoulder, turned her around, and came face-to-face with dozens of red bumps. Bug bites? "Laura, you were in the water, too, and you don't have any." I began calculating mentally. Julie had been exposed to friends with the same symptoms two weeks before. Incubation period? Twelve to twenty days. Usually fourteen.

Yup! Chicken pox!

"At my age?" Julie whined as we tucked her into a sleeping bag, with chills and a fever that climbed higher with each passing hour. We thought of going home.

"Let's wait until morning. I'm not breaking camp in the middle of the night," Kent said. "If she's better, we'll stay the weekend. What's the difference if she lies in bed at home or at camp? Let's not spoil it for the whole family."

Early the next morning we awoke to the music of trees filled with birds. Laura crawled out of her sleeping bag, covered with identical red spots and sporting a low-grade fever. She refused breakfast. Within an hour we were on our way home.

Despite all my efforts to make them more comfortable, the girls complained loudly about the itchy pox that rapidly sprouted all over their bodies. I hoped library books would take their minds off the scratching and discomfort.

Early in the afternoon I struggled up the stairs and plopped fifteen books onto my bed. Laura lay there with four pillows stuffed behind her. She watched me stack the pile of books while she savored a root beer popsicle. "Thanks, Mom. That should last me a few days. You know what I like best about books?"

"What?" I asked absentmindedly.

"There aren't any commercials. If I have to go to the bathroom, I won't worry that I'll miss anything."

I chuckled at her observation. "Enjoy," I said, handing her three books from the stack. Then I headed down the hall toward Julie's room.

As soon as she heard my footsteps, she yelled from her

bed. "Mom, there are two letters on your dresser. One's from Grandma."

"I don't want any letters from Grandma today." I rounded the corner and stood in the doorway.

"Then can I read it?"

"No. Absolutely not."

"Why not? It's not fair," she whined.

"Because it's none of your business what Grandma has to say." I crossed the room and yanked the window shade. "Just leave me alone. Read your books." I was amazed at the harsh sound of my voice.

I didn't want to open my mother's letter. I knew what it would say. I felt my childishness emerging, as it had so often during this pregnancy. I yearned for the approval of my mother in the same way I had as a child. I would take great pains drawing and coloring a picture for her, only to have it met with indifference. Would she be indifferent to me now?

Here I was, thirty-seven years old, mother of three and a crusader for social change, wanting a letter from my mother telling me what a great person I was. And in seeking reassurance from my own mother, I was incapable of mothering my own children—snapping at them angrily. Grow up, Mary Beth, I thought. Isn't it about time?

I had become so consumed with the notion of creating a new family that I had not considered my mother enough; she might be grieving for the grandchild she was about to lose. Never mind that she already had seven grandchildren and another woman in Kentucky had none. I was asking my mother to give up her own kin.

I dabbed at the perspiration sliding down my temple with the back of my hand and sat on the edge of Julie's bed. "I'm sorry, Julie." I felt her hot forehead.

"For what?" She was already absorbed in her book.

"For taking your head off."

"You do that lots of times." She looked up now, her face impassive.

I sighed heavily, knowing I had probably hurt my children over and over.

They needed me more than ever. That was my job—mothering, being sensitive to their needs. If I had learned anything from my own childhood, it was that I should listen to my children, try to understand them, see their problems, and not judge them but help them make their own decisions. I decided I would try harder to appreciate them and not to reject them verbally and physically during that difficult time for all of us.

I leaned across the bed and gave Julie a big hug, holding her tightly for a minute.

"I love you, Julie. You know that, don't you?"

"No."

"You do, too."

"Yeah. But if I admit it, you might think I'm bragging."

"No, I wouldn't."

"Okay. Yeah, I know you love me. I love you too, Mom." We hugged each other with her book between us, and I thanked God for her.

It was not until almost four years later, at a family reunion, that my mother and I sat down to talk about the pregnancy. When she recalled Kent's phone call on the day the baby was born, the tears she was able to shed in front of me healed the wounds instantly. I knew then how much pain she had suffered as a result of her never being able to see him. And I ached for her and for what I had done to her. The only things I have left to share with my mother are the memories of his growing inside me and the photographs of an impish brown-eyed boy I receive from Louisville once a year. She cherishes each one as much as I.

Chapter 12

June 13, 1980

The soft knit maternity top slid off the hanger. I slipped it over my head and smoothed it over the now obvious pregnancy, and picked a tube of lipstick off the dresser.

A car door slammed. I pulled the sheer bedroom curtains to one side and saw Kent walk around the side of his car to the trunk. He was followed by a large, sullen hulk of a man with thick, dark hair. The sleeves of his white dress shirt were rolled up to reveal thick, muscular forearms. He stood, hands on hips and legs spread, watching Kent dive into the trunk again and again to pull out personal belongings, which he neatly stacked on the sidewalk in front of our driveway.

Another man, stockier and shorter, stood next to the driver's side of the car and leaned against it with his arms folded across the roof. He stood in the blazing afternoon sun, his eyes roving up and down the street scrutinizing the neighboring houses and professionally groomed lawns. He didn't pay much attention to the activity at the rear of the car, though his eyes never stopped moving.

I frowned, puzzled. Why was Kent emptying his company car? I listened for conversation and heard only the thunk of Kent's golf clubs hitting the cement. Who were those men?

I drew a quick line of pink across my lips and hurried down

the stairs to open the front door. Intense heat invaded the air-conditioned house. A scream of tires, then Kent's car spit pellets of gravel into the air and disappeared down the quiet street.

"What's going on? Who took your car? Who were those men?" I asked. Kent dragged himself toward the house, loaded with briefcases and a bag of golf clubs over his left shoulder.

I reached for a briefcase and shut the door behind us. He dropped everything at once just inside the door and sat heavily on the piano bench nearby.

"Who dropped you off?" I asked.

"My boss, Morgan."

"He looks like a bear."

"I can think of a better name for him."

"Spare me. Now tell me what happened."

"There's not much to tell. Morgan and this other guy from the home office drove down to take me to lunch. While we ate, Morgan told me I was through. I asked him for a transfer to another district."

"What'd he say?"

"He said, 'No one else wants you.' "

I gasped.

"But I reminded him that according to production figures, I'm running a better office than he is. Damn it, Mary Beth, I'll have my pension vested in five months. I don't want to give up that easily."

"He can't fire you without a reason. It's only been six weeks and he said you had two months. Did he come right out and say it was because of what I'm doing? Because of the baby?"

"Are you crazy? He'd never admit that. Even though this all started two weeks after "Donahue" aired, I can't prove it. What he said was, 'You no longer fit the image of a company manager.' "

I sat down beside him and sighed. "Now what?"

"They'll give me severance pay. I'll have a few weeks to look for another job. Jesus, I never thought I'd see the day I'd be looking for work at the age of forty-five. Do you know, I haven't been unemployed even one day since I graduated from college?" Kent shook his head. "He even took the keys to my office. The kids' pictures are still on my desk."

I slipped my arm around his waist and hugged him. "We knew it was coming, but it's still a shock, Kent."

He jerked his head sharply to look into my face. "*I* didn't know! I thought they took me to lunch today to pat me on the back and tell me what a great job I've been doing for the company. I've been busting my ass for them for almost ten years."

I looked into his gray eyes and saw the cold fear.

"I'm sorry, Kent." I leaned over to kiss his cheek.

He cleared his throat loudly. "Hey, it's not your fault. Morgan never liked me from the first day on the job. It had nothing to do with your pregnancy."

You're a bad liar, Kent, I thought. And thank you for trying to shield me from the truth.

During my first interview, I had told Dr. Levin that I wanted to have an amniocentesis. I knew that a woman my age ran the risk of delivering a child with Down's syndrome. Richard had been noncommittal, telling me he would speak to Margo and Adam about the test, and if they approved, I could go ahead and have it done. At the time I thought it would be a simple matter involving maybe an hour at the local outpatient clinic. I was wrong. I called hospitals and doctors in my hometown and those of a larger city twenty-five miles away, and the answer was always the same. To ensure that the amniocentesis was done properly, we would have to travel to Chicago, a four-hour drive from home. The days before the test were spent arranging for a baby-sitter to stay twelve hours and scouring the shelves of our local library for information about the procedure. But the bits of knowledge I collected didn't ease my apprehension about the test, the needles, and the imagined pain. From the moment Richard had handed me a scrap of paper with the name of a genetics specialist scribbled across it, I was anxious to have it over with.

The dreaded day finally arrived, June 16, 1980. We awoke at dawn, tiptoed through the house in the dim light, and whispered hurried instructions to the sitter before we backed quietly out of the driveway. The early morning temperatures already promised another smoldering day.

We arrived in Chicago almost four hours later, and crawled up and down narrow streets filled with cars parked in NO PARKING zones until we found a garage four blocks from the hospital. Once there, we wandered through a maze of hallways on the eleventh floor until we discovered a secretary behind a tiny desk.

"I have an appointment with Dr. Elias for genetics counseling," I said. She looked up from her book and nodded toward an open door. We entered a windowless cubicle crammed with books, two Leatherette chairs, a small cluttered desk, and a tiny plant that was barely alive in its plastic pot. I paced the cramped office and scanned medical titles on worn books. Kent slouched in one chair, seemingly content to wait.

"Help me fill out this form for my job application. You know I can't spell."

"Why did you bring that thing along?" I looked at the sheets of paper on his lap.

" 'Cause I knew we'd have a lot of waiting. It'll give me something to do."

I pulled over the empty chair next to his and peered at pages and pages of a psychological test.

"They want to find out if I'm mentally stable," Kent quipped.

"By the time I complete all ten pages, I won't be anymore."

I craned my neck to read the first question. "What do they want to know?"

Kent chuckled. "Listen to this one: 'Which would you rather do? Stick your head into a lion's mouth or jump out of an airplane at thirty-four thousand feet?' "

"With or without a parachute?"

"Without."

I slapped his arm playfully. "You're making that up."

"No, I'm not. Now come on and help me with this." He poised a pencil above the next question and read: " 'Are you a perfectionist?' I would say yes, wouldn't you?" He looked at me so earnestly that I collapsed with laughter, both hands crossed over my abdomen for support.

"Anyone who can ignore a leaky toilet for a year and leave a hole in the ceiling for two years is definitely *not* a perfectionist."

He grinned sheepishly. "I guess you're right."

We looked up at the same time to see a short, small-boned man in a knee-length white coat standing in the doorway. His face did not respond to my smile. "I am Dr. Elias. Follow me," he ordered. He pivoted and we rushed to follow him through the maze to an office only slightly larger than the one we had just left. Except for a few family photographs and several thriving plants, the rooms were identical.

Dr. Elias began by taking my family history. When I stopped to mentally gather information for an answer, he seemed impatient and would interrupt with another question. He briefly discussed birth defects, chromosomes, and genes in a mechanical tone of voice.

He informed me that the chances of having a defective child at my age were one in one hundred seventy-seven. He drew little diagrams and pushed them across his desk while he tapped them with the eraser of his pencil. Finally he leaned back in his chair, raised his chin, and peered down at me through small rimless glasses. "Are you aware of the risks of amniocentesis?"

"Risks?" I stiffened. "What risks?"

"One out of two hundred abort. You understand, of course, that the needle is a foreign object. There is always the risk of bacteria being introduced, which could start an infection. Or the needle could rupture the amniotic sac." He held up an eight-by-ten glossy photograph of a newborn with a dimple in its behind. "Punctured by a needle," he stated flatly. "Also a risk."

"If I'm one of the two hundred who abort, will I go into labor on the way home? It's a four-hour drive." My throat felt very dry.

One corner of his mouth turned upward, in what could have been a smile. "It has never happened that quickly before."

"Well? How long would it take?"

"One to two weeks." He leaned forward, elbows on his desk. "Another question. Is there any Jewish blood in your family?"

Kent and I thought of an old family joke at the same time and exchanged a meaningful glance. "I don't know."

He continued. "Is the father of the child Jewish?" I answered in a small, quiet voice. "I don't know."

In a voice like dry ice, he informed us that if there was the slightest chance of Jewish heritage on either side, I would have to agree to a Tay-Sachs blood test. He explained that Tay-Sachs disease is a risk for babies of couples of Jewish ancestry, affecting one out of twenty-five hundred births. It attacks the central nervous system and first becomes noticeable at the age of six months. The baby dies before the third birthday. There is no known cure.

At some point during our conversation I became more aware of misgivings while my mind wandered in and out of the doctor's lecture. I heard Dr. Elias as though through a tunnel, instructing me to watch for signs of cramping, bleeding, and leaking of amniotic fluid. I forced myself to listen.

"Why would amniotic fluid be leaking? Because the cervix was dilating and I'd be going into labor?" I eyed him suspiciously now and leaned toward him.

"That's right." His voice was as cold as his eyes. I glanced over my shoulder to look longingly at the door, wondering if I would ever forgive myself if the pregnancy ended as a result of this test. I knew it was a blessing for thousands of couples with rare genetic disorders. I also knew that if it were Kent's and my child, I would choose to have the test because of my age. But how could a couple make the decision to abort if their child was defective?

I pulled myself back to reality. "How many couples receive abnormal test results? Say, out of every hundred?" My hands rested on the edge of his desk while I waited.

Dr. Elias watched my face, unblinking. "Three or four. That's a pretty low average when you stop to think that all the couples who have it done are having the test for a very good reason. It's not a test you do just to find out what color to paint the nursery. It's still a fairly new medical procedure and it is considered serious, yet low-risk."

"Out of all the people you know who have amniocenteses, how many choose to abort the fetus when the results show an abnormality?" I had to ask.

"All of them."

Only the sound of my sharp inhaling interrupted the silence that followed. Dr. Elias waited for the words to sink in. He took off his glasses and pinched the bridge of his nose between his thumb and forefinger. When he looked up again, his gaze met mine.

"Well, that's why they're here. People come to me from all over the world to have this test done."

"Let me ask you something." I spoke softly. "If the test

shows a chromosomal abnormality, it could mean anything from a harelip to Down's syndrome. But we wouldn't know the exact problem. Or the extent. Right?"

"Correct. Although if there is a chromosome missing, it usually means something quite serious. If there's anything in the genetic history, or if the age of the mother warrants, as in your case, the test should be done."

I leaned back into my chair and gripped the arms. "I don't want to have it done. At all."

"You don't have to."

"I don't have a choice. It was my idea originally, but I'm not so sure anymore." I was thinking about the contract—about Adam and Margo.

Dr. Elias stiffened, pulled his shoulders back, and looked at me with eyes the color of steel pellets. "No choice?" he asked contemptuously. "I find that very hard to believe. I am sure you discussed this procedure thoroughly with Dr. Levin even before you made the appointment to see me. It's simply not true that you don't have a choice. It's your body and I would think the ultimate decision is yours."

I jiggled my head in agreement. Dr. Elias wouldn't believe me if I told him that Richard had handed me a scrap of paper with his name and phone number written on it, and told me to call for an appointment. Thoughts and feelings pulled and twisted in all directions like a hopelessly snarled ball of yarn. I watched Kent rip a hangnail with his front teeth, then concentrate on the injury. Dr. Elias tapped his pencil rapidly on the desk, marking time.

I ignored them both and began to consider my options. I wanted the child to have a good start in life. But most of all I wanted his parents to have a normal, healthy child. If he was not—then what? And if the needle started the chain reaction leading to a miscarriage, how would Adam and Margo react? Should I have the test and take the one out of two hundred chance of aborting their child? Or should I leave the office now and take the single chance out of one hundred seventy-seven that their child could be abnormal? The risk was about the same either way. Dr. Elias did say that only about one half to one percent abort. That was nothing, I realized.

"Let's get on with it." I stood abruptly and pushed my chair away with the backs of my knees. Dr. Elias rose abruptly and headed toward the door. "Do you have any further questions? If not, meet me in Ultrasound." And he was gone.

We met his dark-haired secretary in the hallway. "Hurry," she urged. "You have an appointment at Children's Hospital for a Tay-Sachs test in fifteen minutes."

She whipped a heavy curtain across the doorway of a cubicle the size of an outhouse while she gave instructions she repeated dozens of times each week. "Get undressed. Everything off. Gown opens in the back."

I grabbed a folded gown from the pile on the narrow bench, slipped it over my bare skin, and stepped barefoot into the sterile, rectangular brightness. An auburn-haired beauty with tresses almost to her waist waited for me. She indicated a small room, followed me in, and pointed. "Up on the table," she ordered.

I hiked myself up, legs dangling awkwardly over the side.

"Lie down." She reached for a bottle of clear liquid, squeezed it over me, and cold gel snaked over my bare abdomen. I inhaled sharply from the sensation. She slathered the liquid over my belly, then placed a long, flat instrument resembling a trowel on my right side. The tool's cord was attached to a large machine on my left. She twisted the dials and turned knobs.

"Will I be able to see the baby, too?" I whispered.

"Shhh. Just let me finish my work, honey." The technician moved the instrument across my stomach very slowly, then pointed a pink, oval fingernail toward a small screen near my feet.

"There's the head and the heart," she smiled. "See it beating?" We watched the blurry outline together. I was dumbfounded at the sight of a real baby inside my body.

"Where are his legs?" I gasped.

She moved the instrument and a new image appeared on the screen. "There's one." She pointed again, sharing my delight. "The other one must be hidden from view."

"Are you sure he has two?"

She smiled patiently, as though she had heard the question hundreds of times. "Yes, he has two. It's not uncommon to be able to see only one."

I watched a tiny leg about the size of my middle finger kick gracefully in the fluid of its home. The technician moved the monitor back to the tiny, rapidly pulsating heart and we watched with fascination. The baby's heart appeared to be the size of a peach, larger than his head. Fourteen weeks pregnant, and I had witnessed the miracle on a television screen. My elation spread to thoughts of Margo and Adam and their excitement, could they have been able to share the moment with me. I sat up and chatted happily with the young technician.

Dr. Elias soon announced his presence by speaking to my back. "Lie down and relax," he commanded. I obeyed immediately while he fingered a tray holding the dreaded needles.

The technician dug her fingernail into my skin, making an indentation about four inches below the navel.

"She's making a mark so I know where to put the needle. I would like to miss the baby." For a brief moment I thought Dr. Elias was making a mild attempt at humor, but he wore the same masklike expression I had seen in his office earlier.

He deftly swabbed the exposed skin with iodine, draped a paper sheet with a square peephole over my abdomen, and reached for a large syringe with a long needle.

"Sometimes we can't draw the amniotic fluid. If that happens, you'll have to return in two weeks." He tugged on the paper to straighten the square over my orange skin.

If you think I'm coming back here, mister, you're wrong, I thought. You'd better strike oil the first time.

Swiftly he plunged the ominous-looking needle into my abdomen until the steel shaft was buried. I felt as though I had been punched hard from inside. A childhood memory passed through my mind. My older brother would bully and tease me mercilessly with a strong wallop to my thin upper arm. The result was a dull ache that hurt for a day or two. I had expected pain during the testing, but this was nothing.

I peered down to see a circular tube of plastic protruding from my abdomen, to which Dr. Elias attached a small plastic syringe. Yellow fluid the color of urine began to fill the tube. I had always imagined amniotic fluid to be as clear as water.

Soon the syringe was filled and quickly replaced by another, much larger tube. It filled slightly, then stopped. Dr. Elias pulled back on the plunger. Nothing. He tugged harder. The syringe remained almost empty.

I watched the ceiling tiles in silence while I mentally reviewed the trip back to Chicago in two weeks, baby-sitter fees again, more testing, and the hot, monotonous drive home late in the evening.

He tugged again and again, tight-lipped. Unexpectedly the syringe began to fill quickly. I whistled softly through pursed lips.

"The baby must have had a knee or an elbow against the needle," Dr. Elias offered.

"How much fluid are you going to take?" I asked. I wanted to know if there would be enough left for the baby to live in, and how long it would take my body to replace what had been removed. These questions were next.

"Every time you talk, your stomach muscles move. Please remain quiet," he chastised me.

In another moment he was peeling off thin surgical gloves and labeling the test tubes. The entire procedure took less than ten minutes.

The technician turned toward me, smiling with enthusiasm. "Let's turn on the machine again and get your husband in here so he can see his baby."

Dr. Elias turned slightly to answer her briskly. "That will not be necessary. They're late already."

I stared fixedly at his back. "I'm sure one or two more minutes won't make any difference." I turned my attention to the technician and smiled in gratitude. "He'd love to see the baby."

Dr. Elias eyeballed me and stalked from the room.

When Kent caught sight of the baby rolled into a ball with his little rump topside, he grinned like a kid at the county fair.

I slid off the table, hurried back to the cubicle, and threw on my clothes. After slipping into my flats, I glanced quickly into the small mirror above the bench. The haggard woman who stared back stunned me. The makeup I had applied in the predawn darkness of our home had done little to cover the strain of the long day. Kent waited in the car while I had blood drawn for the Tay-Sachs test and received a printed page of statistics on the disease.

Now, Kent eased the car onto the freeway and stepped on the accelerator. The '67 Ford responded instantly, and we glided along for several miles in comfortable silence.

The tension of the day lifted somewhere on the expressway outside Chicago and we began to talk freely, sharing a closeness and warmth we had not felt in weeks. Having the entire day without the children to distract us lent much to this special mood. Yet the one thing I could not, or would not, discuss with Kent was a thought so distracting that I pushed it aside each time it started to wriggle into my mind.

I had fallen in love with my baby that afternoon.

Several hours after we returned home from Chicago, I lay in the tranquillity of our bedroom, too exhausted to sleep and conscious of the dull soreness in my abdomen.

I eased out of bed, relieved at Kent's snoring, and crept down the carpeted stairs in the dark. Groping for the familiar outline of my favorite chair, I reached for the afghan Kent's mother had crocheted for us years ago, and wrapped myself tightly inside.

The darkness and serenity of the night were as comforting as a close friend who listens but never passes judgment.

A torrent of tears caught me off guard and I tried to suppress them, as I had done many times in the past. But something deep in my being told me the time had come to cry and purge myself of my secret demons before they destroyed me completely.

I sobbed until my throat felt raw and my head pulsated. In the stillness I made a mental list of my fears.

I felt a lack of concern from Richard; I had pleaded with him over and over to let me meet the parents of the baby. I had asked often for even just a letter from them. Did they think of me only as some incubator without emotion? There were so many parts of the pregnancy I yearned to share with them.

I had been worrying over Kent's job situation and our lack of giving to one another. Kent was distant and would only grunt in reply to my inquiries. I knew he was not totally committed to backing me in the surrogacy. He often reminded me of his refusal to be in Louisville when I delivered this child, or of the fact that he lived only for the day he could drive down to Louisville after the birth and bring me back home. My pleas to convince him I needed him in the labor room were answered with a turn of the heel as he left the room.

I could only guess at plans he was formulating for his future. I seemed to have no control over mine. The controversy surrounding this pregnancy and the publicity had drained me. I had nothing left to give anyone.

I missed my friends who had drifted away. But I wondered, had I pushed them away, or was it that they simply did not know what to say to me?

Dr. Elias's words were branded into my brain: "One half to one percent of women having amniocenteses abort the fetus naturally as a result of the procedure." How could I justify risking an abortion simply to find out if the child was healthy? Would I ever forgive myself if I started to bleed and lost the baby? Where on earth did common sense end and foolishness begin? There was a very fine line between the two. I drew it that day.

Tears slid down my face as I came to terms with the worst fear of all. The truth I had never admitted to myself, thinking smugly it would never have to be dealt with—my intense love for the tiny child inside me.

He had been in my life and my heart for almost four months now. In another five months the tiny child I had seen on the screen would be propelled into a warm, bright room in a Louisville hospital, where two strangers would be waiting to welcome him into their lives.

Kent padded down the stairs and stood quietly near my chair. He reached out to touch my arm, and for a brief second, we were close again.

"Honey, are you bleeding? Are you losing the baby? Why are you crying?" His voice was filled with tenderness and concern.

I pulled my arm away. "No, I'm fine. I just need time to

think. Please—just leave me alone," I whispered hoarsely. He turned reluctantly and went back upstairs.

I struggled to think clearly. If the amniocentesis revealed a chromosomal defect, who would make the decision to expel the infant from my womb? Richard and I had never discussed or even thought about having to cope with something like that.

I knew the baby was mine despite the legal contract I had signed. And he would be until I terminated my parental rights in the courtroom six days after his birth. Yet morally he belonged to the two people who should have the right to choose whether this child must be aborted. By the time we got the results of this test, the child would be only four months from his birthday. If the child was not perfect, who decided whether he should live or die?

I asked the same questions over and over while the minutes slipped into hours and the thick blackness began to fade. Whom could I ask? Whom could I trust to help me make this decision? I began to pray for guidance.

I sat folded until the fragile light of predawn, alone with my thoughts and prayers. Suddenly the baby awoke. He kicked strongly against me as if to greet a new day, as if he had felt my suffering through the blood we shared.

Damn the test! Damn the doctors!

What exactly did a chromosomal defect mean? I wondered. Did it mean that the baby would never respond to love or to a gentle smile? That the baby would not have silken hair and eyes that gleamed? Did "handicapped" mean he would be incapable of bringing love to a family?

"Damn you all for putting me in this position," I cursed out loud. "No. Damn yourself, Mary Beth. It was your idea." I was the one who had emphasized flippantly during the first interview with Richard that the parents had the right to a perfect child after all those years of waiting. How different those words had sounded when I was not pregnant, not attached to the fetus.

If the test results were positive, a decision would have to be made quickly. And if the parents decided to eliminate the child, I would have to intercede. But how could I ask Kent to raise another man's handicapped child? The financial and emotional burden would destroy him. And our marriage.

Yet I could not make the decision to snuff out the child with a surgical instrument or an injection of saline. I could not proclaim this child completely useless because he was flawed.

Never mind the way he looks or his intelligence, I thought. I love him. If his parents decide to have him removed, if they feel no responsibility or love for this baby, I cannot demand the medication that will mark the beginning of labor. His lungs are still too tiny to take that first breath. He must not be put to death before he can breathe life.

Only God will decide. If this child is handicapped, he will learn to love. He will grow and live as normal a life as he can. He will give what he can and teach others more than he can learn. I must say NO to all of them.

When the pale morning light shone through the window, the load lifted. "I will not kill my baby." It was the day I knew I loved this unborn child as much as I did my other children. This child was mine! I would fight for his life if I had to.

Chapter 13

Kent's feelings about my pregnancy remained a mystery. Most of the time he was encouraging, urging me to do publicity whenever I balked at having to leave the children again. Or he would laugh when I complained about looking like a giant egg. He would gently remind me he had heard the same complaints three times before, and then tell me how quickly my figure had returned to normal each time.

When I was too tired to clean away the clutter after a large meal I had cooked, he would suggest I lie down for a while. From the bedroom I could hear him whistling tunelessly while he put the leftovers in the refrigerator and cleaned up the kitchen.

Yet we didn't seem to be on the same wavelength anymore. I knew Kent worried about finding another job. When I chattered about the baby and the effect he had on my life, Kent would interrupt with a comment about his lack of job prospects. We shared a house separated by the walls of our own thoughts. I often wished we could stop talking long enough to listen to ourselves and to each other.

Tom and Helen were close friends who had moved to another state several years before. We were sorry to see them leave, but we wrote often enough to stay current with family news. Helen's letters were always sunny and full of humorous anecdotes about her family and shaggy pup. Even though she wrote only twice a year, I cherished each letter. Her sense of humor uplifted me every time I reread one of them.

The letter I received that summer had a different tone. It was full of support for my decision to have the baby. Helen ended by telling me she and the surgeon she worked with in a large hospital had been discussing surrogate motherhood. The surgeon expressed surprise when she told him she had known me for many years, and proceeded to grill her on the following questions: "Why on earth would any woman put herself through the agony of a nine-month pregnancy and a long labor and delivery if she doesn't have to?" "Why would any woman give up nine months of her life for people she's never met?" "What kind of a person is your friend anyway? A nut?"

Helen went on to tell him that of all her friends and the people she knew, I was the only one she could visualize having a baby for strangers, that it seemed right and completely natural that I be the one.

"Then she must be a real dog," he had responded.

Helen did it again. She made me laugh.

Another woman I knew, the sister of a neighbor, had two lovely children, a girl and a boy. She knew our neighborhood was in an uproar, and she tried to defend surrogate motherhood. "If people didn't believe in giving away babies, I wouldn't have a family. Both of my children are adopted." Her confession caught me off guard; there was a mixture of sorrow and joy in her eyes when she spoke.

A woman executive I barely knew commented to me on the telephone, "I think it's wonderful that you can be a surrogate mother, although I can't imagine what it feels like to work for someone else twenty-four hours a day, every day of the week for nine months, with never even an hour off. You wouldn't want to hear the salary I would ask to do such a thing." How many times I wished I could have taken an hour off in the middle of a fitful night to rest in a normal sleeping position!

I remember being with a friend who held her severely handicapped four-year-old daughter as if she were an infant. The child's head hung limply to one side. Her mother sat on my sofa while her seven-year-old, a healthy, curious child, played quietly.

"You're nuts," Jody had scowled. "You couldn't pay me one million dollars to do this for anybody, whether I knew them or not. My pregnancies were miserable. Both of them. I would not put myself through that again for anything. And what about you? You're no spring chicken anymore. You can kiss your figure good-bye. I think you need a psychiatrist."

I didn't bother to mention the two psychiatrists I had seen before the insemination. I never saw Jody again after that morning, and I barely thought of the incident for months.

Sometimes the comments came from unexpected quarters. I found a letter on Julie's bed one morning when I went in to change her sheets. I placed it on the marble top of her walnut dresser and stopped when I saw a reference to me. I broke my own rules about snooping and read her letter, addressed to a relative.

> Connie,
> Hi. How are you? I'm doing fine. I truly think you don't understand what Mom is doing. She is giving a couple who can't have children a child. They already have one adopted child but one that is half theres is better. Mom did not have an affair with another man! And what she is doing is not the same thing, that's plain silly. If you say that if Mom knows what she is doing, you will back her up, then why haven't you started? Mom knows what she is doing. Why are you even bothering to write to her? She does not need to

be bald out. She needs encouragement and praise. She isn't going to change her mind either. (About keeping the baby.) That child can come back and see us when it's an adult, if it wants to. Mom has had the joy of three babies, now its there turn. I'm sorry you missed Donahue. It was on April 22 in Dallas. If you had really wanted to see it you could have looked it up in the T.V. Guide.

Mom spent months thinking about doing this, she didn't just do this at the spur of the moment. That is enough of this subject. I am doing okay in school. I can't believe it will end in four to five weeks. Mom doesn't have anything to say to you so if you want to reply, write to me. I am 12½ and I understand better than you may think I do.

Julie

I sat down on the rumpled sheets and wept.

My sister Kathy, who is four years younger than I, called me one afternoon to remind me not to forget our parents' anniversary. As if I ever had! During the strained conversation, I asked her feelings about my pregnancy.

"I won't know what to say until I talk to God. I have to find out if it's His will or not."

I reminded her that the conception itself after only one insemination *was* His will or it never would have occurred the first time.

Kathy's tone grew angry. "Look what you've started with this surrogate motherhood thing. There was some man on 'Phil Donahue' today who wants a surrogate to bear him a son. He wants to separate the sperm so he has a boy. And he's single," she sputtered.

That's my fault? I wondered.

The twelve-year-old son of a neighbor who no longer allowed her small daughter to play with Jeffrey stood at the bus stop with Julie one morning.

"You sure have a strange mother. She has to go to a sperm bank to have babies." Then another neighboring child joined in. "Yeah. What's the price for the babies these days?"

Julie laughed in their faces. Then she came home and cried.

Another neighbor instructed her sons, who were classmates of my daughters and who stood at the same bus stop each morning: "What Mrs. Kane is doing is absolutely wonderful. If anybody at school gives her daughters a hard time, you defend them. And fight for them if you have to. This is the only time you have my permission to hit another child." When she told me, I was only able to smile and say thank you.

And another neighbor called shortly after the publicity started. "Congratulations—is that the right thing to say? How do you feel? I think what you're doing is wonderful, but I wouldn't go through it again for anything. I would have ten children if I never had to be pregnant or endure those deliveries!" I laughed with her, knowing she meant it.

And then my mother-in-law finally wrote to me. "I can picture you doing this with no trouble. When I heard about it, I was not at all surprised. You have always gone out of your way to help others. I think it's a wonderful idea." She was eighty-two years old.

It was so easy to take the praise. I saved it for those moments the cruel, derogatory remarks threatened to defeat me.

I remember quite clearly the ringing of the telephone one morning. It was the friendly, uplifting voice of a man whose name was unfamiliar, yet he assured me he knew me well, that he attended our church regularly and had seen our family many times.

He talked for a long time about his wife's infertility and lauded my courage and foresight in this venture. "I wish you had been around forty years ago when my wife and I were trying to have a child," he sighed wistfully.

A warmth spread through me while he talked. His appreciation swelled my ego until I blurted, "Thank you for calling and telling me these things. Next Sunday, would you please introduce yourself to me so I know who you are? I'd love to meet you."

His flustered, pleading voice came after a long, thick silence. "Please don't ever speak to me in church if you find out who I am. My wife would never allow it. She would be very upset if anyone saw me talking to you."

Letters from old friends and relatives in Wisconsin trickled in at the rate of one or two a month. How heartwarming it was to receive their news and their words of loving support. I wish they knew how much it meant to me to have them take the time to write, to tell me they were thinking of me. I was so grateful for every letter, yet I seemed incapable of returning the favor. I could not write to anyone.

It wasn't that I wanted to hold back. I yearned to communicate with these friends, to tell them how much their messages of love held me together. At night, before I drifted into unconsciousness, I would think of old friends who had written recently. In my mind I would compose pages and pages of wonderful prose, and just before I went to sleep I would promise myself to put those words on paper the next morning. To reach out. But I could not. The pen would rest in my fingers and refuse to write even a simple salutation. The letters remained bundled, labeled "To answer, someday."

At first, I was so enthusiastic about the pregnancy and the expectations of the new parents that I never hesitated to bubble that I was a surrogate mother when any stranger commented on my bulging midriff. But I soon learned it was easier to lie than blurt the truth.

Faces would sag with puzzlement or disapproval, and I would be forced to parrot the same speech about my motivations for having a baby for a couple who could not have their own.

When a salesperson in a store would notice my swollen belly, she would bend over to crow to Jeffrey, "Oh, I'll bet you're so tickled about your new baby. Are you going to help Mama?" She would stick her pale, powdered face into his little face and wait expectantly for a clever answer until he finally shook his head no.

I would stroke his hair like he was a kitten and interrupt, "Oh, sure he is. He's just being silly." Or I would change the subject, saying something about the person's lovely dress or becoming hairdo to take her mind off the question just asked.

Laura and Julie were also instructed to play the game when we were in public. And I was greatly relieved to become a normal pregnant woman carrying her fourth child. Strangers in a restaurant would glance at our family and ask, "Is everything ready for the new baby?"

I would sing with enthusiasm, "Almost," and think of Margo and Adam preparing the nursery in Louisville. It was much easier than talking about surrogate parenting in a tape-recorded tone while "hyperthyroid" eyes stared at me as though I were mad.

One day in July a phone call from Richard interrupted my morning routine.

"Would you like to talk to Adam on the telephone? He's so excited about being a father, I think the guy's going berserk. He asked me if you would talk to him on the phone so he could express his gratitude."

Although I had been pleading with Richard for months to let me meet the parents of the child, the thought of a telephone conversation with the father suddenly paralyzed me. "No. Please, Richard, don't make me do it. I don't know how I'd react."

I felt that if I talked to Adam, he would become a real person instead of a faceless shadow. I was carrying his child and we were married to different people. If I talked to him and he became real, would it be harder for me to carry his baby and remain objective?

I felt uncomfortably close to this man I had never met. And I could not define those feelings. It was certainly not love, but definitely a bond of some type. We shared an intimacy neither one of us had created intentionally. And I was not yet ready to face that.

"Please, Richard," I implored, "make him understand. I don't want to hurt his feelings. But I can't listen to his voice and hear him say, 'Thank you, Elizabeth.' "

My relationship with Margo was also extraordinary. To me, she was a woman whose physical characteristics I could not know, yet I did know she would be caring for my child for the rest of his life. I had no vision of hair color, height, or features. Yet she had seen me on television and in newspapers and magazines many times. She had watched me gesture and speak about my feelings to an audience. She had seen my smile and the warmth and love I felt during the pregnancy. I was real to her, as was the mound of her child under my maternity top.

I ached to meet her. We had feelings to share—she, too, was an expectant mother. Like the darting flash of a lightning bug on a hot summer evening, it occurred to me how threatening I must be to her. In her mind, was I a rival? Her womb would never feel a fullness of life or her breasts the familiar tug of her own hungry infant. And her husband's fertility had been proven by another woman.

Chapter 14

July and August 1980

The summer was bringing us record heat waves, with many days of 100 degrees or more. As the temperatures increased during the morning, my energy level decreased. The weight of the baby created continual back pain, and I thought longingly of cooler September days.

Early in July Richard arranged a publicity tour for me, with Katie as my companion. How I dreaded going. Three cities in three days on the East Coast. The original arrangements had been made for four cities, but I flatly refused to be gone from home for longer than the three days that that tour would take, or to miss Laura's eleventh birthday. And the thought of spending all that time with Katie Brophy . . .

Richard knew we couldn't stand the sight of each other. How could he do this to me? I refused to pack until the very last minute.

Soon after takeoff I began to experience diarrhea, a cutting pain in my lower back, and regular contractionlike pains across my abdomen, from hip to hip. I tried to remain calm, searching for a reason. It was three weeks after the amniocentesis. Could it be—? No, the doctor had said one to two weeks. Maybe it was the stress of rushing to get ready to leave. The last-minute instructions, pages of handwritten notes for Kent, all the food shopping and preparation, housecleaning, and a multitude of other details only a mother would be aware of. The tightness continued with regularity, and I soon began to recognize the symptoms from my miscarriage six years earlier.

Panic rose in my throat like floodwater. I began to breathe slowly and deeply, forcing myself to remain calm and to think clearly. Premature labor would be the worst thing. If that's what it was, I would ask the flight attendant to have an ambulance meet me when we landed in Baltimore. I would check in under my legal name. Not Elizabeth Kane. My greatest fear would be to have Margo and Adam hear about the loss of their child on "NBC Nightly News."

But the symptoms did not increase in severity. When we landed, I met Katie at the hotel, feigned exhaustion, and ignored her disappointment at my not joining her for dinner at a marvelous restaurant. She could go alone. Or not at all. I simply did not care.

By the following morning all symptoms had vanished. But I promised myself right then to do little if any publicity in the future. I was not going to risk my health or my baby's just to tell people about surrogate motherhood.

During the three-day tour, Katie and I spent hours dragging our luggage in and out of dilapidated taxicabs and waiting in airports. We were led into tiny over-air-conditioned rooms until it was time for our turn on a talk show. When we missed lunch, we would eagerly accept the offer of cheese and crackers on the small commuter planes. On each show we smiled brightly and chattered about surrogate parenting. And each night we fell into a new bed in a different city, too exhausted to care about the strangeness.

I soon grew used to Katie's barging into my room asking for shampoo, a razor, or some other article she had forgotten to bring. It was similar to the scenario each morning in my bedroom with Julie and Laura.

By the end of the third day of our trip, I had discovered a new friend with a deliciously dry sense of humor—who was an easy traveling companion. Our banter became comfortable, warm. Soon there was only one more talk show to endure. We spoke eagerly about going home as we waited in the studio.

On the air, the studio audience asked predictable questions about this new form of parenting. They were open-minded, friendly, and intelligent. I spoke confidently as the interview drew toward a close.

"We have only one minute left, Mrs. Kane. I'll ask you one more question, if I may?" The host flashed me a ready smile while he stood in the audience clutching a microphone.

I nodded permission and returned his smile.

"Isn't it possible the only *real* reason you're having this baby is just so you can get free publicity and have the glory of being on all the television talk shows?"

I was perched on the edge of a tall three-legged stool, directly in front of the audience. My legs dangled awkwardly in front of me. Gravity tugged at my bulk. When I opened my mouth to speak, my brain was empty. There were no words.

"I mean, you have to admit," he continued when he saw my plight, "all of this attention must be flattering. Being asked to appear on television, seeing your name and picture in the papers, flying all over the country." He sneered the words in my direction.

I turned helplessly to Katie to see her delicate features twisted in anger.

"Let me answer that question." Her Kentucky drawl seemed more pronounced when she raised her voice. "We were on the 'Phil Donahue Show' several months ago at *their* request." She crossed her legs and hooked a high heel onto a rung on her stool for leverage. "At the time of Elizabeth's insemination, we all thought we would be doing it for just this one couple. But by the time we returned from Chicago, the requests for surrogate babies were flooding in from all over the world. The press inundated us. We've turned down many more programs than we've accepted."

She shook a slender finger at him for emphasis. "Like this one. We didn't call you asking to be on this show. You called us. Remember?" She glowered at him, never dropping her eyes for a moment. The red signal light on the camera died suddenly. If there hadn't been an audience, I would have hugged her.

The day after I arrived home, I checked my calendar and shivered with anticipation as I dialed the phone.

"Genetic Counseling. Will you hold?" A nasal voice ran the words together and clicked me on hold before I could reply.

The silence thickened until I was positive we had been disconnected. I redialed slowly. The nasal voice spoke less rapidly. "Genetic Counseling. Will you hold?"

"No!" I shouted.

She replied with a push of the button and silence. I began to mentally calculate my telephone bill for the month and consider writing a letter.

At last. "Can I help you?" A disinterested female voice.

"I'm calling for the results of an amniocentesis."

"Name." It was not a question.

"Kane, Elizabeth."

"Spell it."

"K-A-N-E."

"One second." She sighed. Within moments she was back. "We have only the preliminary results."

"What does that mean?"

"The chromosomes are all in order. The results from the Shriver Foundation for spina bifida prove negative." She exhaled loudly.

"What do you mean, 'The chromosomes are all in order'?"

"There are forty-six chromosomes present."

A moment of silence followed until I was forced to reveal my ignorance.

"Yeah?"

She spoke slowly, as though I were eight years old. "That means that there are no serious birth defects evident, and the test for Down's syndrome was also negative."

I leaned weakly against the back of our bed and mumbled, "Thank you."

"Uh huh."

"Wait a minute," I shouted, gripping the phone. "Don't hang up. Is it a boy or a girl?"

She was very cool, very detached. The answer had been right in front of her all the time. "This test indicated a male."

I watched a spot on the wall above Kent's dresser. "A male?"

"That's right."

"A boy?"

"Yes."

"This baby is really a boy? You're telling me, a healthy baby boy?"

"That's right, ma'am."

My throat clamped shut and I tried to thank her. Instead I hung up and burst into tears.

Twelve hours later I tucked Jeff into bed, kissed the bridge of his nose, and when he didn't stir, tiptoed from his room and down the stairs.

Kent unloaded the dishwasher while he watched television. I began talking over the noise of the program. "Kent?"

"Hmmm?"

"Are you sure you won't change your mind?"

"Huh?" He slid plates into the cupboard and turned toward me.

"Are you sure you won't change your mind and be in the delivery room with me?"

"Nope." His attention was focused on the set.

"You could always get gowned and masked at the last minute. I still remember how thrilled you were when you saw Jeffrey being born."

"Nope." He looked directly at me now. "Mary Beth, I've told you before. I don't want any part of it. I'm not even going to Louisville with you."

"What if I need you?"

"You won't."

"But what if I do?"

"Richard will be there."

"He'll be too busy to give me moral support."

He threw spoons into the silverware drawer, and I listened to the rhythmic chink for a while, then turned away. "I'm going for a walk."

He followed me to the door. "I'm almost finished with this. Would you mind if I came along?"

I paused a moment, seeing his eager smile. "Yeah, I would. I'll see you later." I slammed the door lightly between us and stepped out into the inferno of another summer night. A sliver of golden moon ducked in and out of ragged clouds and followed me down the street.

I looked back only once to see if Kent had followed me to apologize. For what, you fool? I thought. How can he be sorry when he doesn't even know he's hurt you?

But what could I do? Demand he be there with me? Tell him how much I would need him to hold my hand in a roomful of strangers when the pain got unbearable and I couldn't go on for that last hour?

No! I can do it alone if I have to. I will.

I strolled along our quiet street with only the chime of neighborhood church bells. Eventually the dogs along the way began to exchange husky barks. I walked for a long time. Thank you, God, for a healthy baby, I thought. Surely this is a sign of your approval.

Finally I crossed the street and turned toward home. I sat on the front steps and contemplated the past five months. The worry over a miscarriage, the amniocentesis, the loss of old friends and of Kent's job—I caressed my abdomen lovingly.

"Now that I know you're perfect, little one, the next four months will be a breeze. Nothing else matters."

The next afternoon Jeffrey picked at his lunch dejectedly. He nibbled at his sandwich, then slipped it to our new Irish setter pup while I looked the other way. His normally hearty appetite had disappeared as the heat increased with each hour.

While he sat at the kitchen table, his left hand propping his small, tanned face in a posture of gloom, I realized that at the age of four, he had no one to play with. The parents of his two friends in the neighborhood no longer allowed their children in our yard or home. He had already colored pictures, worked his airplane puzzle, and played cowboy on his rocking horse. The puppy wanted to nap in the shade and Jeffrey needed to play outside. But not alone, again.

"Jeff, let's go out."

"Really?" He snapped to attention.

"Sure. That's what summer days are for. My work can wait. I'll read in the lounge chair while you run through the sprinkler."

As I helped him into his swimming trunks, he put his arms around my neck and kissed me on the cheek with silky lips. "Thanks, Mom."

I was jolted by that one, soft kiss.

I'm giving away your brother, I thought. You have no one to play with and I'm giving away your half brother. His only male sibling, who could become as near and dear to him as any full-blooded brother could ever be. What made me think the child I carried would mean nothing to my children?

I was carrying a brother Jeffrey might have enjoyed hunting with someday. They might have swum in a lake on a hot summer day, or wrestled in the living room until they broke my favorite lamp. All of the things that brothers should do together.

Jeffrey would never meet his brother. I wondered if he would resent my decision when he was old enough to understand why his brother would not be a part of his life.

Within the next week Kent accepted a job offer from a large company headquartered in Indiana. It meant more traveling for him, but we were so relieved that that didn't seem to matter. He was to be the zone manager for the state of Illinois. The offer included excellent insurance benefits and a company car.

By mid-August I was back in Los Angeles doing publicity for Richard's surrogate parenting clinic. He and I stood one morning in the brightly lit tiled hallway of a Los Angeles hospital. High-pitched cries filtered through the thick glass window of the nursery. Cameramen wove around us, readying their equipment to film us for the news that night.

We stepped back, out of the way, and watched the now-familiar scene of sound, camera, and lighting technicians scurrying about, always mindful of time and their next assignment.

An attractive couple in their mid-thirties stood near us, holding hands. She was stylish and pert with blonde curls. He was a head taller, professional-looking in his expensive gray suit.

They walked toward me, smiling expectantly.

"There's something we wanted to tell you before you leave," the man said and began to shuffle awkwardly.

"What?" I listened only distractedly.

"We want to thank you for what you're doing."

"Why?" I focused on his face now, confused. The gratitude in his eyes surprised me.

"For giving us the opportunity to have a surrogate baby someday. If it weren't for you, we never would have known about Dr. Levin or Louisville. We might not have had a chance to ever—"

"Do you know," the woman interrupted him, "I never read the newspaper, but for some reason, one morning I picked it up while I was having a cup of coffee before I left for the office, and there was your picture. I read the article and was so excited I called my husband at the office right away."

Gratitude lay on their faces like a gift. I shifted from one leg to the other.

"Thank you, I really appreciate it." And I returned their beaming smiles.

September 1980

I began to appreciate nature even more during my pregnancy. I took great pleasure in seeing the dark sky before a thunderstorm, listening to the low rumble of the thunder and watching distant flashes of lightning, admiring the water slashing at the earth, then surveying with wonder when it was over.

I began to spend more time watching my children play, instead of burying myself in the kitchen doing endless tasks that could be done long after the children were grown.

I would sit outside on the front porch in the evening after the children had been read to and kissed good night. It was the hour of the day I enjoyed most. The smell of cool, freshly cut grass and the still-blooming flowers filled the air. It seemed as though everything alive and growing was thanking the heavens for September nights.

Kent's shadow filled the door frame. "Can you come inside? It's cold."

"No, it's not. I'm not."

"Can I join you?"

"No, I need to be alone."

He murmured his understanding and closed the door behind him.

Many people had been curious about the viewpoint of our church regarding my pregnancy. I was as unsure as anyone else how our senior minister felt, since he had thus far chosen to ignore my obvious pregnancy and the controversy surrounding it. But we continued to attend services each week, and the maternity dresses I wore elicited no comments from the parishioners. I assumed they all knew by now that the child I was carrying belonged to another woman. It was easy for me to duck in and out of the church each week, hurrying to pick up the children from Sunday school classes and not stopping to chat with anyone. We had been attending the church for little more than a year, and since we had not yet gotten involved in the social activities, I had very few people to exchange pleasantries with on Sunday mornings.

By mid-September, Julie was about to begin a two-year session of confirmation classes, and we had received a letter in the mail asking us to attend a supper meeting for parents and students. There was no way out of this social function, and I arrived at the church with a pan of brownies in my hand and a great sense of foreboding. The church basement was crowded with families who seemed to know each other and were chatting comfortably. Kent and Julie followed their sweet tooths to the dessert table and I found myself alone. I stood near the doorway feigning confidence and searched the crowd for a familiar face. The young people skipped back and forth boisterously as they eyed the long tables full of cakes, pies, and chocolate brownies.

A tall, hefty man in his early thirties strode toward me. His eyes glinted with curiosity. "Are you the surrogate mother?" His voice was big and warm.

I stepped back, as though he had threatened a physical attack. His mouth turned in amusement. "Did I pronounce it right?"

"Yes." I scanned his face warily.

"Good." He thrust out a large hand. "I'm Steve Michaels, the new assistant minister." He grasped my hand, shaking it firmly. "Now tell me. Are you?" His soft brown eyes were fixed on the middle of my maternity top.

"Yes." I hesitated. "How did you know?"

He chuckled softly. "Look around you. Everyone here knows."

I glanced about guardedly. The room was dotted with faces of every age. Many watched us intrusively, and I could not help but squirm.

"My wife and I have three kids. I can safely say you're due in about two weeks, right?" He watched my face, his back turned to the crowd.

I laughed at his bad guess. "Nope. More like eight."

"Oh, my. Are you carrying twins?"

"Nope. The sonogram said one." I shifted to another foot to ease the pain in my lower back. "Are you new here?"

"Yes, I am. This is my second week. Say, it looks like we're ready to get started. We'll talk more later." Pastor Michaels turned to leave, then stopped and put a long arm around my shoulders, hugging me to his chest. "I want you to know that whatever you need, you can count on me." He looked down at me, and when our eyes met, I was filled with relief and wonder at his openness. I felt an overwhelming trust in him, at that moment, something I could not begin to understand.

Several days later I called him at his church office. He remembered me instantly. "Pastor Michaels, NBC's 'David Brinkley's Magazine' wants to bring a crew to my house to do some filming for their program in October. Would you object if we also filmed at the church and maybe did a scene with the two of us having a consultation?"

"Sounds great!"

"It does?"

"Why do you sound so surprised? Of course!"

"I was planning to spend some time convincing you. I called my obstetrician a few minutes ago to ask him the same thing, thinking we could work the filming in with my next prenatal visit while he took my blood pressure. He said no."

"I don't understand why," Pastor Michaels answered.

"He told me he's spent twenty years building a practice in this town, and he doesn't want to risk his reputation by being publicly associated with surrogate motherhood," I continued. "But, I can understand that, too. He was polite but emphatic."

"That might be," Pastor Michaels clucked sympathetically, "but as your minister it's my duty to stand behind you and support you in your decision."

I did not remind him that my decision had been made months earlier and that we had met each other only several days before.

He asked me to come to his office on Saturday afternoon, stating we should become better acquainted before the filming.

Several days later I sat stiffly on a small gold vinyl chair in Pastor Michaels' office. A picture of Christ wearing a crown of thorns hung on the wall behind his cluttered desk. I fidgeted in the uncomfortable chair until he finished his telephone conversation.

He hung up and leaned back in his chair, adjusting the knot on his brown knit tie. "Whew," he whistled softly. "That reminds me of something one of my professors once said. 'The world is a mountain of shit and we all have to fight like hell to keep our noses above the top of the pile.' " He smiled and watched me closely. I did not know how to respond.

He finally spoke again. "Tell me about your faith."

"Well, I guess I'm like a lot of people," I answered quickly. "I use it like a water faucet. I turn it off and on as I need it. When things are going well, I feel as though I'm doing a great job of managing my life. But when all hell is breaking loose, I'm the first one to look to the heavens and ask, 'Where are you, God?' He's not the one who strays. I am." I spoke without shame. "I admit it. I use my religion sporadically."

His gaze softened and he smiled gently. "Tell me about your marriage." The questions continued, one following another: "Tell me about your childhood." "Tell me about your parents." "How do you feel about them?" The barrage lasted for almost two hours before he stopped.

"What are you?" I gasped in amazement. "A psychiatrist or a minister?" My head was reeling from our conversation. Pastor Michaels had not once touched on the subject of surrogate motherhood or my motives. Why was I here? I'd come to discuss the filming we'd be doing—didn't he want to know why I had made the decision to have a baby for another woman, and how I felt now, two months from delivery? I kept my thoughts inside. I was too intimidated and awed by his authoritarian tone and manner to say anything.

Several times during the interrogation, I glanced nervously at the clock opposite my chair and murmured that I had to leave soon. He took little notice of my apprehension and I finally rose awkwardly from my chair, firmly insisting our conversation was over.

He walked me to the parking lot, and we began chatting animatedly about the filming NBC would be doing the following week.

I finally opened the car door and ducked in, lowering the window to say good-bye. "One nice thing about this pregnancy, Pastor Michaels, is that it will soon be over. The day after I give birth, the whole world will say, 'Who's Elizabeth Kane?' and I can finally go back to being a normal wife and mother. I can't wait to start my Christmas shopping and baking. It will be a relief to be a regular person again."

Pastor Michaels bent low to speak and his tone was serious. "If you really believe that, then you're being terribly naïve."

"Why?"

"Because in the first place, the public won't let you forget what you've done, and in the second place, you've started a mission. It must be finished. It is *your* responsibility to answer the demand for knowledge and to help infertile couples in any way you can by continuing with the publicity."

"Oh, that's nonsense." I laughed up at him nervously and started the engine, anxious to leave.

"Think about what I've said," he warned, backing away from the car. "You're a pioneer. You can't quit now."

I pulled into the driveway to find Jeffrey and Kent on the front lawn playing catch with a large, colorful rubber ball. Kent walked toward the car. "I was worried about you. I thought maybe you had a fender bender or something. I just called the preacher's office to find out what was taking so long."

"It was a long talk."

"About what?"

I scooped Jeff up into my arms for a kiss, but he wriggled away to show me his new ball. "I don't know. Everything and nothing. It's hard to say. I feel as though he threw me into fifteen feet of muddy water and now I have to fight my way to the surface for light and air. He makes every simple thing sound so complicated."

Kent looked at me oddly, studying my face. "It must have been heavy."

"Do you know—" my voice trailed off as I caught sight of Jeffrey. "Get out of the street, Jeff."

Kent glanced toward the curb. "He'll be all right. Go on."

"Do you know, Pastor Michaels offered to drive me down to Louisville in his van and to stay with me for the entire birth and recovery period!"

"Really?"

"Yeah. When I mentioned you wouldn't be there, he offered to take your place. He even insisted on being in the delivery room. Kent, I don't even know the man. I don't want him in the delivery room, for pete's sake."

"I think it's great. He can be around to keep the reporters away, and if you're not in the mood for an interview, he can guard the door. And if you really don't want him in the delivery room, I'm sure he'll understand."

"I don't think so. He's so enthusiastic about it all. He wants to wear his clerical collar and be at the press conference with me. When I protested about his being at the birth, he insisted it wouldn't be anything new for him. He seems to have everything planned out already."

"Hmmm. That's strange. It seems odd that he would take such an interest in you so quickly."

"You're not kidding. I think I need a few days to sort some of these things out." I shook my head, trying to comprehend the entire afternoon. "Do you know, Kent, if it were legal to have this baby here in Illinois, I wouldn't have to cope with any of this worry about traveling to Louisville."

Two days later I stood barefoot on the cool lawn in front of my home. The September sun warmed me as I read a letter Pastor Michaels had just handed to me. He had taken it from his shirt pocket, waved it around while he spoke indignantly about the contents, and warned me not to read it.

"Don't be ridiculous. I have a right to know what's going on," I demanded. The letter was in answer to Pastor Michaels' request to the church council to have NBC film the two of us in his office. It was a searing reply from the president of our congregation, a priggish-looking woman in her mid-forties. I read the letter again, stunned by the words in perfect script.

She had accused me of making a mockery of the Lord's temple and stated I was putting a price tag on the emotional stability of my children by being a surrogate mother. She said

I was a publicity seeker and a grandstander. She wrote that I would make money on the publicity. She closed the letter by stating she could not condone my behavior by allowing any filming to be done in the church building. As president of the congregation, she forbade Pastor Michaels to use the sanctuary for publicity purposes.

As I finished reading, my spirits sank. I knew she had a tremendous amount of influence in our church. I remembered she also taught Julie and Laura in their classes at the local school. Would she punish them, too, because of me?

Part of me did not want to believe what I had just read. "Surely what she's saying is a personal reaction. I mean, this is just her opinion, isn't it?" My voice quivered with each word.

"Unfortunately not." Pastor Michaels shook his head glumly. "You have no idea how many women from our congregation I've had in my office this past week. Women sobbing because they just don't know how to handle their reactions to you."

Anger surfaced suddenly and I shouted, "They don't react to me at all! They all ignore me! Not one of them will even say hello to me on Sunday mornings!"

"You're right. I know it. But I'm trying to teach them that even if we don't like what a person is doing or what a person believes in, we should still try to love that person. I am trying to teach these women to separate the behavior from the person."

"What does that mean?"

"Let's say a man murders his wife. You might not approve of his behavior, but as a Christian, you must love him anyway."

To me, the idea sounded hypocritical and impossible. But I kept that opinion to myself. I did not have the energy to start an argument with the only friend I seemed to have at the moment.

I looked up at Pastor Michaels' round, boyish face. And I felt sorry for myself. I felt sorry for Kent and the children.

"It looks like for some of the people in our church, Christianity ends with the benediction each Sunday." There was bitterness in my every syllable.

We stood in the warm breeze, and Pastor Michaels took a step forward and put his arms around me, hugging me tightly with the mound of baby between us. A saw buzzed loudly from a neighboring yard.

"Give us time, Mary Beth. Don't judge us for judging you," he said softly.

"Pastor Michaels, please don't get involved in this. You're so new in this church and in our city."

"I have to. I promised you I'd be in Louisville with you when you have the baby. I'll stay with you for as long as you need me. My clerical collar will keep the reporters away. They'll respect me."

"Please don't risk everything for me," I pleaded.

He reached out and stroked my hair tenderly. "I want you to learn to trust me, Mary Beth."

I can't, I thought. For some reason I felt uneasy about this pastor's subtle psychological aggression. My fears were confirmed. I soon learned that he was relaying my most intimate confidences to people within our church community. I had no qualms about calling him several weeks later to tell him there was no need for him to accompany me to Louisville for the birth.

October 1980

Eighteen women, all showing signs of advanced pregnancy, sat Indian-style on the floor and eyed each other cautiously. Next to each woman sat a man. Their shapes and ages varied slightly but the looks on their faces were the same—wide-eyed with wonder and apprehension.

Only one man in the room was different. He was old enough to be a father to most of the people already seated. He looked more uncomfortable than the others, as though he would rather be anywhere else. He leaned over and whispered against my hair. "Jesus, they're all kids."

I looked at the smooth, soft skin on their faces and the swollen midriffs. "Not all."

The instructor spoke rapidly in a high-pitched voice with a heavy accent. I strained to decipher each sentence and felt a throb in the back of my neck.

"Everybody introduce yourselves." Her eyes were full of enthusiasm.

Kent and I looked at each other warily, sending silent messages while each couple recited their names in soft, shy tones. They talked about their children already at home or beamed proudly when they announced this was their first baby. For most, the pregnancy was an awesome, frightening experience.

It was our turn. I cleared an imaginary frog from my throat. "I'm Mary Beth and this is my husband, Kent. This is my fourth pregnancy." I offered no other information. Our instructor smiled at me knowingly, then nodded to the couple seated next to us to continue.

Several weeks ago I had called the Pekin Memorial Hospital to register for Lamaze classes. The instructor had returned my call a few days later, refusing me admission to her class. She was polite but adamant. Because of my "unusual situation," she felt I would be disruptive to the class; my presence would create discomfort among the other couples, and they would be unable to concentrate and learn.

"You understand, don't you?" she asked coldly.

"Yeah, sure," I fibbed.

I asked for the name of another instructor and called her at home. Her name was Mrs. Park. I explained the situation and she readily accepted my application. We both agreed it would be wise to withhold information about my pregnancy for the six-week class period and simply pretend we were a normal couple having our fourth baby.

When the introductions were over, the room burst with conversation as couples chatted more comfortably.

"What are you doing here?" the young man sitting next to me teased. "You should have the procedure down pat by now." I laughingly agreed with him.

I remembered the first class the week before. It was short and mainly for the purpose of registering, paying the forty-dollar fee, and receiving booklets. I had dreaded going.

Kent was traveling and unable to be with me. It was a cold, windy evening, and by the time I had served the children their dinner, my back ached with fatigue. I loaded the dishwasher and sighed at the thought of driving downtown alone on the blustery October night.

"Let me go with you. Please, Mom," Laura had begged. She picked up a plate and plopped it into the lower rack without rinsing it. Chunks of potato fell through the rack. "I'll be your coach tonight. I'd love to. Please, Mom." She wriggled with anticipation.

I studied my tall, slender eleven-year-old. Memories of my pregnancy and her birth filled my thoughts, blocking out everything else. I remembered our two hours together in the nursery at night while she was a baby. Her chubby cheeks would split in a wide, toothless smile. She had always been cheerful and patient as an infant.

I could see her as a toddler again, her diaper-clad body with its round, bare tummy and fat little legs strutting down the sidewalk on a warm July evening. She loved to wear her Indian bells strapped to each ankle and to watch each foot hit the ground with a jangle. Then she would chicken-walk with wide, flat feet across a scraggly lawn and pluck a dandelion to present to me as though it were a long-stemmed rose.

Laura did go to the meeting with me, and afterward we hurried to the car, heads bent against the wind.

"That was fun, Mom. Can I go with you every week? Even if Dad goes, too?"

She had often asked if she could drive to Louisville with me to be part of the labor and delivery. She wanted to hold the baby after he was born. She wanted to bring him a plush teddy bear. She wanted to study his face to see if he looked like our Jeffrey.

I didn't have the heart to remind her that that night would be the closest she would ever come to being a part of her brother's life.

Every Thursday night for two hours, Kent and I sat on the hardwood floor of the fourth-floor hospital conference room. Often the room was filled only with the sounds of our deep breathing during imaginary contractions. The concentration intensified when we counted to ten and sighted in on our focal points.

The young expectant mothers spoke earnestly about choosing the right crib, shopping for tiny cotton clothing, and buying soft crib toys with little bells inside. They interrupted each other often in their eagerness to compare information. I remained quiet.

Self-pity began to invade me while their conversations grew more animated. I was the only woman in the room who would go through the discomfort of labor and not have a child in the end. I foresaw depression, soreness, and fatigue after the birth, with no one to share my feelings. There would be no elation while I waited for a nurse to bring my baby to breast-feed, no anticipation each morning of holding him against me, sweet-smelling and warm from sleep. There would not be any relatives calling to congratulate me, begging for details of his every feature.

Good grief, stop feeling sorry for yourself, I thought. I shook my head to scatter the morbid thoughts and came back to the bare, bright conference room. I knew very well the reason I was sitting there in that roomful of strangers. I had no right to envy these women. I had had my turn three times. Now it was Margo's turn. I was warmed by the thought of my son in her arms. She was the one shopping for baby things like the women in my class.

I pictured a pretty, cheerful nursery filled with adorable tiny clothes and irresistible toys. The thoughts reassured me and the self-pity fled.

Part of the purpose of Lamaze classes was to educate the father about his wife's emotions, physical condition, and reactions during different stages of labor. He was told his wife might curse or cry out near the end of her labor and that she might plead with him to stay near her, but would become angry if he tried to speak to her or touch her. He learned not to be offended. This was a normal reaction near the end of her long journey.

"Now, Father," our instructor began her singsong instruction. "When you get home from work every day, I want you to feel your wife's tummy. Then when she's in labor and having a contraction, you'll know the difference in the way her abdomen feels. Come home every night, give her a hug and a kiss. Then when you put your arms around her, you'll feel the kicking. Ask her, 'How's my baby today?' " Her cheeks lifted in a grin, almost closing her tiny eyes. "Okay, fathers? Okay?"

Kent shot a glance in my direction and gave a half smile. I swallowed a chuckle when I saw his face. What was he supposed to say when he put his arms around me and felt the baby kicking against him? "How is Adam's baby today?" I knew what he was thinking and I looked away.

I listened intently to the lecture on cesarean sections. Mrs. Park stood at the blackboard scratching numbers on it with chalk. "Twenty percent of the women in this room will have a C-section, mothers. Listen closely."

I did. My baby was in a breech position, one of the main reasons for a C-section. Despite Dr. Kasten's reassurances that the baby would probably rotate to a head-down position before birth, I added another item to my list of worries.

Chapter 15

October 12, 1980

Kent and I were looking forward to a weekend without the children. Richard had called several days earlier, inviting us to Louisville to be part of a French documentary being filmed at his office. He asked us to drive down on Friday afternoon, do the filming that night, and have dinner with him and his wife, Pam, on Saturday night.

"If we have time on Saturday, I'd like you to see the hospital and the birthing room." I greeted Richard's suggestion with enthusiasm, knowing it would quell my fears about giving birth in a strange hospital.

We soon discovered that the one-hour documentary filming would take four or five hours. The crew from France spoke little English and had difficulty working the rented camera equipment they had picked up that afternoon. I waited anxiously for them to finish and sighed impatiently from where I was perched on the edge of an uncomfortable sofa.

Kent found the scene amusing; there I was rubbing my aching back from sitting in a ramrod position, with an ever-ready smile in the event they would be able to film for another few minutes. The producer finally sighed in defeat and politely asked us to return early the next morning. He promised to have his equipment working properly. I breathed a sigh of relief.

The crew kept their promise and the filming went quickly the next day. They thanked me graciously and walked into Richard's office to film Katie behind Richard's massive desk.

Kent and I leafed through magazines until Richard joined us in the small waiting room.

"What are you doing this afternoon?" he asked, reaching across Karen's desk for his pipe tobacco.

"Katie's boyfriend, Charlie, has a hot-air balloon for the afternoon and he promised us a ride. We're going out to a farm near here. I can't wait. I've wanted to ride in one of those things for years," I answered.

Richard watched me out of the corner of his eye while he filled his pipe. "You're not going to go up, are you?"

"No, I'm going to just stand in it while it's tethered to the ground," I said sarcastically. "Of course I am. They're not dangerous."

"They can get pretty bumpy," Richard disagreed. "I don't think you should."

"Don't be an old lady, Rich. I'll be fine," I protested, but I was soon outnumbered when Kent sided with Richard and insisted I stay on the ground.

"Well, what am I supposed to do all afternoon while Kent's having fun?" I pouted.

Except for the sound of Richard sucking deeply on his pipe, the room was silent. He looked thoughtfully into the distance. Before long he said casually, "How would you like to come back to my house after lunch and meet Margo and Adam?"

"Sure. Fine."

"You don't believe me, do you?"

"Nope."

He grinned, and I saw mischief in his face. "Well, it's all arranged."

"Oh, my God, Richard. Really?"

"Yup."

"Why didn't you tell me sooner?"

"I just now got off the phone with them."

I turned to Kent to share my elation. "Oh, Kent, I can't believe it. After all these months. Do you wanna come along?"

"No way. I don't want to meet that guy. Besides . . . I'm not passing up a ride in a hot-air balloon." He put his arm around me. "You and Richard go. Have a good time."

"A good time? You're crazy," I answered. "Oh, Rich, I'm so nervous."

"Good. It serves you right for bugging me about it for eight months."

"Rich, what would you do if I didn't want to meet them? If I changed my mind?"

"I'd put my hands around your skinny little neck and squeeze." His dark eyes flashed playfully and he made a wringing motion with his hands.

"Well, what if I don't like them?"

"You will."

"What if they don't like me?"

"They're stuck with you anyway." He threw back his head and laughed with pleasure at his own wit.

After lunch, we sped down the highway in his dark brown Corvette and, within twenty minutes, turned into a quiet subdivision with winding streets. We moved through the maze of perfectly groomed lawns and luxurious homes until we screeched to a stop in a curved driveway gracing the front of a massive two-story house. I sat in the car not wanting to get out. Suddenly the front door opened, and four small girls spilled onto the lawn and into their father's arms. Pam followed them, giving me a knowing smile. "I promised the kids hot fudge sundaes. We'll be back in an hour or so."

I followed Richard into the house through the red brick foyer, and he strode into the kitchen, assuming I would follow. He picked up a telephone on a small kitchen desk and dialed.

He spoke softly, with his back to me, then hung up and turned toward me, looking serious. "They'll be here in a few minutes. They're leaving now."

I touched the round bulge protruding from beneath my light blue maternity top and stroked it lovingly. "This is it, baby. Five more minutes and I'll know who your parents are."

I poked around the first floor until I found a half bath off the family room. Richard stood in the doorway, leaning jauntily against it while I peered into the mirror. The wind had teased my hair into a wild fluff. Oh, why hadn't I had it cut before we drove down here? I dug through my purse for a hairbrush, found a tiny glass bottle and held it to my wrist.

Richard grinned, watching every move. "Perfume, too?"

"Leave me alone."

He obeyed and began to pace the length of the carpeted family room, walking from the red brick fireplace to the stereo on the other side of the room. Back and forth, back and forth, like an animal in a cage. He began to search for his camera and pipe, chattering at me. I heard only the noise he made, not the words. My jaws were locked while thoughts raced through my head.

What if I don't like her? She's going to raise him. *Will it be embarrassing to meet the father?* Our relationship is so intimate, yet so distant. *How will we react to each other? What if they don't like me? Oh, why did I ever argue with Richard about wanting to meet them?*

I tugged at my curls with the small brush and shoved it back into my purse. Then I scowled into the mirror at my image.

Richard dropped onto the sofa and leaned against the soft cushions, sucking hard on his unlit pipe. His long legs and cowboy boots stretched in front of him and reached halfway across the cozy room. He began to rub his stomach absent-mindedly, in a circular fashion as though he were in pain.

"Just watch Adam blurt out his last name when he meets you," Richard said.

I plopped onto the sofa opposite him. "Don't be silly."

"Watch and see." He nodded his head for emphasis. "Not on purpose, of course, but I can guarantee it will happen."

"Oh, Rich, stop being ridiculous. The last thing on earth this couple wants is for me to know who they are." I scoffed at his sureness.

How many times in the past months had I felt as though their reluctance to meet me was an indirect rejection? I had tried to visualize their faces hundreds of times. Over and over, I had asked Richard for a picture of them. Earlier, I would have been satisfied with that. But later my curiosity and desire to meet them had turned into a burning obsession.

I jumped off the sofa and returned to the bathroom. My hands trembled as I applied lip gloss. I heard Richard leap off the sofa and rush past me into the foyer. I started to follow and he put up a hand as a signal to stay where I was. I ignored his warning and followed him across the family room, stopping at the edge of the foyer. My eyes searched the screen door, straining to see their faces. Voices floated into the house, and then a refined, petite blonde woman stepped daintily across the threshold. Her canary yellow sweater and slacks accentuated her femininity. Satisfied, my eyes flew to her husband's face. I had expected—no. All these months I had visualized a dark-haired, plain-looking man of average height with a pronounced paunch. The man before me was blond and boyishly attractive. His blue cashmere sweater did not hide his trim, athletic body. The blue in the sweater matched his eyes perfectly.

He grinned shyly at me, with teeth even and white against a deep tan. It took me about four seconds to reach the conclusion that the baby would be adorable!

Silence hung for a moment in the room, and then I approached Margo and embraced her briefly. Adam walked toward us, and I impulsively grabbed his hand and placed it on my protruding abdomen.

"Look at how big your baby is already, Adam. Feel him!" I blurted. His face filled with distress and confusion. I drew back instantly and mentally kicked myself for being such a clod. The three of us walked stiffly into the family room while Richard held a camera in front of our faces, clicking furiously and recording every emotion. Finally Margo put a tiny, slender hand over the lens. "Richard, stop. That's enough," she said firmly.

I watched openmouthed as he obeyed her, returned the camera to the top of the stereo, and joined her on the couch. I curled into a leather rocking chair next to the fireplace while Adam lowered himself gingerly onto a love seat to my left. I looked from one face to another, feeling gawky and out of place. The weight of the baby pressed against my lungs, and I inhaled deeply and shifted position in the chair. I stole a glance at Adam and saw a smile whip across his face so quickly, I wondered if it had been there at all.

Hopelessly uncomfortable, I tossed my shoes toward the fireplace, drew my legs up onto the chair tailor-fashion, and wriggled until the bulk of the baby was squarely in my lap. All eyes were fixed on my wriggling.

I grinned with embarrassment. "This is my Lamaze position. It lets me breathe." Adam cleared his voice with a low growl. "How have you been feeling, Elizabeth?"

Should I tell him about the sleepless nights when the baby kicks, the painful pressure from tiny hands and legs in my groin and bladder, the shortness of breath that results in constant fatigue? The pesky heartburn and continual back pain? I stole a glance at Margo's tiny waistline and a stab of envy shot through me.

"I feel fine," I lied cheerfully. "I'm a little bit tired, but

I guess all pregnant women feel that way near the end." I rested my right hand on the mound. "One more month and he's all yours," I beamed.

I looked at Margo expectantly, but her smile was gone. Her body language revealed nothing to me, and I changed the subject quickly. "Have you picked out a name for the baby yet?"

Adam answered for her. "As a matter of fact," he interrupted, "we have narrowed it down to five."

"Five!" I laughed. "You call that narrowed down?" I rubbed my hands together briskly. "Come on, let's hear them. We'll all take a vote."

"Well," Adam drawled, smiling shyly. "I like Winston."

I shot forward in my chair. "Winston!" I shouted, then fell back in mock helplessness. "Is that a joke?" I turned to Margo.

She threw back her head and laughed and clapped her hands, rejoicing. "Oh, Elizabeth, thank you. You're wonderful. See, Adam? I told you that was terrible." She smiled at him lovingly, teasing.

He dropped his eyes, looking as hurt as a little boy who had just goofed on an easy math problem and who was now being ridiculed by the other kids in the class.

"Adam," I said tenderly. "You wouldn't do that to your son."

"I thought it was nice."

"Let's try another one," I encouraged him.

"Justin," he beamed. "Justin Maley."

"That's not bad," I fibbed. Where did "Maley" come from? A grandfather? Or maybe Margo's maiden name? The sunny, cozy room was quiet.

Adam continued without hesitating. "Or we were thinking of Jonathan Andrew Maley."

My eyes riveted to him while he went on innocently.

Margo impassively, unabashedly watched me. When I looked at Richard, I knew immediately his prediction had been confirmed. He leaned back into the cushions. His eyes rolled toward the ceiling and he bit down on his unlit pipe.

"Adam, did you just tell me your last name?"

"Oh, yeah! I guess I did."

A joyous rapture slowly spread through me, and I clamped down on the inside of my cheek, trying not to show the unexpected delight. The name "Maley" was already fixed in my memory. There was a thick silence while I waited. And waited.

"Richard, please don't be angry," I blurted.

"I'm not. Don't worry about it." He struck a match and casually drew on his pipe stem, concentrating on the dancing flame. "Didn't I tell you it would happen?" he grinned. "You're all too comfortable with each other to be on guard."

The remainder of our meeting felt like a family reunion. The bond was inevitable when I remembered how often Margo and Adam had been in my thoughts since last February. Even though their faces were unfamiliar, the long-repressed sentiments were there. We had too much to share and so little time.

Margo asked how the children were reacting to the pregnancy, and I quickly relayed Laura's fears of never being able to become a part of her half brother's life.

"Would you mind if the children gave the baby a gift? They want him to have something to remember them by."

Adam cut in. "Now you know us better than that. Of course we wouldn't mind."

I searched their eyes, looking for true feelings, and saw only genuine smiles radiating from their faces. How *would* I know you better than that? I thought. I don't know either of you at all, though I love you both. You are the father of my son, Adam.

Margo sprang to her feet after glancing at her wristwatch. "Adam, we're already fifteen minutes late for the party and it's a twenty-minute drive. We really must leave."

The hour had slid by too quickly. I wanted to cry out in protest; I needed more time. Privately I wanted to embrace them and reassure them everything was going to be fine.

"Come here, Margo. Feel my stomach. The baby's kicking now."

She crossed the room and placed her fingers delicately across the right side of my abdomen. A smile opened her face during the next thrust and she gasped. "Was that a foot or a knee?"

"I think it was an elbow." I placed my hand next to hers, ready for the next push from a tiny limb.

Richard crossed the room and joined Margo. He bent over me and drew imaginary lines on my abdomen with his fingers to show the baby's position. He talked to Adam and ran his hands up and down my body. "See? His head is already down in the pelvis preparing for birth."

Adam cleared his throat again and stared past us, engrossed in the blue and yellow flames skipping over the logs in the fireplace. He looked so naïve and self-conscious, I wanted to hold his hand. How could I feel so united with this sweet man and so detached at the same time? I would have given anything to know how they felt about me. He was probably as bewildered as I. And Margo? How did she feel, seeing me large with the weight of her husband's child?

Margo wrapped her arms around me in a warm hug. "I can't tell you how wonderful it was for us to be here this afternoon, Elizabeth. I feel so much better now."

Now we were circled in the driveway, with the October breezes tugging at our clothes. I might not see them again. My invitation to them to be in the delivery room was met with a momentary hesitation, but then Adam promised that they would be there if I really needed them.

Richard's presence seemed to loom like a threatening cloud. It was difficult to say the words we needed to say or to share an intimate moment before we parted.

"Go ahead, Adam," Richard teased. "You can hug her. She won't break."

Adam timidly draped his arms loosely around me while Richard watched in obvious amusement.

They were standing beside their large black sedan. I mentally pulled them back to me and clutched at them, begging them to stay. "Please don't dart in and out of my life this quickly," I appealed to them silently. I craved only another fifteen minutes.

"Margo," I called after her as she settled into the front seat of the car. "Is the nursery ready yet?"

She poked her head through the open door and spoke, her gaze steady. "Just the clothes." Her voice faltered. "There isn't any furniture. I'll wait until just before I bring him home before I have it delivered." Then her eyes misted and I was startled.

"Margo—if you think—if you have any ideas that I might try to keep him—"

"Oh, no, Elizabeth," she quickly denied. "It's just that when we adopted our first child, it took his mother nine months before she decided to sign the papers. I lived in terror every day of those nine months fearing my son would be taken from me. Then when she finally agreed, I waited in the car at the attorney's office for four hours. It took her that long to decide to sign the termination papers. I can't go through that hell again."

I visualized her suffering. When I looked at Adam, the wrenching emotions of those nine long months flashed across his face like a neon sign.

My child would not disappoint them in any way. Nor would I. I would sign those papers gladly five days after the birth, and if not gladly, at least promptly. I could never knowingly hurt this loving couple waiting for my son.

The car backed out of the driveway swiftly, and Margo and Adam waved good-bye. I turned toward the house before they rounded the corner. With a stockinged toe, I scuffed at the weeds growing between the red bricks that lined Richard's front walk. "Pull these weeds, Rich," I growled. "They look terrible." I poked at them again sharply with my foot and climbed the four steps to the house.

I paused inside the screen door and peered through it at Richard who stood on the front porch. "They really love each other, don't they, Rich? After all these years—" I looked at him for a long moment. "Rich, I know we agreed this meeting would be an experiment, but don't ever do it again. Don't ever let your surrogates meet the parents. I'm glad I did, but I'll soon wish I hadn't."

I was alternately filled with elation and depression at having met them, but the moment their car turned the corner, the depression reigned supreme. My son was going to live with two people who were no longer nameless or faceless. And I envied them. I envied their close relationship, the love and respect they had for each other after all those years of marriage, their financial security.

I knew they would be good parents. Adam would be a perfect father. Firm but gentle and not afraid to show his love. He would be a good role model. And Margo? I couldn't have handpicked a better woman. She was attractive and sensitive, caring and intelligent. She would put her own ambitions aside to raise my son.

She would be the one to encourage him when he staggered across the room on short, chubby legs and fell into her arms in triumph at those first steps. Within a few weeks he would be awakening her at night instead of me. She would cuddle him to her breast. She would rejoice in each accomplishment as he shed childhood and entered adolescence. And even if someday he and I would meet again, we would always be strangers. The months he spent with me would mean nothing to him. There would be no memories.

My feelings of self-pity fled quickly when I remembered the joy on their faces as they spoke of him. He would bring happiness into their lives.

Yet I was filled with a strange new fear. I had thought it would be easier to let go if I didn't know the names of his parents or where they lived. How easy it would be for me now to pick up the telephone on the days his absence overwhelmed me and severed all rationality. How easy to intrude into their lives through telephone calls and letters, making demands for pictures and asking for accounts of his progress. I did not want to be a threatening reminder to Margo that another woman had given her son life. I told myself that once the umbilical cord was cut, I would force myself to cut the emotional attachment as well.

Chapter 16

The kitchen calendar had become my enemy, an ominous monster lurking on the wall. The induction date drew closer and closer—Three weeks more! Three weeks more! At times I was barely aware of the days blending into one another. Other times I would stare at the numbers on paper and fiercely try to will them back to April.

There were days when I would have welcomed the first pains of labor and the freedom from my burden. Justin's weight on a nerve made it difficult to walk, and often my legs would fold under me until he shifted position. Many times I stood in the aisle at the supermarket, leaning on the cart for support until the feeling returned to my legs. At first I found it humorous, but as time passed it became less so.

Other days, thoughts of labor and the pain of delivery would consume my mind—I could think of nothing else. I was reluctant to part with the little friend who had shared my body as well as my thoughts for the past eight months. I began having nightmares that haunted me into the daylight hours. I would fight secret demons in my sleep as Justin twisted and turned inside me. I sorted endlessly through my thoughts—dissecting and analyzing my feelings. And then I would awake early, damp with the turmoil of my dreams, and I would try to scare them away by rushing to ready the children for school. But the dreams seemed to drag along behind me as I did the housework, hanging on relentlessly.

Then there were Margo's words when she called me a few days after we had met. Her voice was filled with emotion as she told me she had felt empty when she saw me pregnant with her husband's child. Her voice had trailed off and we were both wordless.

We were all paying a price for the giving and receiving of life.

Kent's new job required more and more travel, leaving me to cope with the daily travail of raising children and maintaining a home. One minor crisis followed another in those final weeks—problems at school with unfinished homework, frantic calls to the veterinarian, plumbing leaks, and the last-minute scramble to make Halloween costumes.

When he walked in the front door after being gone for days, the only welcome Kent would receive was a long tirade on the difficulties I had encountered that week. His only answer was to remain mute, which would infuriate me more. The fury would build until I was ranting accusations about his job being the only thing that mattered to him anymore. I insisted I was nothing to him but household help, someone he ignored as long as his laundry was clean and all the chores were done. Even as I spoke, I knew I was being unreasonable. But I needed to vent my anger.

I couldn't communicate with Kent. I couldn't scream at Richard. I surely wouldn't admit anything to the press, who were calling me daily with requests to be present at the birth. But I felt the demands from everyone during those last weeks.

My pouting and accusations replaced normal conversation and loving communication, something that had always suffered in our marriage. But never as badly. Until now.

One morning I awoke bursting with newfound energy. I didn't question the source of this unlikely spurt, but began to strip dusty curtains from bedroom and kitchen windows until the house looked oddly bare. I spent the morning washing windows and curtains. I ironed and rehung the crisp material over shining glass, moving slowly under the pressure of the baby's weight.

When I passed our collection of Hummel figurines in the curio cabinet in the living room, I stopped and slid the glass door aside. It would be the perfect time to pick out a figurine for Justin, I thought.

After Margo and Adam had agreed to accept a gift, the children had decided on a Hummel. It was something they felt he would appreciate, and it would grow in value over the years. They wanted to give something that would remind him of their love for him. A gift he would cherish when he was older, whether he ever knew them or not.

I studied the figurines, one by one. The handpainting done so painstakingly in Germany seemed to give each tiny figure a personality all its own. There was an aura of love surrounding that cabinet; the children were often drawn to it. They would admire the figures, creating stories for each little porcelain child, and then pick out their favorites.

It'll have to be a boy, I know that, I thought. I reached toward the glass shelf and picked up *The Photographer*, with his little dachshund by his side.

No, Margo and Adam don't have a dog. I replaced him gently on the shelf and looked at another. *Ride into Christmas* was a beautiful child riding down a snowy slope on a sled loaded with a tree and gifts.

No, I can't—that's my favorite. *Easter Greetings*? No, that's Jeff's. He was our Easter baby.

The Doctor? It was adorable. He stood in a white coat, a broken doll at his feet. Maybe . . .

The Skier? Definitely not. A wedding gift from a relative. How about *A Letter to Santa*? I reached toward the back of the bottom shelf and pulled out one of the larger pieces. I scrutinized it carefully, thinking. Justin was due around Thanksgiving, even though he would be induced on the sixteenth. That was about the time little boys started thinking about writing to Santa.

The porcelain figure stood on tiptoe in the snow, trying to reach a mailbox. His mittened hands gripped a large envelope. A stocking cap covered tufts of windblown blond hair. The child's earnest brown eyes were filled with determination as he stretched his little body that last inch to drop the letter through the slot. It was enchanting.

Justin might have brown eyes like mine and blond hair like his father, I thought. I knew for certain he would be a determined child. It was perfect. This was the one.

Without warning, tears began to sting my eyes and the figurine's coat and leggings blurred. I kissed it lightly and put it back on the shelf. I slid the glass door shut and slipped into the antique rocking chair next to the cabinet. The tiny lump that had formed in my throat grew until I could not swallow. "What's the matter with you?" I chided myself aloud.

The house was too quiet. My ears began to ache, and I wished the children were there, their laughter and happy chatter filling the emptiness. I sat in the afternoon sunlight that filtered through the sheer draperies, and made no attempt to wipe the tears that ran down my cheeks.

Would my giving away that porcelain boy signify the giving away of the child? Was I already terminating my parental rights?

The thought frightened me. If I loved him this much now and had never seen him, how would I feel when he was gone? I started to ache from his absence, even while he lay quietly inside me, resting on my lap.

An hour later I startled myself back to reality. Surrogate motherhood would work if I made it work. I had publicly announced over and over what a wonderful idea it was, what a tremendous breakthrough it had been for infertile couples. But what if I failed at the end? If I crashed now, or in the hospital, the whole world would be watching me. The media would record it all. Some would say, "I told you so. It serves you right, too, for your half-cocked notions."

All right. I chose to set an example for the surrogate mothers of the future. I would do a perfect job of it.

I rose from the rocker and walked slowly out of the room to look for a box for the little porcelain boy.

The following day Jeffrey and I sat on beige chairs in a shoe store.

"Please, Mom." Jeff's brown eyes begged until I felt my resistance begin to melt. "Me like the tan ones best."

"Jeffrey, the dark ones are dressier looking and won't show scuff marks as easily. Let's buy the brown cowboy boots," I reasoned.

He stood up, very sure of himself. "No," he announced. "Me taking home the tan boots. See how good they walk?" He goose-stepped around the red shag carpeting like a Russian soldier until he was the center of attention.

"Okay. But for what they cost, you'd better *love* them, not like them," I teased.

We drove home with raindrops splattering the dusty windshield. The sky was dark and the wind came in loud gusts. We pulled into the small corner grocery. I grabbed Jeff and we dashed into the store just as the water seemed to gush from the sky.

I helped Jeffrey into the grocery cart and headed toward the dairy counter. The girls would be home from school soon. I glanced at my watch, noticed a special on peanut butter, and placed two jars in the cart. When I looked up, I saw that a fragile elderly woman, wearing what was probably her "good black coat," had been watching us. She smiled, her eyes resting on Jeff. She reminded me of my grandmother with her sweet, pleasant face and her white curly hair neatly arranged under a hair net of the same color. A thin plastic rain bonnet trailed from her coat pocket.

"My, you certainly have some good-looking shoes on your youngster, missus." Her voice quivered with age.

I chuckled, realizing she probably had not purchased shoes for her children in thirty years. The prices today would astound her. "Those good-looking shoes just cost me thirty-two dollars without tax. Jeff insisted on wearing them home. He's so proud of them."

Jeff beamed and stuck both feet in the air for her to see the shiny new leather. The woman watched his cherubic face, and her expression grew even softer.

I began to swerve my cart around her, stopping at the dairy counter. She stood behind us while I stooped over for a gallon of milk. "Is he your only child, missus?" she asked timidly.

I sneaked a peek at the bulk that emerged from beneath my coat. "Heavens, no," I replied patiently. "I have two girls at home, eleven and twelve."

She nodded, smiled at Jeff again, and pushed her cart slowly down the aisle a few feet, as if to leave. But she stopped and turned toward us once again.

She began to speak very quietly now, almost to herself more than to me. "All my married life I wanted to have a baby and I never did get one. No, ma'am, I never did get that baby." She stared past me and I sensed her despair, even after all those decades of her infertility had passed. She looked so vulnerable.

I broke the silence, feeling like an intruder. "I'm having this baby for a lady like yourself. She can't have any children either. I'm having a baby for her and her husband. I'm their surrogate mother."

She studied us for a long minute, glancing from me to Jeff. He smiled angelically at her, and her pale blue eyes filled with tears.

Her voice was only a whisper now. "God bless you, little lady. God bless you."

She turned away and shuffled down the aisle of canned goods. Long after she was out of sight, I thought about her pain and how she must have suffered all those years. I imagined her longing to celebrate a Mother's Day. Life had cheated her.

November 1, 1980

Two and a half weeks before the day I was to be induced, the children piled onto my bed with their trick-or-treat candy and began to argue over their favorite Sunday morning cartoons. The kaleidoscope of flashing colors and long-legged characters soon mesmerized them, and they lay wrapped in a cocoon of blankets in front of the TV.

Jeffrey unwrapped a Tootsie Roll. "Mama, when you come home, where will your baby be?" he demanded.

The girls were instantly attentive. Their faces studied mine as I slowly explained for what seemed like the three-hundredth time.

"The baby will go to his new home. There's a mommy in Louisville who couldn't grow a baby in her own tummy, so we're going to give her this baby to take care of and to love. She needs a little boy as sweet as you are." I grabbed him and kissed his neck with loud smacking sounds and he squirmed away, seeming satisfied.

"Okay," he answered.

The room rippled with laughter. "Gosh, he's sure casual about it," Julie said.

Laura spoke truthfully then. "That's because he's the 'king' in our house and he doesn't want to be dethroned."

Julie leapt onto the bed and knelt next to my hips, placing her hands on my huge abdomen. "Let me feel him."

We watched together in wonder as the mound under my nightgown began to move from one side to another, and then finally a small knob popped up beneath the stretched skin. The girls squealed with delight, grabbing for the bump. "Oh, it's a knee, Mom. It's his little knee." Laura beamed with the discovery.

"No, I think it's his rear end," Julie insisted.

"Nobody has a pointed rear end, stupid." Laura mocked her. "I think it's an elbow 'cause it's so little and bony."

Julie flopped onto her belly next to me and looked up wistfully. "Mom, do you think they'll love our baby as much as we love Jeff?"

Laura interrupted. "I think Margo will be jealous of the baby because he's yours and Adam's and not hers."

"She'll never think about that once he's in her house, Laura," I replied.

"I hope not," she mused and turned back to the noise coming from the television.

"Mom?" It was Julie.

"Hmmm?" I laid my newspaper across my knees and looked at her.

"What will you do if this baby looks just like Jeffrey?"

My answer came so easily, without the usual stab, that I was taken by surprise. "Then Jeff will have a little brother who looks just like him, won't you, Jeff?" I bent over and lightly kissed his round pink cheek, marveling at the sweet smell of him.

Julie plopped onto the floor next to Laura and began to dig through her trick-or-treat bag for a chocolate bar.

"Coffee?" Kent pushed through the door, backside first, holding two steaming mugs.

I took one gratefully and sipped the hot liquid. "Hey, Kent, guess what? I'm making progress," I announced.

He patted the large mound under the blanket. "You sure are. Three weeks to go, and then you can get up early and make *my* breakfast."

"No, not that kind of progress, you tease. I'm talking about feelings. I just had a conversation with the kids that would have sent me into tears a couple of weeks ago."

" 'Bout what?" He edged onto the bed and reached for the newspaper.

"The baby. What he'll look like, where he'll live. Things like that."

"There's no point in dwelling on what he'll look like. He's not yours," he reminded me, not unkindly.

I hugged Jeffrey to me and held him too tightly. "I never let myself forget that for a moment. I don't dare."

Kent's words, spoken to a reporter only weeks earlier, echoed through my mind: "I admire Mary Beth for what she's doing. I think it takes a lot of courage." Even though he had been unable to say those words directly to me, I treasured them as much that day as I had when I overheard them.

Where is it coming from, all this courage? I wondered.

Several days later on a rainy afternoon, I prepared lunch for Kent. That evening's dinner was on the stove: chunks of roast beef simmered in a thick vegetable concoction that was more stew than soup, just the way Kent liked it. "Stewp" was the family name for my creations. I held a wooden spoon and stirred absentmindedly while I thought about the telephone call I had received that morning.

Kent hung his raincoat in the closet, kissed me on the cheek, and bent low to inhale the aroma of meat, vegetables, and herbs.

"Mmmm. It's nice to come home for lunch once in a while."

"This isn't lunch. We're having grilled cheese sandwiches."

"That's okay." He walked into the half bath off the kitchen. "How are you?" he called over the noise of tap water.

I didn't answer, knowing he wouldn't notice anyway.

He lifted Jeffrey into the antique high chair, poured milk from a gallon jug, and asked in a vague tone, "Did you get any interesting phone calls this morning?"

My head jerked up to look at him. "What do you mean, 'interesting'?"

"Nothing special. I just wondered if Karen called you. You know I don't want you doing any more publicity before the baby's born."

I slid a cheese sandwich onto his plate and handed him a sharp knife. "I got one phone call from a reporter today."

"Who?" The curiosity was unmistakable.

"Sarah Moore Hall called from *People* magazine." He bit into his sandwich, nodding, while I continued. "She wants to come to the house next week for an 'exclusive,' as she put it."

"Is that soup ready? I'd like a small bowl, if it is."

I ladled soup into a bowl until Kent held up a hand as signal to stop.

"What does she have in mind?" he asked.

"She wants to write about my feelings and how they've changed during the pregnancy, especially now that the end is near. She also wants to be in the delivery room with me, so she can write about my feelings during the birth. She wants to stay around until we go to court, so she can record what I have to say about giving the baby back to his father." I hesitated and watched Kent lift the spoon to his mouth in a steady rhythm, slurping loudly at each spoonful.

"You promised her a follow-up story after the insemination," he said, his eyes riveted to the bowl.

"I know. You don't have to remind me. I just don't want to do it."

"Then don't. I don't blame you. You don't owe anybody anything." He shoved the last bite of his sandwich into his mouth and wiped his lips on the linen napkin beside his plate.

"She offered me five thousand dollars."

He stopped chewing, one cheek bulging. "*Five thousand dollars?*"

"Yeah, you heard me. Five big ones. Five grand to sell my soul."

"This is the first time anyone has offered to pay you for any publicity. You realize that?"

"I don't care. I don't want to do it."

"Why not?" His words were sharp.

"Because I don't know if I want the whole world to know how I feel. Not now or after. What if I'm depressed and feel like hiding under the blankets all day? Do you think I want some reporter sitting next to my bed recording my most intimate thoughts about the labor and delivery? *While* I'm going through it?" My voice had risen and I did nothing to restrain the sarcasm. "I don't expect you to understand, Kent. But a birth is a very private and personal time for a woman. I don't want an audience when my legs are in the air."

Kent was completely controlled and spoke softly. "We could use the money. You haven't worked for almost seven months."

"I know that. Do you think I don't know how much we've taken out of our savings account since I quit my job? But I will not sell my soul to that magazine for five thousand dollars."

"Why not?" His face twisted bitterly. "You've been doing it for Levin all these months for nothing. You've done it for every reporter and television studio that's asked you. You've done a dozen telephone interviews when you should have been getting supper for the kids. The only difference this time is you'd get something out of it."

Kent's tone chilled me. He had never spoken to me that way. Ever. I gawked at him in disbelief, then bolted from the room. I took the steps two at a time, oblivious to the cumbersome load under my breasts. Tears blinded me as I slammed the bedroom door with all my strength, locking it behind me. Damn you, Kent.

When I heard the screech of rubber on the street, I knew

he was on his way back to the glass cage in his office. To safety and solitude.

His words cut into me, slicing deeper than I could have thought possible. All these months, all this time he'd gone along with the publicity. There was never bitterness and anger until the magic word erupted: *money*.

A timid knock at the door and a tiny voice brought me back. "Momma?"

I opened the door and fell back onto the bed in exhaustion as Jeff sat down next to me, confused by my tears. He quietly rubbed my back with his small hand while he muttered soothing words to comfort me.

I lay there for a long time and tried to sort out everything Kent and I had said. Should I swallow my pride, do the magazine article, and take the money? I was terrified of what I might feel after the birth. How would I react? It wouldn't be a thirty-minute talk show, where I could almost predict the next question. What if I was severely depressed? It would be a reporter's dream. I could just see the headlines: ELIZABETH KANE, PIONEER MOTHER, TAKES A DIVE.

That day I was obligated to no one. But if I signed a contract with *People* magazine, I would have to reveal everything. For weeks they would want to record every event and do God knows what with the photographs, twisting my words into any kind of story they wanted. I would have absolutely no control, and Kent and the children might have to suffer the repercussions for months.

My head began to swim as I recalled that Richard had actually mentioned camera pools in the delivery room; and there would be major networks clamoring for a story; press conferences; foreign reporters calling me at home, begging me to allow them to be present at the birth.

It was all tearing me apart. I hated it. I felt like a whittling project at Girl Scout camp. Chipped and gouged and dug at, until nothing recognizable was left. Only a small, mutilated piece to be tossed into a roaring fire. Just an experiment.

If I did the story and accepted the money, it would mean a much-deserved vacation for the family that winter in Florida. Kent and the children had endured so much as a result of the pregnancy—my ever-changing moods, the endless fatigue, the loss of companionship. I thought of all the things I should have done with the children that summer and hadn't been able to do. They had rarely complained, but did they resent me for it? Did I owe them this opportunity to pay the bills and give us a vacation? The kids needed dental work; Julie had been waiting impatiently for braces that would cost $2,500. How much did I owe my family?

I rose from the bed, kissed Jeffrey, and wrenched at his thin little smile. A glance in the mirror revealed red, swollen eyes and a pasty complexion. I thought of all the people who called me a publicity seeker and a celebrity. *Celebrity*? I sneered at my reflection. If this was the price I must pay, they could have it all. If they only knew the truth before they judged me so harshly.

Maybe I did owe a piece of myself to the world and, most of all, to the children. But I could not do it. I could not prostitute myself for $5,000. I hugged Jeffrey to me.

A short time later we were in the kitchen. The telephone rang, barely audible over the drone of the mixer. I turned it off and grabbed the receiver.

"Hello, Elizabeth." Sarah's voice was easily recognizable.

"I've thought about your offer, Sarah, and—"

"Good," she interrupted.

"And I've decided—"

"I've just talked to my editor in New York City—"

"Sarah, I'm not—" I tried again to finish my sentence.

"He's withdrawn the offer," she gushed cheerfully.

"Oh, good!" I was relieved, puzzled, and disappointed at the same time.

"What he wants to do now is to have a photographer come with me to your house for a few days next week. He wants pictures of you and the children during your last days at home, and he wants some shots of you packing for the hospital and of the children saying good-bye to you when you leave for Louisville on the fifteenth. The photographer will be in the delivery room with us to take pictures of you and the baby after the birth. It will be an exclusive with no other photographers present. You will not be allowed to give any interviews to anyone else for seven weeks—and we'll pay you $15,000! If it sounds all right to you, we can have a contract sent out this afternoon." Her voice rose with enthusiasm.

I groped for the closest chair and fell into it. I told her I would let her know in a few days. There was so much to consider.

First of all, there were legal considerations. Since the case would set precedent in the Kentucky courts and since surrogacy had never been legal anywhere in the United States or been processed through any judicial system, the publicity could draw adverse reactions from the people of that state. It was also an election year. The judge might decide that his career was on the line, that he might have to bow to public opinion and rule the surrogate procedure illegal. He might even put the baby in a foster home. He could refuse, according to Katie, to let Adam or me have possession of our son.

People magazine would not promise to hold the story until after the legal proceedings. And, after caring for the baby all these months, I could not take the smallest chance that the surrogacy procedure might become hopelessly tangled as a result of early publicity. The baby belonged to his father. We had to ensure that the process went smoothly.

Kent and I would be listed as the legal parents of the baby at birth. Only after we both signed the termination papers in the judge's office in the Jefferson County courthouse five days after the birth would a new certificate be issued with Adam listed as the father and me as the mother. And then, six months after the birth, Margo would be able to climb the same steps at the courthouse and have her name written into the space marked "Mother." Justin would officially be her son at that moment, as though he had been born to her.

I reread a letter I had received from our attorney several months before:

> I'm concerned that the amount and degree of media interest will serve to alert our circuit judges to the termination and adoption proceeding, which will be filed here [in Louisville]. Perhaps I am being overly conservative and cautious but I feel that a judge can evaluate this matter much more objectively if he does so without the glare of camera lights or under the scrutiny of the press. These matters by statute are intended to be private. I only hope that we can proceed in anonymity. My intent is not to alarm or disturb you, but only to alert you to possible repercussions from too much exposure and publicity. You are the vanguard of a movement that ten years from now might be taken for granted.

Several days later it was not difficult to tell Sarah that all the money in the world wasn't worth risking a delay in the court proceedings. I turned down the $15,000 offer.

Having to cope with this problem restored Kent's and my abilities to communicate, and a feeling of closeness was renewed. I was delighted when he casually mentioned one night after a Lamaze class that he would be driving me to Louisville and coaching me in the birth.

Chapter 17

November 8, 1980

I awoke with a bitter taste of acid rolling into my throat, choking me. I rolled over, slid heavily off the mattress, and knelt on the floor next to the bed. The nausea erupted suddenly. I hoisted myself and stumbled to the bathroom in the dim light. I sat on the cold tile floor and waited for the next rush. The bathroom window was dark. I had no concept of time as the nausea continued to ripple through me.

Some time later, I became restless and crept down the stairs to the kitchen. Every muscle ached with weariness, and yet I paced the kitchen floor like a nervous animal.

"What's the matter?" Kent squinted against the bright lights, rubbed his eyes, and yawned. "Are you sick?"

"I guess so. I feel awful."

"You look terrible." He leaned toward me and touched my forehead with the tips of his fingers. "Do you think you're in labor?"

I pulled away from him roughly. "The baby's not due for another two and a half weeks! You know very well I've never had a baby early."

Within minutes Kent was dialing the phone frantically, trying to reach Dr. Kasten at the hospital making his early morning rounds. I wrested the phone from his hands.

"Just relax. Jeff already has an appointment today with Dr. Kasten for his chest cold. I'll go in with him at ten o'clock. I can wait another few hours."

"You haven't started to dilate yet." Dr. Kasten peeled off lightweight rubber gloves and dropped them into the small sink. "But that could change almost instantly in any woman who's already had several children."

"Do you think I should go down to Louisville today?"

Dr. Kasten pulled a three-legged stool toward the foot of the examining table and straddled it. "That has to be your decision. But as far as I'm concerned, two and a half weeks is pretty early for a baby to be born. If you go to Louisville today and it turns out you're not in labor, Dr. Levin will probably induce."

"I don't know what to do." I shifted on the table. "I've been arguing with Richard for weeks now about inducing me too early. I even thought the sixteenth was too soon. If I'm not in labor, I don't want to go today. But legally, I can't have this baby in Illinois."

Dr. Kasten stood in front of me now, looking grim. "You'll have to figure out what to do. All I can tell you is, you're not dilating yet."

I tugged pink slacks over my huge abdomen, slid a flowered maternity top over my head, and joined Dr. Kasten in the next room. I closed the door quietly behind me and watched him examine Jeffrey while he repeated our conversation to Kent, who frowned in thought under the brim of his brown felt hat. I started to remind him to take it off and stopped myself. After fifteen years of reminding, did it really matter?

I heard Kent speaking. "I think we'd better get home and get packed. We can drive down to Louisville later today."

Dr. Kasten removed his stethoscope from Jeff's narrow chest and looked up. "Drive?"

"Yeah. I hired a private pilot this morning to fly us down there when I thought Mary Beth was in labor, but I think I'll cancel it when we get home," Kent replied.

Dr. Kasten stood and faced Kent, inches from his face. "I forbid it." The words were a brusque command. "I absolutely forbid Mary Beth to sit in a car for seven hours. If you drive down there, Kent, you're asking for serious trouble." Dr. Kasten's brow creased and his voice was more firm than I had ever heard it. "Do you realize the baby could be born on the freeway?" He stared Kent down like an angry professor chastising a student. The fact that they were the same age seemed to make little difference at the moment.

Kent leaned against the door frame, still wearing his hat and appearing unconcerned. "She isn't in labor."

"She might not be," Dr. Kasten argued, "but that could change quickly. Once she starts active labor, it could be a matter of an hour before the baby is born. I insist you stay here in this state or fly down to Louisville." The mild manner I had seen all these months had been replaced by a tone of authority that left no room for argument. I sat quietly, as though I were an inanimate object in the small examining room. Only my eyes moved from one face to another, a passive observer at a Ping-Pong tournament.

Dr. Kasten turned his back to Kent and began to concentrate on Jeffrey's chest sounds. I watched him slide the stethoscope expertly over pale skin while Jeffrey coughed hoarsely.

I inhaled sharply, held my breath, and focused on my body. A tightness began to form near my hips. It pulled toward the middle of my belly and began to mount higher and higher like a cresting wave. Then it peeled back and drifted away with such gentleness, I thought it might have been my imagination.

Within five minutes the tightness began to twist upward

again. I grabbed Dr. Kasten's hand and placed it firmly on my stomach, waiting. Kent looked at me quizzically.

"Shhh." I put a finger to my lips to insist he remain silent.

Dr. Kasten's face froze as he bent over me, one hand resting on my tight flesh. He straightened slowly, his eyes met mine, and his cheeks bunched into a triumphant smile. "Well! *That*, young lady, was a contraction. You are in labor!"

Back home, I tried to block out the frenzy in the house. The children clamored for attention, Kent dialed the telephone frantically—calling Richard, the airport, the baby-sitter. One question demanded an answer before anything else: What if the labor was fast, three hours like Jeff's, and I didn't make it to Louisville?

I found the Lamaze book and flipped to the chapter on emergency childbirth. The baby would come easily on its own, without help if need be. But what would *we* need?

I padded down the hall toward Jeffrey's room, making mental notes. Rubber pads, bath towels, blankets, a warm clean blanket for the baby. I rummaged through boxes of outgrown baby clothes in Jeff's closet. Keepsakes. No time to wash and dry them. Better than none at all.

I knelt on the carpet in the closet and touched a hand-crocheted cream-colored baby blanket and another edged with delicate lace. Much too beautiful for a bloody birth in an airplane. Oh, well. I stuffed them into the large plastic bag and grabbed another, the best, for wrapping the baby.

The junk drawer in Jeff's bedside table was open, and I dug through cars, marbles, puzzle pieces, half a chocolate chip cookie. I found the small blue suction bulb used to remove mucus from Jeff's nose and mouth after his birth. Plastic bags, a large stainless steel mixing bowl for the placenta, a box of Kleenex, a small bottle of water, damp washcloths—the list went on until the bag was full. I went to the front door, about to ask Kent to put it in the car. It was the first thing I had packed. The most important item.

Kent grabbed the bag from me, muttering something about taking out the garbage before we left. I stopped him. "It's not the garbage. It's my birthing kit." He paled visibly and shook his head. I didn't try to decipher what he said.

Jeffrey had clung to me while I tossed clothes into a suitcase. "Mommy's going away. Mommy's going away," he chanted, tears streaming down his red cheeks. I hugged him tightly, then unwrapped him from my leg, and stood in front of the closet so he wouldn't see my sorrow.

"What should I take to wear after the baby is born? Richard wants a press conference after we sign the papers in court. What do you think will fit me, Jeff?" It was senseless conversation to a four-year-old, but it helped fill the emptiness.

"Jeffrey, please don't cry. Mommy will be home again soon," I lied.

I found a favorite plum-colored maternity dress that had fit me only until the fifth month. It was perfect. Heels, panty hose, a slip, another maternity bra. I tossed in a book and a tape recorder.

The girls stood in the doorway, shoulder to shoulder. Their faces were filled with apprehension. For eight months I had dreaded the thought of having to leave my children with a baby-sitter for a whole week when this day came. I wanted to remind the girls to be careful on their bikes and to stay out of the street, but when I opened my mouth, I knew the words were unnecessary.

"Mom, you can't be in labor. The baby's too early," Julie wailed pitifully.

"I can't help it," I said too gruffly and pulled slippers from my closet floor.

"Mom, will you take lots of pictures of him so I can show my friends at school?" Laura smiled eagerly, waiting for my answer. I couldn't tell her there would be no pictures. There wasn't time to explain. There was nothing to do except kiss them and say good-bye.

"Six—seven—eight—nine—ten," I exhaled softly through pursed lips, as though blowing out candles on a birthday cake. The tightness eased, and I loosened my grip on the stair railing and continued down toward the kitchen, my suitcase in my other hand. Kent stood with his back to me, the phone receiver hooked over a shoulder. I heard only his half of the conversation, but the pitch of his voice told me he was near panic.

"What do you mean, you can't find our pilot? Where the hell is he, out on the golf course? He promised he'd fly us down there.

"Did you call his home? His wife can't find him either? Great!

"Find us another pilot. Now!

"She's in labor.

"Eight and a half months.

"I told you, she's in labor. Who the hell cares when she's due?

"Five minutes apart.

"Listen, goddamn it, I'm telling you she's in labor. Is there someone around there who knows how to fly a plane?

"Good.

"Tell him to skip the shower and meet us at the airport in twenty minutes. I don't give a crap how he smells—just so he knows how to fly the damn plane!"

Kent smashed down the receiver and wheeled around, his face gray. "I can't find Levin. All I get is that stupid recording and he doesn't answer his private number." His shoulders slumped in defeat.

"Kent, don't get so upset." I sat down next to him and put my arm around his shoulders. "Everything will work out all right." I wanted to believe it, hoping the forced control in my voice would make it true.

We opened the front door and called the children. Kent grabbed the birthing kit and tossed it into the backseat of the car. He rushed back into the house, reached for my suitcase, and jerked it toward him. The spring snapped and the suitcase yawned, spilling clothes and books in all directions. I ignored the new contraction and leaned against the wall for support, holding my stomach and roaring helplessly with laughter.

At Byerly Aviation, the middle-aged overweight man in jeans and a flannel shirt bent over aerial maps, eyes hard and concentrated. A pencil lay between his full lips.

"How long will it take?" I asked.

"About ninety minutes or more."

"Why so long?" A cool November breeze teased the front strands of my hair. "It shouldn't take that long with a twin engine." I squinted in the sunshine at the rust and white Rockwell Commander parked near the hangar. A teenage boy with skinny legs clad in faded blue jeans stood on the nose, washing the windshield.

The pilot's face was somber. "This plane is designed to fly at twelve thousand feet, but the baby won't get enough oxygen at that altitude. We'll fly at five thousand. It will take longer, but we don't have a choice. How far apart are your contractions?" He narrowed his eyes and stared blatantly at my middle.

I shifted my pillow to the other arm. "Right now, five minutes. But my doctor told us that I could go from three minutes to birth within an hour."

"Listen, Bob." Kent moved between us, facing the pilot squarely.

"Bill."

Kent ignored the correction. "If this baby is born in the airplane, don't radio the tower until we cross the state line.

We can tell them it's just been born and make up a time. He has to be born in Kentucky, preferably Jefferson County."

Bill nodded his assent with a quick jerk of the head. The flesh under his chin wobbled. He stepped toward the sleek little plane and held out his hand to me. "Get in," he said tersely. "There's no time to waste."

How often I had thought about this day, imagined it while I should have been sleeping. The pain of leaving the children thirty minutes ago was still fresh. Why hadn't I taken the time to pack their pictures? I smiled at Kent's words from a few days before, when I had complained about missing the children. He suggested I set a tape recorder on the supper table to record their bickering.

"Then when you're in the hospital, you can play it back and you'll know what you're missing," he had teased.

When we stood in the doorway those final minutes, I had wanted to cling to them for comfort. I wanted them to assure me everything would be fine. What lay ahead for us? For the whole family? And for the new child, about to begin his journey, what did the future hold? Whatever else happened, he must emerge smoothly, beautifully, and perfectly formed. For his parents. For me.

I shivered under the chilly blue skies, wishing time would suspend itself. All I wanted was just one more week.

"Come on now," the pilot urged. He touched my arm, as one would to soothe a distressed child. "The plane's ready to go."

I trembled under the touch that brought me back to reality and climbed reluctantly into the backseat. I felt the plane shudder eagerly when the engines began to rumble. We inched toward the runway, and a sense of loneliness began to invade me.

Watching the colors in the sky as we rose into the air, I knew with a peaceful assurance that my son would be born the next morning. A Sunday's child.

It was on a Sunday afternoon that Margo had driven to

Richard's home to plead with Richard to find a surrogate mate for her husband. A Sunday news article had sent my mind whirling with the possibilities. On a Sunday the child had been conceived. And on a Sunday he would be born.

And the child that is born on
the Sabbath Day
Is bonny and blithe and good
and gay!

I glanced down at the can of 7-Up balanced on top of my mound. The baby initially had objected violently to the roller-coaster motion of the plane, but the turbulence had ceased and he was quiet now.

I leaned forward to peer through the windshield as we approached the Butler Aviation airport in Louisville. I could see the runways. Flashing lights zigzagged crazily in the eerie twilight, shooting strips of red across them. Emergency vehicles were on the ground and red flags signaled us to taxi slowly. Our pilot turned in his seat, grinning widely.

"Looks like they really put out the welcome mat for you." He seemed impressed by our reception committee.

Kent and I exchanged dumbfounded stares. "What on earth is going on?" I asked.

"Bill must have called in a landing code to receive clearance before any other aircraft," Kent offered. "Look." He pointed out the window, craning his neck. "There's a cop car, an ambulance, and the crash-control truck."

"Good grief." The dramatic reception embarrassed and delighted me. With all the conviction I could muster I demanded, "Kent, send them away. I am not riding to the hospital in an ambulance."

A male voice spoke through the static on the radio. "What is the extent of the injury?"

Bill put the microphone to his lips. "There is no injury. There's a woman in labor aboard. Roger." Then we taxied to a stop.

I ducked my head low under the wing as I got out, and stood quietly while another contraction gripped me. I breathed deeply and counted silently, keeping watch on the last of the crimson sun that slid between the hills.

Twenty minutes later we stood in the crowded doorway of the same birthing room Richard had shown me in October. I noted again the comfortable luxury compared with the stark, tiny rooms I had labored in four times before. A small television camera on a tripod seemed to dominate the room.

"What's with the camera, Rich?"

"For pictures of the labor and delivery." He was deliberately nonchalant and looked even more youthful in loose brown scrubs.

"We've talked about this before, Mary Beth." His voice rose in unmasked irritation. "You knew I was going to have a photographer here after we canceled the NBC camera pool last week."

"Rich, you told me you might have someone here to take pictures of the admission to the hospital and during the early stages of labor. But you promised me there wouldn't be any pictures until the delivery was over and I was cleaned up."

Richard waved his hand toward a tall, slightly balding man who stood shoulder to shoulder with him, whose eyes were intelligent and gentle, almost sympathetic. There was strength in his face, but he looked uncomfortable while we discussed him.

"Don't worry about him. Paul's my cousin. He'll be discreet. He's a lawyer, too." He added this last quickly, as though that would correct everything.

I wanted to say: He might be your cousin, Rich, but I've

never seen him before in my life—who asked him to be here? But I already knew the answer.

Why was I always the last piece in the puzzle? Richard always changed the plans we'd talked about and then expected me to simply jump into place.

It looked like the other pieces fit. Margo and Adam were waiting anxiously at home, the nurses were hovering around us like honeybees over soda pop, and Pam, Richard's wife, was there. Katie was there with her boyfriend, Charlie, who had driven us to the hospital in his squad car. Even Karen was there. And now there was Paul with his camera, too.

Well, here I am, Rich, I thought. The puzzle is complete. I won't ruin it for you. I wanted to shriek in protest at the lack of privacy I would have for the birth. Instead I smiled and went into the bathroom to undress while they filled my birthing room. As another contraction began to bind me, I knew I would have to save my strength for the baby's journey. There was no energy to fight with Richard.

Half an hour later, two wide straps decorated my bulging abdomen. A fetal heart monitor stood guard. The large rectangular room seemed more like a hotel suite than a birthing room. A combination of comfortable lounge chairs, a sofa bed, lamps, end tables with current magazines, an assortment of lush plants, and a stereo filled the room with brightness. A color television set stared blankly from a shelf high on the wall opposite my bed. There was a large braided rug on the floor.

I rested quietly against a stack of pillows while Richard watched the fetal heart monitor. He reached absentmindedly into the cellophane bag lying near my knees, pulled out a lollipop, ripped the paper away, and popped it into his mouth.

"Richard!" I sat upright and pulled a sucker stick from my own mouth. "Don't you dare eat another lemon lollipop. Those are for me. I brought the grape ones and the candy bars for you."

The white stick rested between his lips. "I like lemon," he protested, talking around the candy on his tongue.

"So do I and I'm the one who's in labor. My Lamaze instructor told us lemon quenches thirst. All you'll let me have is those stupid ice chips to suck on. Now get your hands off."

"What does your Lamaze instructor know?" he teased, glancing at Kent who returned his elfish grin.

I turned to the monitor, which beeped continuously. Red numbers flashed on the screen: *161—160—159—158—161.*

"You know, Rich, wouldn't it be a gas if this baby turned out to be a girl? I know the amniocentesis said it was a boy, but in Lamaze classes—" I ignored the dramatic rolling of his dark eyes, "—they told us if the heart rate is over 140 beats per minute, it usually is a girl. And if it's below 140, especially around 120, it means a boy. Some of the new parents from earlier Lamaze classes came back for the last class and told us it's true."

He leaned toward the monitor, watching it closely. The slender white stick dangled from his lips like a cigarette. "Sounds very scientific to me."

Kent guffawed without restraint and Richard joined in.

"All right, you two. I know when I'm outnumbered. I'll just shut up."

"Fat chance," Richard winked at Kent.

My contractions had increased in intensity during the two-hour plane ride, pulling on me as if an eight-inch-wide rubber band were tightening around my girth every five minutes, but shortly after I entered the birthing room, the contractions diminished to almost nothing.

Richard ordered Pitocin, which should have speeded things up, but the contractions were mild and discouraging. I eagerly waited for the pain I once dreaded.

My "fan club" passed the hours by watching the monitor

and listening intently to the rhythmic notes of the baby's heartbeat. Many emotions were present in that small room—excitement, apprehension, anticipation, impatience.

The hours dragged on like days and we chattered to each other about nothing, not communicating but merely filling the space with words. People drifted in and out for dinner or to smoke a cigarette, something like an open house. Eventually pizzas were delivered to feed my "guests."

I cocked my head toward the monitor and tried to block out the banter of Kent and Karen, who stood nearby. I had long since gotten used to the glow on Kent's face whenever he spoke to her. I was no longer jealous when he openly admired her dark, sultry beauty. I liked her too much to dislike her for being enchanting.

"Pam, listen to this heartbeat." I turned up the volume on the monitor, and a sound like bongos pulsated through the room. "Isn't that something? Gosh, I could go to sleep listening to the sound of his heart."

Richard draped himself sideways across the lounge chair at the foot of my bed and lit his pipe. "Not until you get that kid out of there," he grinned.

An hour later Margo's blonde head peered around the edge of the half-open door. Adam followed, looking justifiably uneasy. "How do you feel?" he asked, working hard to avoid staring at my bare, strapped bulge. I resisted the impulse to cover my naked abdomen with a sheet.

We filled them in on the details of my early labor and our scurrying to get to the airport. They seemed relieved and apprehensive at the same time.

"How do you feel?" Adam asked again. He stood at the foot of the bed and, in his dark suit, looked like he belonged on a page of *Gentlemen's Quarterly*. "You look fine," he added. I knew he was fibbing. My hair needed to be curled and the makeup I had applied hours ago had worn off, leaving my skin sallow with dark circles ringing my eyes. My haggard appearance was not enhanced by the cotton hospital gown that made my long, thin arms look like broomsticks on a snowman.

Margo and Adam were soon fascinated with the fetal heart monitor, as we had been earlier, and Margo squealed with delight when she heard the baby's heart pounding a strong, steady tempo.

Richard began to explain the workings of the machine to them, and when he had finished, he held out a hand to Margo. "Come on. I'll take you upstairs and show you the nursery."

Margo crossed the room with him and stood in the doorway, ready to leave. She was radiant in a long-sleeved white silk blouse and black wool skirt, with dainty pewter-colored heels. I felt more frumpy than ever before. I pulled the thin blanket over the hospital gown and clutched it to my chest.

"Margo, you'll love the nursery," I chimed in. "Rich took me up there in October when I was here to see the birthing room. The babies are absolutely adorable."

Her face brightened perceptibly. "Oh, I know. And just think, tomorrow my baby will be there."

The words *my baby* vibrated through the room.

The baby was still inside me and I wanted to finish giving birth before Margo called him hers. For a few more hours he would be mine. One step at a time, please; I had a lot of work to do before he was ready for any hospital nursery. Or for her arms. At that moment he was still in *my* nursery, and I fervently wished for Margo just to go away.

Many hours later, the head nurse blasted into my room like a drill sergeant. Katie and Charlie had untangled themselves from the sofa and left begrudgingly when I asked them to. Karen went home, also, and Richard, Pam, Paul, and Kent were in the doctors' lounge, resting.

The nurse's skinny silver curls stuck out like little springs from beneath the starched white cap balanced on the back of her head. Her lips formed a straight line as she bent to clean up beer cans and pizza boxes.

"Now that everyone is finally gone, maybe you can put some work into those contractions." She shoved the cardboard boxes into the small, overflowing wastebasket. "Let's get down to business and make some progress." There was a jagged edge to every word, which left no room for questions or disagreements.

An hour later Richard stopped the intravenous Pitocin. "We'll see how you're doing in the morning and then we'll make some decisions."

Thoughts of a cesarean section had been building all evening, and I wanted to discuss the subject with Richard. I tried to jump into it, but he left the room before I could get my questions answered.

Kent slept peacefully on the sofa bed in my room, still fully clothed and covered only with a light blanket. Two nurses who had been assigned to my delivery tiptoed past him several hours later. I welcomed their company in my sleeplessness. The chubby blonde nurse told me how her own last labor of eighteen hours had ended in surgery. She spoke softly and kindly about older mothers and their lack of muscle tone. I knew she was talking about me.

When the nurses tiptoed from the room, there were last-minute warnings about a "C-section in the morning if you don't start to do something soon."

I lay against the firm mattress thinking about the surgery. I can't! I won't! I have to get ready for Christmas. I don't have time to recover from major surgery. It wasn't supposed to be this way.

Then a bitterness took over, and I began to damn the fact that the parents of this child might be cheated out of seeing their son born normally and holding him only minutes after his birth. I prayed in desperation, begging God for an uncomplicated delivery. I fell fast asleep, completely serene, knowing the child was in His hands.

Chapter 18

November 9, 1980

Richard shuffled into the room, still groggy and rumpled from sleeping on the sofa in the doctors' lounge. I had already washed and applied makeup, and felt refreshed from the few hours' sleep.

"I hear you're not doing anything." His voice was light, but concern crept into his words as he donned a thin rubber glove. I winced at the pressure when he examined me. "Kathy, come here," he called to the nurse who had been in my room during the night. His voice was high-pitched and tight.

"Richard, what's wrong?" I propped myself up on both elbows to see his face.

"Nothing." His face was a mask, but a flicker of apprehension showed through before he looked away. "Kathy, put your hand in there and tell me if that feels like the cord to you."

She probed more gently, then peeled the glove off and flipped it toward the wastebasket. "Sure does," she drawled, sounding curiously unperturbed.

"Okay. Watch it. Call me if there's any change," Richard ordered crisply.

"What does that mean, Rich? Is something wrong?" I asked.

"Not yet. Don't worry about it." Then he looked more

relaxed, and smiled. "I'm going to find Kent and get some breakfast."

"Bring me back coffee, two eggs over medium, and a thick slice of that Kentucky ham you're always bragging about. I'm starving," I said.

Kent entered the room just then, and Richard slapped his arm around Kent's shoulders and wheeled him back toward the door. "Let's get breakfast." Richard shot a glance at me, enjoying his game.

"Me, too, Rich," I begged. "Please. Something. Anything." I hadn't eaten since Friday.

"Fat chance." He dragged the two words into the hallway and disappeared.

"You rat!" I yelled after him, and heard him laugh all the way down the hall.

I remembered asking Adam the night before if he would be able to participate in a golf tournament if he hadn't slept for thirty-six hours or hadn't had anything to eat or drink for two days. "Are you kidding?" he had answered, aghast. "I wouldn't even be able to see the ball."

How did Richard expect me to muster the stamina required of an athlete when I had been deprived of nourishment since Friday? By now, I didn't have the energy to participate in a normal delivery, anyway. He might as well knock me out and cut my belly open, I pouted to myself. I sat in bed with arms crossed over my chest, pondering the absurdity of my fast. Any pleas to the nurses for a small glass of water fell on deaf ears, though I was well aware of the rules.

Kathy padded back into the room to hook up the Pitocin. She concentrated on watching it drip slowly through the tubing.

"Tell me why you can feel the cord." I asked.

She fiddled with the needle in my arm. "It's nothing. Don't worry about it."

"Tell me the truth, Kathy. Is the cord wrapped around his neck?"

"Possibly."

A chill shot through every muscle. "Is that what they call a prolapsed cord?"

"Yup."

"But he's not in trouble," I insisted. "Look at the monitor. The heart rate is steady."

"You're not in active labor yet, either."

"What do you mean? Why would that make a difference?" And I thought I knew everything there was to know about this business by now.

Kathy touched my chest lightly. "I want you to lie down and rest. When Dr. Levin comes back, we'll see what he wants to do." She waltzed around the subject, trying to avoid telling me the truth. I had read enough to know that a prolapsed cord could be dangerous, even fatal, to the infant.

"Stop playing games with me, Kathy. I want to know exactly what you're talking about."

She slid her hands into the pockets of her uniform and faced me squarely. I could feel an ominous cloud hanging like mist. "What it means is—when you go into active labor, and when your water breaks, we're going to have to act fast. Right now the baby's still bobbing around in the fluid. He hasn't even moved into the birth canal."

"What happens when the water breaks? What's the rush?"

"The baby's oxygen and blood supply will be cut off. When this happens to obstetrics patients, we get them on a cart and take them down to delivery as fast as we can. One of us would have to sit on the cart straddling you and hold the baby inside until we could get you into surgery."

"You mean a C-section?"

"Honey," Kathy sighed and her eyes narrowed. "I'm talking about an emergency. We'd have about four or five minutes to get that baby out of there alive."

"My God." I fell back onto the pillows.

"Now don't get out of that bed for anything. I'll bring a

bedpan if you need it. I want you to lie quietly and call me immediately if anything happens. If you're not sure, call me anyway. The Pitocin should start to work soon and let's hope for some contractions. Strong ones, for a change." She turned on her crepe soles and was gone. It didn't matter. I had no more questions. How many times had *I* done the same thing to "protect" patients when I'd worked in a doctor's office?

My frustration grew. By the time Kent returned, I was restless and irritable. "I had better contractions than this on the plane," I groused at him.

"Then let's go for another airplane ride." He chuckled at his wit and seemed undismayed by my glare. I refused to cooperate when he attempted light conversation, and to my relief he soon turned to the television for companionship. I had no intention of worrying him by repeating my conversation with Kathy. Instead, I began to pray, asking God for a normal, safe delivery.

An hour later, I shouted over the music coming from the set, "Kent, call Margo and Adam. Tell them I'm still not in labor. I'm sure they were up half the night worrying. Call the girls, too. It's time for them to start getting ready for Sunday school." I still needed to mother my children from a distance. I needed the comfort of knowing they still needed me, and I wanted to touch their lives to ease my loneliness. I also wanted to reassure myself of the normalcy of our lives outside this hospital.

My belly rested on my thighs while I sat tailor-fashion on the mattress. It was difficult to breathe deeply with the baby compressing my lungs, and I arched my back to give my lungs more space.

Will this ever end? I wondered. I sighed and reached for the telephone receiver Kent held toward me. I began giving Julie instructions, and she listened carefully to all the things she already knew by heart.

"Mom, did you have the baby yet?" Laura's voice filtered

through from a phone extension. They both listened to me now.

I tried to sound optimistic during the conversation, but immediately regretted telling them about the possibility of a cesarean section if labor didn't start soon. Laura rattled off a list of questions about scars, pain, and recuperation time. "How long will you be gone, Mama?"

"Not more than a week, I hope. Even with the surgery." I waved Kent away while I talked, but could no longer ignore his gestures to attract attention. I put my hand over the receiver. "What do you want?" I hissed.

Kent leaned toward the monitor, his face only inches from the dark lines on the graph paper. "You're having a contraction. A good one. Look at this." His face was pink with excitement.

"I am not, for heaven's sake. I would be able to feel it," I snapped.

"Look at the tape." He pointed to the graph paper, and I watched the needle rise to the top of a narrow curve.

"Big deal. If I can't feel it, it's not worth a thing," I retorted. "Don't get your hopes up, mister."

Kent bent over the monitor again and began to study the black peaks being recorded, then he reached up and absentmindedly scratched the naked spot on top of his head.

Without warning, a muffled, popping sound like the uncorking of a wine bottle entered the silent room. Warm fluid began to trickle over my thighs.

"Laura," I said into the receiver. "Get ready for Sunday school now. I have to hang up because the nurse is here," I lied. "I love you, honey. Say hello to Jeffrey for me. I love you all. Bye."

Kathy's warning bounced in my head: "If the cord comes down first when the water breaks, the baby could strangle."

"Kent. Get Kathy. Quick. Tell her the water just broke."

He stood planted, openmouthed and staring. "Are you sure?"

"Hurry," I urged, pushing him from me. He ran for the door.

A minute later Kent was back, standing nearby with his hands shoved deeply into his trouser pockets. His pale skin and wide eyes showed his terror while Kathy examined me.

"You're dilated to four centimeters now," she grinned triumphantly.

"But I'm not having contractions," I protested.

"Yes, you are. Look at the graph." She nodded toward the squealing metal monster attached to me.

"I don't feel a thing," I disagreed, still not believing.

"Honey," she said earnestly, "don't argue. You're in active labor. Finally." We remained silent while she bent over me again, gently pushing and probing my insides.

"Guess what?" She began to laugh then, and her musical voice floated through the room, chasing the tension out the door. "That's not the cord we've been feeling. It's his little fist."

A cold chill shot through me and I sank back onto the stack of pillows. He's safe, I thought. My baby's about to be born, and his hand is saluting a greeting to his new world. Thank you, God!

Suddenly a giant wave came over me, knocking away the next breath. The dark ink from the needle on the monitor shot to the top of the graph paper, leveled off, and slowly descended. Fluid gushed, cascading onto the crisp sheets and the floor. The pressure eased and I inhaled deeply with delicious relief. It was nine o'clock on a beautiful, warm, sunny Sunday morning. The room darkened when Kathy slammed the draperies together.

"Don't!" I cried.

"Look at the walkway next to your room," she replied.

"Do you want everyone who passes outside your window to look at your bare bottom?"

"No." I laughed, but still resented that I would be denied the cheery sunshine.

"We have to find Dr. Levin," Kathy barked, racing from the room.

Powerful, surging contractions swept over me, one after another, each lasting a full minute with a full minute in between. I searched for the mental notes I had made during Lamaze class, found as my focal point the heat register high on the wall near the door, and began deep breathing.

Our instructor had warned us we would remember only a fifth of what she had taught us and only an eighth during the stress of labor. She was right. Now the only thing I could concentrate on was my focal point and counting to ten while I inhaled deeply, blowing out through pursed lips after number ten. It had never taken this long to get to ten during practice.

I lay on my left side because I remembered there would be less pressure on the aorta. The increased blood supply to the baby during contractions would cause less fetal heart distress, if any.

"Kent, call Margo. Tell her to get down here now. It won't take more than another hour."

Within minutes Kathy was back. She and Kent became a blur, moving plants and furniture from the room, dragging the soaked braided rug into the hall, and swiping the floor with a mop. I watched in a daze, as though it were a silent film being shown in fast forward.

"Where's Richard?" I asked between contractions.

"I don't know." There were two parallel grooves between Kathy's eyebrows. "I've called his answering service, had him paged in the cafeteria and all over the hospital—I also called his home. I just can't find him anywhere and he's not answering his beeper. I even called the health club in the hospital, thinking he might be playing handball or taking a shower. Where could he be?" she fretted.

"Kent, after you had breakfast, did Richard tell you where he was going?"

"Nope. I left the cafeteria before anyone else was finished." He glanced toward the tripod and camera. "Richard will kill himself if he misses this one," Kent chuckled.

"Kathy, is there another doctor around who can deliver me?"

Her worry lines smoothed and she smiled briefly. "Sure, but we have plenty of time," she assured me. "We'll find him."

Another contraction mounted, rising in intensity. I no longer resisted the nausea, and when the vomiting came, I welcomed the relief. No, we don't have plenty of time, I thought, knowing for me the sickness was a sign of almost-immediate delivery.

Kathy carted in a low stool on wheels, a stainless steel table lined with gleaming instruments, a Kriselman with a warming light for the baby, a stack of gowns and blankets. I was motionless while Kent and Kathy dashed in and out of the room. I tried to draw strength during the now forty-five-second reprieve from the wretched pulling inside me.

"I need a bedpan."

"Forget it. That's no place to give birth," Kathy grinned. "Just lie down now and breathe deeply. Stay on your left side," she ordered, handing Kent a gown.

"I need a mask," he reminded her.

She shot him a disbelieving look. "She's about to drop that baby on the floor and you're worried about a mask? Forget it. Where's Dr. Levin?" she muttered.

She donned a rubber glove and examined me again. Her face remained impassive. I knew I was dilating rapidly.

"I'll bet I'm up to seven centimeters already," I offered from experience.

She rushed from the room, calling over her shoulder, "We might be able to call it eight."

She told me later that I had gone from four centimeters to ten. I was fully dilated and ready to deliver. She was prepared to deliver the baby herself with Kent assisting. Unmasked. We laughed about it later. But not now. Not having Richard with me was a nightmare I had never imagined.

Kathy pulled out the lower half of the bed, snapped stirrups into place, pushed the footstool near the U-shaped bottom portion of the bed, and slipped an extra sheet over my outstretched legs. Kent, Kathy, and I were going to have this baby. We were ready.

Paul, the photographer, crossed my focal point in three long strides. "How you doing?"

I waved silence with one hand and fixed my eyes above his head. "Seven—eight—nine—ten. Whew! Where's Richard?"

Paul bent over his camera and began filming after he nodded toward the door.

Richard had never looked so handsome.

"Where have you been?" I asked, not masking my irritation.

"In the sauna. It's about time you did something for us."

"Richard, get ready. I'm having this baby."

"Just relax." He held up his hand, as if to stop the next contraction. "I *am* ready." He sauntered out the door to scrub.

Kent had been standing guard at the monitor, reading numbers to me during each stab of pain, assuring me constantly that the baby's heart rate was still stable. Then Kathy jerked the plug from the wall and the machine went dead.

"Don't do that," I cried.

"We don't need it anymore."

"How will I know if he's in trouble?"

"He's not. His heart rate is terrific. You'll be seeing him in a few minutes." She stroked my arm, soothing me. A moment later pain hit me in waves. There was no control over the forces deep within me ejecting the baby from the security of my womb. I was only a vehicle through which he was being propelled into a new world. I lay quietly while my body worked to rid me of him, and I wondered, for a brief moment, whatever had possessed me to go through it again. I must have been insane to forget how it felt.

I realized the baby was about to be born and his parents would not be there to welcome him. "Kent, find Margo and Adam. Quick!" I gasped. When he crossed the room to leave, I shouted to his back. "No, don't leave me. Hold my hand. I need you. Here comes another one. Oh, my God, it hurts."

Kent reached for my hand. "Don't touch me!" I yelled. "Just stand there."

He grinned like a ten-year-old. "Hey, our Lamaze teacher said you'd get like this right before the baby was born. She said you might even swear a little," he babbled.

"Oh, shut up. Stop talking to me."

Richard balanced on the low stool while one nurse tied his gown in the back and slipped a mask over his face and another slid rubber gloves over his outstretched hands. I could see only his large brown eyes. They were calm when they met mine. He adjusted the mirror and I saw something white at the edge of my body. Was it the cord after all? I wanted that baby out of there. Fast!

"Push." Richard spoke in low tones.

I made a Herculean effort, pushed, and grunted loudly.

"Don't grunt," he said crisply. I heard his order echo in the silence that followed while he waited for another contraction. Kent concentrated on his wristwatch, counting the seconds out loud. "Thirty—forty-five—sixty. Boy! That was a good one. They're really strong now," he announced, beaming with enthusiasm.

"Goddamn it, stop telling me how long they're lasting. I know how long they're lasting. I can *feel* every one of them."

"It won't be long now, honey. Hang on." He patted my arm while my focal point began to fade.

I felt my lungs losing air. There was no control over the sound that came from my throat.

"Stop grunting," Richard demanded gruffly.

"I have to."

"It uses too much energy. Try not to."

I looked at the mirror and saw the baby's head bulging against me. I began to shake with excitement at the reality of the birth.

I became dimly aware of Kent's voice in my ear, soft and soothing. "Take a breath. Good. Blow it out. Take a breath—real deep. Hold it, hold it. Push!" He squeezed my hand. "Come on, come on. You're doing great." Just when I thought my lungs would rupture, his voice would bring me back. "Let it out," he would command, and I would exhale in one, loud gust.

"How do you always know when it's the right time to tell me to let it out?"

" 'Cause your face is purple." We laughed together and I loved him even more.

"Okay," Richard ordered. "Let's have another one like that and I won't have to use these forceps."

"Don't you dare, Richard." From my half-sitting position, I could see the metal monstrosity, a medieval torture device.

I sat up straighter, clutched each knee, and followed Kent's commands to breathe. I began to push with a new strength from depths that had been hidden for years.

Then, "Richard, it hurts. God, I can't stand it." I was on a wild, terrifying carnival ride and I couldn't get off.

"Keep pushing," he urged.

I strained to work with the powerful contractions that were overwhelming all other senses. The baby slid from my body. Perfectly formed. Two legs, two arms, soft, rosy skin, chubby and healthy. My body was empty. I was soaked with sweat and unmitigated joy. The room exploded with the sound of my son, like the ringing of church bells on a crisp, clear Christmas morning.

The door to the birthing room burst open and Margo bolted in, frantically tying a green mask over her nose and mouth. She ran toward him in stocking feet.

"There he is! I heard him!" she shouted gleefully.

The birthing room was a chorus of voices celebrating my son's life. Margo's voice was soft and unbelieving, and she crossed the room to hold me in her arms.

"Thank you for my beautiful baby." We held each other then, until I no longer knew which tears were hers and which were mine.

When she brought him to me, I closed my eyes with delicious relief.

Thank you, God, for making him a stranger, I thought. My Sunday's child did not look like Jeffrey. He truly did belong to his father. I breathed a silent prayer of thanksgiving and felt the weight and warmth of him against me.

And then I placed him in the arms of his mother as the baby's father ran into the room to meet his son.

November 11, 1980

I shook off the grogginess of sleep and carefully eased my way out of the hospital bed. The room felt different, and curiosity forced me out of my bed to the large picture window still darkened by heavy draperies. I reached for the cord, pulled, and watched the landscape expose itself in the early dimness. Yesterday a lush green and yellow forest had covered the soft, rolling Kentucky hillside. It had been a day filled with warmth and the promise of Indian summer. But sometime between dusk and dawn, the cold, crisp air had sucked life from the earth. The land was now swathed in grays and shades of brown. I surveyed the bleakness in silence.

An impending sense of doom began to fill me as I stood alone in the large, quiet room. I remembered today was my first baby's—Heidi's—sixteenth birthday, and I wondered how she would be celebrating it, and if she was even still alive. Nervously, I began to wonder about the children and what they were doing.

I want to go home, I thought. Now. Please, somebody. Let me fly home today to see my children. I promise I will return on Friday for the drive to the courthouse to sign the termination papers.

The gloom lifted slightly after a steaming shower and a hearty breakfast served on beautiful china, but I began to long for a roommate to ease the boredom of the long day ahead.

The phone rang sharply. I picked it up and recognized Attorney Brophy's voice immediately. "Hi, Katie. What's up?"

"I'm coming up tonight after office hours. There are some papers I want you to sign."

I was puzzled. "Papers for what? For court?" I asked.

"No," Katie said, "just some routine things. I'll explain it to you when I get there."

"Okay," I answered agreeably. "I'll be here."

The morning dragged and I tried to kill time by reading the newspaper and listening to the stereo. Suddenly, a tall dark-haired man with a receding hairline appeared in the doorway. I immediately recognized Paul, Dr. Levin's cousin who had taken the videotape of the delivery. I remembered how irritated I was to find him in the labor room without my permission, but when the time came for the actual delivery I had been too preoccupied to ask him to leave. He had camera equipment with him again. "What are you doing with all your equipment, Paul?" I asked.

He sat down in the rust-colored upholstered chair and his long legs sprawled in front of him. "I'm meeting Richard here in ten minutes," he said nonchalantly.

"You're meeting him here? In my room? For what?"

Paul looked surprised. "To take pictures of you looking at the baby."

"No, you're not. There must be some mistake." I looked at him with a stupid smile on my face trying to comprehend what he had in mind.

"Didn't Richard tell you? He told me he was going to stop in to talk to you about it."

"Paul, I haven't seen or heard from Richard since he delivered the baby. I don't know what you're talking about. In any case, I don't know if I should see the baby, Paul. Richard promised me right after the birth that I could see him any time I wanted to, but I need to think about this. Nobody told me about photographs. Besides, my stitches are killing me. And I look terrible."

"Oh, you look fine. Really," Paul said.

Without saying a word, I grabbed my makeup case and headed for the bathroom, locking the door behind me. Right now it was the only place in the world with some privacy. Now, even my hospital room was a public meeting ground. I threw on some makeup and plugged in the curling iron.

I put on my white satiny lounge robe, grumbling inwardly at the way I was being taken for granted. Before long, Richard came striding into the room, still wearing his green surgical uniform. He flopped into a small vinyl chair, while I began curling the front strands of my hair.

"Hi, Rich," I said coolly from the bathroom. "Thanks for telling me about the pictures."

"You don't have anything else to do today anyway," he said.

"You're right, I don't. But I look terrible. If I had known, I could have done something to my hair and face." Richard and Paul got up and started walking out the door, signaling for me to come.

We went down the hall together and entered the nursery quietly, peering around the corner of the door marked "Private" as a nurse checked to make sure our presence was allowed. She asked Dr. Levin who Paul was and he assured her Paul was with us and it was okay. It was clear the staff was being very careful about who they let into the nursery to see my baby. Even I could not get in. As I soon learned, I was not even allowed to see my son through the glass of the nursery window. Richard had promised he would change the rule immediately. But he had not.

I caught my breath as I peeked through the doorway of the private nursery. Justin was lying on his stomach. One round cheek was pressed flat against the printed sheet. His lips puckered, sucking instinctively while he slept soundly. I gasped at the sight of him. A beauty had emerged in my son overnight just as surely as the landscape outside had grown ugly. The last hint of newborn redness had disappeared, leaving him with a rosy beige complexion and a perfectly shaped oval head with downy hair. Instinctively I reached toward his crib to caress the smooth skin of his face, then stopped. I had no right. He belonged to someone else. I could only stand at a distance, admiring the perfection of him.

I studied the angelic face, memorizing every detail. Are you soft, Justin? Are you warm? Would you remember my voice if I held you in my arms and close to my chest? Would you recognize my heartbeat?

Paul photographed the baby as Richard examined him by listening to his heart. At the feel of the cold stethoscope, the baby jumped several inches and wriggled under the tightly tucked blanket, but never awoke. I smiled tenderly at him, my heart aching. "I'll wait out in the hallway for you, Paul," I said, as tears stung my eyes. I walked away quickly and headed for the doors.

He called after me, "Don't go back to your room. I want to take pictures of you looking in the nursery window." I didn't answer him. I didn't trust my voice. But I stopped. Several minutes later, Paul motioned to me to look in the nursery window, and he filmed me looking at empty cribs. All the babies were being fed in their mothers' rooms at that moment, so the general nursery was completely empty. I felt like an idiot looking at empty plastic bins, smiling, pretending "they" were adorable. He finished filming quickly, much to my relief, and the three of us walked back to my room. Richard was saying something about his five hours in surgery that morning.

I interrupted, "Rich, let's go back to the nursery and ask the nurses to let me see the baby whenever I want to."

"I don't have time now," he said curtly.

"Come on," I urged. "It will only take a minute. If you write it on the chart when I'm with you, they'll have to let me come when I ask. It's ridiculous that I can't see my own child. He *is* mine until Friday, you know."

"I said *no*," Richard snapped.

"Richard, you lied to me! You promised before I had that baby that I could see him when I wanted to. I think they've got people from the secret service working in that nursery! Nobody can get in to see him. I know if you write the orders right on his chart, the nurse will let me in."

"Listen, I have not lied to you. I just don't have time right now, and I don't like the way you're talking to me. Sometimes, Elizabeth, you treat me like a child." He was shouting.

"You treat *me* like *I'm* twelve years old. And I don't like the way you take me for granted either. I'm nothing but your guinea pig, Richard Levin!" I shouted back. By this time all the nurses at the station were standing and staring at us open-mouthed. Richard strode away angrily, leaving me standing there with Paul. I was fighting tears, angry, and humiliated. Paul walked me back to my room, picked up the rest of his equipment, mumbled something about Richard having a bad day, and quickly left.

My breasts began to ache with the fullness of milk that had come the moment I had caught sight of the baby. I climbed into bed, pulled the blankets tightly over my head, and ignored the throbbing. Eventually I fell asleep.

I awoke an hour later, feeling more hopeful. Perhaps by now Richard or Katie had called the nursery and instructed the nurses to allow me to hold Justin. Richard had previously asked me to choose a code name to be used in the hospital to confuse reporters and to enable me to receive phone calls from Kent. I had chosen the name Sarah Leigh, a takeoff on the famous bakery, because everyone seemed to want a piece of me.

I dialed the nursery extension and gave my room number. "Is the Leigh baby awake?" I asked the nurse.

"Yes, and he's just eaten."

"Did it stay down this time?" By now, I had learned Justin was having a hard time digesting the formula.

"Yes. A little better." She was kind and patient.

"That's wonderful. I'd like to see him now. Can I come down?" I asked eagerly.

"Fine. We'll be ready for you."

Oh, bless you, Richard. I quickly thanked her and hurried to repair my makeup, run a brush through my hair, and grab my bathrobe. My heart pounded with anticipation as I thrust my feet into slippers. The phone rang and I hesitated, hoping it would be brief. No telephone conversation was going to keep me from my son.

"Mrs. Leigh?" A female voice.

"Yes?" I answered warily, wondering if it was a reporter.

"This is the nursery calling. You just called asking to see the baby?"

"Yes. I was told to come now because he's awake."

"There's been a mistake. We thought you were his mother." And the phone went dead.

The pain was excruciating.

I *am* his mother, you damn fool! My head was on fire.

"I hate you, Richard!" I bellowed at the wall. "You deliberately lied to me to get me to do what you wanted. Now you think I'm dumb enough to roll over and play dead." I grabbed a pillow and walloped it, yelling. "I hate you, Richard Levin! Damn you! I hate your guts!" I smashed the pillow again and again, unleashing a fury hadn't realized existed. Not until Kent called was I able to calm myself. He promised to call Richard and ask him to change the orders.

Late in the afternoon, I heard a knock on the door. It was the head nurse from the obstetrics section. "Hi, Elizabeth." She noticed the darkened room and apologized for intruding. "I have some papers I want you to sign. I'll be right back with them," she said, as she ducked out of the room. Linda returned a few minutes later with Kathy, the nurse who had helped deliver the baby. They stood there and looked at me expectantly. Linda had a folder under her arm and a pen in her hand. "Attorney Brophy asked me to have you sign these papers before I went off duty. They have to be signed today. Kathy will witness your signature." I sat tailor-fashion on the bed and read the documents.

"These papers terminate my parental rights to the baby," I said. I was surprised. I had not realized I would be asked to sign anything before Friday. I reread them. "What I'm doing here is signing the baby over to Attorney Brophy."

"No, you're not," Linda said. "The termination papers don't get signed until Friday when you go to court."

"I realize that," I said. "But this paper states I am releasing the custody of the baby to Attorney Brophy. That means she can take the baby out of the hospital if she wants to." I was starting to panic. "Is she going to have him moved to another hospital? Somebody had told me she was going to do that. Is that true?"

"No, Elizabeth. It's not. She can't take the baby out of the hospital without your permission. You are still the mother of that child until Friday when you go to court." Linda handed me a pen. "Sign the papers. They're just routine in adoption cases. They don't mean a thing." I signed the papers reluctantly, knowing full well I was releasing the baby to Katie's care and from that moment on, I had no control over him. He was no longer mine. He never had been mine to keep, I knew that, but I had hoped for just a little time. Now it was legal. I no longer had custody of him.

Why didn't Katie come up here herself with those papers and explain the procedure to me instead of sending a nurse to do her dirty work? To think they had the gall to call the papers "nothing" and pretend I wasn't signing anything legal. They were treating me like an imbecile, not a mature woman of thirty-eight. I would have signed happily if Katie had taken a few minutes to explain things as she had promised. But to be misled about the legality of it was degrading.

Later, when they were gone, I reached for the ringing phone and pushed my supper tray out of the way. I recognized Katie's voice without her telling me who it was. "I signed the papers you wanted me to sign, Katie," I told her, "and I gave them to Linda."

"What papers?" she said. "I'm coming up tonight to have you sign some."

"If they were the papers releasing the baby to your care, I've already signed them," I said. There was a long silence and finally I heard Katie say softly, "That nurse was not supposed to bring those papers to you. I told her that I would bring them in myself and that she should leave them at the nurses' station for me." It was obvious there had been a misunderstanding of some sort or that someone was not telling the entire truth. I was not going to argue about it.

"Nevertheless, Katie, they were papers releasing the baby to your care, weren't they? Why didn't you tell me what they were when you called this morning? As you can see, I would have signed them for you."

"I told you," she said emphatically but somewhat nervously, "I would bring them up tonight and talk to you about them."

"Okay," I said, "so talk. What were they?"

"They were just some papers you had to sign so Justin can go home tomorrow." Her voice sounded hollow in my ears, as if she were very far away.

"Tomorrow?" I repeated, stunned. "He's going home tomorrow?" I could not believe it. I'd never see him again. My heart raced as my throat closed, making it difficult to continue. "I thought he was going home Thursday. I'm not leaving until Friday."

"Well, the pediatrician examined the baby this morning and said he's in great shape and there's no reason why he can't go home tomorrow if his bilirubin count stays down."

"Okay," I said weakly, "I'll see you tomorrow, then. I want to rest now. 'Bye." I hung up before she could say more. I lay there feeling tricked, used, and cast out with yesterday's garbage.

The phone rang again. I reached for the receiver and answered with a dull hello.

"Hi." It was Richard, sounding cheerful. "How are you?" he asked.

"What do you want?" I grumped back.

"I just thought I'd call to see how you're doing."

I knew very well he was only reacting to Kent's phone call earlier.

"You know very well how I am. You looked at my chart this morning." I tried to sound as angry as I felt, but he ignored my sarcasm.

"I know I looked at your chart, but I really haven't had a chance to talk to you. It's been so busy at the office. My schedule really got fouled up."

"Don't worry about me, Richard. I'm in perfect health," I said sarcastically.

"Are they taking good care of you?" he asked.

"Of course they are . . . Why were you so angry this morning, Richard?"

"I just had a bad day in surgery and felt terrible from standing over the operating table all morning."

"Well, you didn't have to take it out on me," I said emphatically. The sting of our argument this morning was still fresh.

"I didn't mean to. People who work with me know how I am. By the way," he added, "I called the nursery and you can now walk down there anytime to see the baby."

"Boy, I've heard that before."

"No, really. I just talked to them and everything has been cleared."

"It's too late, Rich. He's going home tomorrow."

"Well, you can go see him tonight if you want to. I'm sorry it took so long for the nursery to get their orders straight, but once a person makes a rule, it's hard to break. Everything's been settled now."

"Okay," I said, suddenly cheerful. "I think I will go down now. Thanks for calling. 'Bye." I hung up, eager to be able to see the baby, knowing that even though it would be the last time, tonight he belonged to me.

I hurried down the long hallway as fast as my stitches would allow. My breasts tingled with fullness at the thought of holding him to me.

A middle-aged nurse in crisp cotton guarded the entrance marked PRIVATE. She recognized me instantly and nodded for me to enter.

The scrub room held two large stainless steel sinks. A row of shelves near the door held stacks of sterile gowns and masks to be worn over street clothes or uniforms. I quickly scanned the instructions for the scrubbing procedure taped to the ceramic tile between the sinks. I pulled out a paper packet, ripped off the covering, and began to scrub with the small disposable brush. The five-minute procedure seemed endless while I yearned to hold and kiss my son, to smile into his eyes. That night I would talk to him privately and stroke the softness of his body. I would look into his eyes and tonight our souls would meet.

I glanced over my right shoulder as I spread the lather in wide circles over my hands and wrists, hoping to get a glimpse of him through the nursery window adjoining the scrub room.

And then, every muscle in my body turned to stone. I could no longer feel the steamy water pouring over my soapy hands. Two people in green scrubs and masks filled the small space of the nursery, and I recognized Margo and Adam. My right foot groped for the floor pedal to stop the stream of hot water, and I moved out of sight, hands dripping onto the immaculate tile floor.

Adam was seated in a maple rocking chair with his newborn son in his arms. He stroked the round, smooth curve of the baby's cheek. Margo stood beside them protectively, her hands draped across Adam's back. Long, slender fingers with perfectly polished nails curled around his left shoulder.

Justin slept peacefully while they admired him, talking and smiling at each other. There was so much love and tenderness, pride and awe in their expressions, I instantly felt like an intruder. Then Adam bent to kiss Justin. He held his son firmly in both hands, raising the tiny bundle until his lips touched the baby's forehead.

A cameo; their profiles were identical. They were a family, linked together after years of waiting for that private moment. I had helped them achieve it, but now my part was over. I no longer belonged there. The warmth of satisfaction rippled through me, and I quietly slipped through the doorway without their ever knowing what I had observed. I knew I would never see my infant son again.

I walked rapidly past the large nursery, down the hallway, and through the double doors that separated the maternity ward from the rest of the hospital. I made no attempt to brush away the tears that began to slide down my cheeks. A mixture of pride and accomplishment, sorrow and love for the child I had conceived and nourished, given birth to and loved, swirled through me. I would never again have the opportunity to hold him close to me. The next day his tiny Isolette in the nursery would be empty. It was almost impossible to comprehend.

I shut the heavy door to my private room, took out several sheets of paper, and began to write Justin a letter, my thoughts and emotions moving faster than my pen.

Dear Justin,

I saw you for the last time this morning. Tonight I saw you being held in the arms of your father, protective, loving, disbelieving you were really his flesh. I was struck by your beauty the moment I saw you. Do not be offended, Justin. As a young man you will be handsome, but as a newborn child you are beautiful. You are purity in its highest form.

You slept peacefully this morning, unaware of my presence while I marveled at the smoothness of your skin and the perfection of your coloring. Like mine.

I ached to pick you up and hold your tiny, soft body against mine, if only for one precious moment. Just to be able to cherish forever the way you would feel outside me. But I could not. I knew you would melt into me and snuggle your velvet cheek against my neck. I would have listened to your small sucking noises while you sought nourishment with your eyes closed, rooting for the breast milk you were forbidden.

If I would have held you, Justin, I would not have put you back. Ever. But you do not belong to me. I could not touch you with my hands. I had to be satisfied to embrace you with my heart. I want to remember the way you looked forever.

I have lost a friend in you, Justin. A part of me has died. I will grieve alone, for who would understand the loss of you? Yet I am reminded, even though your leaving me feels like a death, that you are a gift of life. You are healthy and alive and have simply been placed from my womb into the arms of another woman. Just remembering her elation when she held you after birth still swells my heart with pride.

I love you, Justin. If we could have been together, I would have held you tightly and whispered those words into your tiny ear. They would have been burned into your subconscious forever so you would always remember you were not given away but simply relinquished to another woman who needed you more than I.

You will always be my son, Justin. I am part of your soul. Pictures of your grandparents are in my photo album. Even though I have to share you with another, you will always be inside my heart.

Sleep peacefully now, baby boy. Make them very happy, but never forget that your mother loves you. Good-bye, my darling son. I can no longer be a part of your precious little life.

With all my love,
Your First Mother

My eyes felt hot and dry. I wanted to keep them closed for a long time and relieve the horrible burning inside me.

When the anguished sobbing ended, the aching for him was gone. I fell asleep peacefully, knowing my job was finished. My son was with his parents at last.

Epilogue

What lies behind us and before us are small matters compared to what lies within us.
—Ralph Waldo Emerson

Seven years after that famous birth was announced in newspapers all over the world, I am still hailed as the nation's first legal surrogate mother. A pioneer. I continue to be inundated with requests for television and radio appearances, and for interviews in magazines and religious periodicals. The requests—"Just a few minutes of your time"—I often turn away, but sometimes I ask, "Why? What does it matter, all these years later?"

The reporters are insistent, persuasive. "You spent over a year crusading for surrogate motherhood. Now you've done a complete about-face, asking for surrogacy to be banned. *That*, Mrs. Kane, is newsworthy. We want to know why. What happened in those years to change your mind, Mrs. Kane? You owe the world an answer."

Part of me shrinks back and rebels. I have just begun to recover from my experience battling infertility by promoting surrogate parenting. My husband is happy in his new executive position where no one knows his wife is "Mrs. Kane." My children and I are trying to return to living normal lives. We collect fewer stares in public today than we have in years past.

I am enjoying the routine of a peaceful, predictable existence as wife and mother. The name I used in the press, Elizabeth Kane, has begun to sound odd to me. Yet when I hear a voice in a public place call "Elizabeth," the familiar ring turns my head. Part of me still remembers the unexpected and uninvited intrusion that local, national, and international media made on my family.

I wish the story were simple to tell. I wish I could report one lightning-bolt revelation that explains how I finally saw the light. The issues associated with surrogate motherhood are a tightly woven canvas of psychology, ethics, religion, science, and the law. Recently, it has begun to unravel. If I made the first stitch, the surrogates now involved in litigation are seeing the flaws in the fabric—the ramifications of exchanging babies for dollars.

For several years I tried to ignore the trickle of stories that arrived secondhand. Dark, disturbing tales of surrogate mothers becoming obsessed with tracking down their children, of children with emotional problems, of psyches so damaged that marriages could not survive the strain. One surrogate mother in Michigan lost custody of her three children during a routine divorce proceeding after her husband revealed to the judge that she was carrying a surrogate baby. The judge declared her to be an "unfit mother" because she was able to sign away her unborn child. Her decision to help an infertile woman fulfill a dream of having a baby of her own had ended in the catastrophic loss of her own entire family.

I now believe that surrogate motherhood is nothing more than the transference of pain from one woman to another. One woman is in anguish because she cannot become a mother, and another woman may suffer for the rest of her life because she cannot know the child she bore for someone else.

It has been a long journey since November 9, 1980. The road I traveled has been filled with more twists and turns than I ever imagined. When the path grew perilous, I would rely on Kent to bring me back to reality and get me through my self-pity.

For months following the birth I was euphoric. I would get high just remembering the look on Adam's and Margo's faces as they held their son in the delivery room. To my surprise, I was still in almost constant demand from major networks and talk shows to expose my deepest feelings about giving a son to an infertile couple.

But as I attended press conferences, chattered away on television, and gave interviews to radio stations and magazines, my children were being cared for by a baby-sitter. I could no longer ignore the looks on their faces when they felt a reporter was more important to me than they were.

I was forced to make a decision. I knew there were innumerable couples who had not yet heard there was hope for childless marriages. And I was well aware that after every television appearance I made, Dr. Levin would receive many telephone calls from potential surrogates or infertile couples asking for applications. Yet I felt I had completed my mission. I notified Dr. Levin that my celebrity status had to end, that it was not nearly as important to me as mothering my children through their fragile years of adolescence.

I made my decision in June 1981. My son Justin was almost eight months old and I was unable to push away the thought of him. Memories of his parents in the delivery room in silent awe no longer enraptured me, and I began to acknowledge the dull aching in the middle of my chest. I was relieved I no longer had to continue the facade of proclaiming to the world that surrogate parenting was the ideal solution to infertility. Never again would I have to look into the guileless eye of a television camera to parrot my feelings of having had no regrets. Deceiving the public did not appeal to me. I yearned for anonymity and peace.

I understand now that it was important to me to project

an apple-pie image to the public. I wanted to make surrogate motherhood work so much that I refused to let myself feel or think negatively about my decision to have Justin. Now that I have the freedom to look back, I realize I should have talked about the emotional impact this pregnancy had on me and my family. I should have had the courage to let my family see my tears on Christmas and Mother's Day, but I was incapable of speaking the truth to them and, most importantly, to Justin's parents.

My fears of being labeled a failure by the media or incurring the wrath of Justin's parents and Dr. Levin silenced me. I would remain the perfect case so others might follow my example. At that time, I had no idea there would be a price tag attached to this deception.

Time lost all meaning after June 1981. I cannot honestly say how long my depression lasted. It could have been six months or twelve. Perhaps eighteen. I became obsessed with Justin's absence. I knew where he was, but I could not reach out to him. He belonged to another woman and my heart was slowly turning to stone.

I have vague memories of my inability to mother my children properly, to keep the house in order, or be a companion to Kent. I had no interest in making friends or being presentable so I remained in the house day after day. I was incapable of even answering my mail. Evenings were the worst. I only remember putting the children to bed and then lying in front of the stereo listening to Mozart with a glass of wine, drowning in self-pity. I could think only of my infant in the home of Margo and Adam. At times, Kent's shadowy figure would stand by helplessly, watching me mourn.

The depression soon grew into fantasies of my death. I had assured myself Kent and the children, as well as Margo and Adam, would be better off without me. I was a blight that needed to be removed. I planned and replanned my death, rational enough to want to end my life in the cleanest, least expensive yet most effective method. I yearned to seek professional help and recalled the words of Dr. Stein during our initial psychological counseling in Louisville. "If at any time during or after the pregnancy either one of you needs anything, please let me know. I will not abandon you." I knew he was there. I wanted his help but I was terrified he would betray my confidence.

Pastor Michaels, in whom I had confided and whom I trusted during the pregnancy, called a reporter while I was in the hospital after the birth. Imagine my chagrin when I arrived home and saw newspaper headlines revealing family confidences. There was no one left to trust. I felt fragile, completely alone, and betrayed.

Just as I cannot say when the suicidal fantasies began, I cannot recall when they ended. But I clearly remember the desperate struggle to begin thinking on a rational level again.

I had two choices. I could destroy myself with cancerous thoughts or I could rejoice in the fact that Justin was here on earth. I chose the latter.

I took aerobics, and embarked on a sensible diet to regain my size-eight figure. Shortly afterward, Dr. Philip Parker, a psychiatrist, asked me to speak at Wayne State University in Detroit, Michigan. I informed him I was no longer enthralled with the idea of surrogate motherhood, but he encouraged me to speak the truth. "As the first legal surrogate, you were a social and psychological experiment. Your opinion will be invaluable."

Four weeks later I stood behind a podium with a trembling voice and told a large group of physicians and attorneys about my feelings.

"Surrogate motherhood has nothing to do with logic but everything to do with loving and caring and emotions. Stop treating us like we are a disposable uterus. You're tossing away our feelings with the placenta. We are *not* human incubators!"

My words had little impact, if any. The press did not seem interested, and the number of surrogate parenting clinics continued to grow throughout the world.

I returned home and resumed my campaign to heal myself. I dove into community affairs and church activities, helped organize a fund-raiser for teenage alcoholism and drug abuse, and enrolled in our local community college to exercise my brain. Despite Kent's protests, I signed up for skydiving lessons, which I had wanted to try for many years. That imaginary brush with death was an experience so exhilarating it served only to whet my appetite for living each day to the fullest.

The effects on my family were dramatic and undeniable. For months after the birth, Julie would come home from school in tears, angry at those who waved newspapers in her face, taunting her with my picture on the front page. She became withdrawn, resenting the remarks in the lunchroom, at the bus stop, in the hallways between classes.

"Why don't they leave me alone?" she would wail. "I want to be a regular kid again."

She is now twenty years old. We talk often and openly about recent years of our life. She has been able to face Justin's absence much more realistically and has suffered no apparent long-term scars. She made the dean's list in her first year of college. I have hope that she has survived almost unscathed, yet she readily admits she enjoys being anonymous at college and has confided only to her roommate the events that surrounded her adolescence.

Laura has suffered the most. Shortly after the birth, she sat at the breakfast table, unable to eat the Cheerios floating in her bowl. She covered her face with both hands and sobbed, "I never got to hold my baby brother!"

In speechless terror, I watched her thin shoulders shake. I knew I could try to deny he was my son. I had told the world he belonged to another woman. But Laura knew the truth. He is her brother. Nothing that is said or done can ever change that fact. They share the same blood, the same grandparents, and the same mother. I was unable to stand there and tell her she was wrong. I put my arms around her and held her against me as her tears dampened my bathrobe. There were no words. Justin's absence was like a death. We had to mourn it together.

During succeeding months, she was able to verbalize her anguish, but as the years passed, she grew pensive and withdrawn, retreating to her bedroom every time we received photographs of Justin. Any effort on my part to talk about the surrogacy or Justin would result in a stream of obscenities and a wall-shaking slam of her bedroom door. Through counseling we attempted to resolve our differences and her alleged loss of respect for me. The effort was short-lived and futile. Today our conversation remains stilted and veiled. In spite of my sadness over our damaged relationship, I have learned not to feel guilty. I know I cannot be responsible for the way she perceives my actions.

I tried to see the events from Jeffrey's perspective. I left the house in labor, frightened and enormous with the weight of the child within. One week later, I returned home slimmer, tired, trying to be cheerful. The child had disappeared.

Jeffrey would look at pictures of babies and grow sad. "Oh. Baby's gone." He would shake his head sadly and stroke my flat abdomen, no longer able to feel a tiny foot kicking against his hand. It was impossible for him to understand.

Today at the age of eleven, he is in a self-contained special education classroom for learning-disabled children. He is a clinging, fearful child plagued by constant nightmares. Recently he has become afraid of death—especially mine. He will cry and be unable to fall asleep if he hears of the death of an unknown person on the evening news. His behavior completely bewilders me.

In May 1987, while I was on the way to Lansing, Michigan to testify at a Senate committee hearing against surrogate motherhood, my plane was delayed for three hours due to severe thunderstorms. I sat next to a man and waited for the storm to subside while we chatted about his career and personal life. He was a well-qualified psychologist specializing in training special-education teachers. Eventually, I told him about Jeffrey's behavioral problems and he kindly gave me his interpretation.

"Your son is undergoing classic symptoms of grief and loss. It's as though you gave birth to a dead child, came home empty-handed, and never mentioned the baby again. There was no funeral, no family grieving, and little mention of the loss of his brother. Promise me you will get immediate professional help to draw out the denial in this child. Once he becomes an adolescent, the task will be that much harder."

He looked at me with gentle, pale blue eyes. "Find a counselor who specializes in loss, and grief, and death. Promise me you will go with him. You both need help understanding what you've been through."

For a long time I have felt that the difference between losing a child through adoption procedures or surrogacy and losing a child through stillbirth or infant death is like the difference between divorce and widowhood. One is a choice, long considered in advance. The other is an unexpected ruthless blow. With one, you receive only criticism and rejection. With the other, you have sympathy, love and support, and a reaching out from others to soothe your sorrow.

I have lost a child. Kent has not. We no longer relate to each other in the same manner we once did. The closeness and respect have diminished. There is little real communication after twenty-one years of marriage.

Recently, while cleaning out a desk drawer, I found some notes Kent had made during my pregnancy. His feelings about the possible breakup of our marriage and his feigned acceptance of my surrogacy—his fears for all of us following the birth—saddened me. He never once revealed those feelings to me.

During these last years, I feel as though I have been riding a giant pogo stick. I have greatly resented Kent for seemingly controlling my life. When his company had financial problems and reduced their staff by forty employees, Kent was one of those laid off. The six months he was out of work, I was deeply, if unreasonably, angry at him, hating the fact that he had lost his job and couldn't be more successful like my friends' husbands. It was impossible for me to admit that my earlier behavior had cost him his first job and he would have been promoted within that same company by now instead of looking for work at the age of fifty. It was easier for me to blame him, to make him the scapegoat, than to accept the role I played in our family drama.

During the first years after the birth, I would shout about divorce, using illogical arguments for not being able to live with him anymore. The children would watch wide-eyed while I would open suitcases for Jeffrey and myself and begin packing. Then minutes later, I would sink onto the edge of the bed and sag with defeat. I had nowhere to go. Whom could I visit? Whom could I trust not to call the *National Inquirer*? I feared the headlines: ELIZABETH KANE AND HUSBAND SPLIT OVER SON. SURROGACY FAILS.

I think Kent realized my frustration but was unable to cope with it. His answer would be to leave the room or the house until I collected myself. When we rejoined each other at the dinner table, no mention was made of earlier events. The problems seemed to be worst on Sunday afternoons. For many years Sundays were difficult and depressing for me, and Kent was always the target of my anger.

The psychologist I talked to in the airport confirmed my feelings about the difficulties that surrogacy had presented in our marriage. "Each time your husband looks at a photograph of Justin, he is reminded of your bond with another man. As though you had taken a lover. Your son by this stranger might very well have qualities that Kent wished his own son had. This could only add to feelings of low self-esteem."

Each day I try to remind myself to be less caustic and more understanding. Sometimes I am almost overwhelmed at the amount of energy and work involved in keeping my marriage together. The thing that confuses me most is the fact that Kent does not seem to be as dissatisfied with me as I am with him. I wonder if the problem lies within me rather than in our marriage. I also know we are growing rapidly in different directions. I am no longer the young submissive girl he married. I can only pray that counseling will give me some answers.

My feelings of helplessness came to a head in the fall of 1986 when I saw a bronze plaque placed among flowering plants in a nearby park. "To sin by silence, when they should protest, makes cowards of men."

The words were Abraham Lincoln's. I was mesmerized by them. I could no longer deny my cowardice by remaining silent about my feelings.

The name Mary Beth Whitehead meant nothing to me until late one Monday afternoon in October 1986. On the advice of my librarian, I bought a copy of *People* magazine. A burning rage spread through me as I read about her nightmare. My most dire fears of women proceeding unwittingly to join the ranks of surrogate mothers had come to pass in the form of Mary Beth Whitehead. Tears of compassion ran from my eyes while I typed a letter to her in care of *People*.

"So, you fell in love with your baby, Mary Beth, and no one told you it would happen. Well, so did I. So do we all!"

My bitterness at the exploitation of young women by unscrupulous professionals eager for an easy dollar spilled onto the page and I sealed the envelope without retracting a single word. Within days, *People* called, asking permission to reprint my letter and promising to forward it to Mary Beth.

Several days later her attorney called to ask for my support and to invite me to New Jersey to meet her. I balked, making no promises. Later that night, the phone rang. The moment I heard Mary Beth's soft, determined voice I liked her. After a two-hour conversation I felt a sisterhood with Mary Beth Whitehead, and I wanted to help her. It was eleven o'clock on a Saturday night and I sat on the edge of our bed, interrupting Kent's movie on television.

"Don't get involved. I don't want any more publicity. She's got a lawyer so just leave it alone," was my husband's response.

"I can't. Don't you understand what she's going through? Do you want her to suffer like I have? That's her baby, Kent. She needs that child. No one has the right to take it from her."

We talked late into the night until he finally relented. "Do what you have to do, but leave me out of it. I like this job and I'm not looking for another one at my age."

"There won't be any publicity," I assured him. I ignored his skeptical look and turned out the lights.

How could I expect him to know how Mary Beth felt? I was the one missing a child, not he.

When I boarded the plane to New Jersey the next afternoon, I knew Mary Beth needed me. What I didn't know was that I needed her even more.

The next day I filed an affidavit through her attorney with the New Jersey Supreme Court, stating my belief that surrogate motherhood should be banned nationwide, that the practice caused unexpected emotional damage to surrogate mothers and their families. The long-term psychological ramifications of surrogate parenting contracts were no longer a mystery. I had seen the damage firsthand.

Later that night Mary Beth and I sat in her pink and white kitchen, immaculate and dainty as a dollhouse. We munched apple slices as we talked; from time to time she reached for a chunk of cheese with long red fingernails. Thick, dark hair framed a pale face filled with weariness.

"Stop calling yourself a surrogate mother, Elizabeth." She raised her normally gentle voice almost to a shout. "You're his mother and he's your son. The *other* woman is his surrogate mother. She's the substitute, not you." Her brown eyes fixed steadily on mine. "You're the one who was in the delivery room, not her. He's your son, not hers. Don't you realize that?"

"Yes, but I can't say that." I answered her in a voice that was barely audible.

Her eyes never wavered from my face. "And why not? It's the truth!"

"Because it's too late, Mary Beth. He's gone. I signed him away."

"Yes, but it's not too late for you to stop other women from doing what we did. My God! How many more innocent women are going to have to endure the hell we've been through before it will all stop?"

It was 3:00 A.M. by the time I climbed into bed. The baby she called Sara and the courts call Melissa had an empty crib standing less than two feet from my bed. It was like sleeping with a ghost.

Twelve hours later we arrived at the airport. There was to be a press conference for us. Mary Beth held my hand to give me the courage I needed. My lunch was in my throat, and I started to choke out the words we had prepared during the long drive. Tears streaming down my face, I admitted to the press that I missed my son, that I had never gotten over the loss of him and that surrogate motherhood was a terrible mistake.

Photographers two-stepped around me, holding Nikons

and Canons inches from my face, clicking away like the steady drip-drip of rain on a roof. I held up my hand trying to regain composure, pleading with them to stop as a crowd gathered. Then Mary Beth and I held each other and wept openly. We had underestimated the depth of our emotions. We cried for ourselves, for the suffering of each other, and for other surrogate mothers who would someday acknowledge the same pain.

Mary Beth Whitehead's case was inevitable from the moment I began carving the word *surrogate* into the American psyche. I never thought I would find myself campaigning against a method intended to help infertile couples, but today with Mary Beth's fight for her daughter fresh in the national consciousness, it is time to reexamine the entire concept of surrogate parenting.

It is important to study the motives of physicians and attorneys running surrogate parenting clinics. They claim every couple deserves a chance to start a family with a newborn, and yet their exorbitant fees ($15,000 for an insemination that actually should cost $324) prohibit a majority of the infertile from hiring surrogate mothers. Infertile couples must be made aware of the risks involved in asking a complete stranger to sign a contract before conception that states she will relinquish the child at birth and agree never to see her baby again. It is against human nature for a woman to psychologically disassociate herself from the child she is carrying. There is a human factor involved that should make the contract unenforceable if the surrogate wishes to change her mind. Even an unwed teenage mother contemplating adoption procedures has an option to keep her child if she changes her mind.

There has to be something wrong with a judicial system that will allow a contract as legal which obligates the natural mother to sign away a child she has not yet conceived in exchange for $10,000. A well-known surrogate clinic on the

East Coast has drawn up a contract stating the surrogate gets $10,000 for the delivery of a healthy child, nothing for a "defective" child, and she must *pay* the father $25,000 if she decides to keep the child. Why should the life of a child suddenly go up in value if the birth mother keeps it, as opposed to the child's father raising it?

Many reproductive engineers now in charge of surrogate parenting clinics refer to the baby as a "product" or as "an investment." When a potential surrogate mother walks through the door of a baby broker's office she is viewed as a healthy uterus worth so many thousand dollars. The fact that the clinic is paid by the infertile couple immediately, while the surrogate must wait until the birth, has never been questioned. Infertile couples who are unwilling to accept the disappointment of life without a biological child may feel it is their right to hire another woman as their breeder, but they do so only after careful screening to ensure she will produce an acceptable product.

I am appalled at the lack of proper counseling, before and after the pregnancy. There are no requirements for the psychological testing of prospective parents. A surrogate mother is supposed to undergo rigid psychological screening to assure she will be a good candidate for the clinic, yet at least one clinic I am aware of sends potential surrogates to any number of interviews until they have two psychologists willing to write positive letters advising the clinic to go ahead with the insemination. This was the case for one unbalanced young woman who is serving a life sentence in prison today in Oregon for shooting her three children, killing one of them and paralyzing the other two, a year after terminating her parental rights to her surrogate child. She told the judge that the only time in her life she felt worthwhile was when she was carrying a child. She conceived another child shortly before she was sent to prison.

I am also concerned about the surrogates from one well-known clinic in the Midwest who are advised not to pay taxes on their fees. Our accountant researched the law and informed us my fee was considered income. These surrogates are being paid in smaller amounts to avoid any questioning by the IRS. They are following the advice of their baby brokers, some of whom are attorneys, and, ironically, may be breaking the laws as a result.

There are, also, the ticklish related problems. Insurance companies are being deceived into thinking they are paying hospital costs for babies of their policyholders; in fact, they may be shelling out thousands of dollars for children of men who have never paid them premiums. Blue Cross/Blue Shield is now considering including a clause in its policies ruling out payment for surrogate births. Women on welfare are having their surrogate births paid for by the taxpayers!

My concerns do not stop with the surrogate mother and her family. I worry about the damage that someday may be inflicted on children of surrogate arrangements when they learn of the circumstances of their birth.

Children are not a commodity. The fact that our society has begun to view them as such by demanding that a surrogate mother be held to her contract reaffirms my belief that we as a public need to be reeducated about the exploitation of women like Mary Beth Whitehead, as well as the surrogate in prison in Oregon, the woman whose husband divorced her because he could not accept her surrogacy, and the handful of surrogates who are beginning to share their tales of horror.

We have to come face-to-face with the fact that wealthy men are taking advantage of women from lower-middle-income families. The baby brokers and judges are well aware of the financial status of women being hired as breeders, smug in the fact that few will have the financial means to engage in long legal battles to regain custody of their own children. This is reproductive prostitution.

For some women, $10,000 might seem like an enormous amount of money, especially if they are financially troubled. But can we really continue to allow women to rent spaces in their bodies and sell their children for profit?

I shudder to think of the loss of self-esteem when today's surrogate children are told they were bought and sold. I can only imagine the scenes that will take place fifteen or twenty years from now when these children—the products of our genetic engineering—are old enough to hire their own attorneys. Perhaps they will sue their own fathers for denying them the right to have relationships with their biological families. Perhaps they will vent their anger and frustrations by suing their birth mothers for signing them away before they were even conceived, deciding long before birth that they were not wanted. Either way, these children have an extended family they will not know until their childhood can no longer be retrieved. Our courts must consider the children above all else.

The *Observer* recently reported (London, April 5, 1987) that Dr. Jennifer Steadman, a Canadian psychiatrist, has completed a study in which she voiced the following concern: "There seems to be no consideration of the effect on the siblings." Steadman predicts that there will be

> an increase in feelings of abandonment, fear, and anxiety among children of surrogate families who see their parents willingly giving away a child after birth.
>
> And what of the child itself? When it learns the truth, how will it deal with the knowledge of a mother who gave it away for pay? And how can it have access to family medical history or be guaranteed a good home? Conventional adoption requires record keeping and a careful selection of the adopting parents. Reproduction without sex does not.

In this age of advanced reproductive technology, I feel we are forgetting ethics and morals. Just because we *can* do something does not mean we *should.* As a society it is time for us to recognize the fact that surrogate parenting can and does create havoc within the family units it touches.

I do not regret having Justin. He is a gift and he was meant to be here. His father and I could not have created him any other way simply because we never would have met. I do not regret that Justin is being raised by his father and the woman he calls "Mother." I am fully aware of the joy and sense of completeness he has given to their family. But I understand now that I am *not* a surrogate mother. I am a birth mother. He is my child and I do not think I will ever get over having given him away.

I do regret that what I had thought or intended to be a selfless act for an unknown family turned out to be a selfish act toward my own. What right did I have to put my husband and children through a test of courage I thought would be only mine to bear? I had no idea my children would bond with their brother during the pregnancy or would spend years aching for the touch and sound of him. We all long to share a tiny piece of Justin's life.

The recent discovery that Justin's adoptive mother has the power to refuse me a reunion with him left me fraught with grief and anger. The turmoil it raised in me made me doubt I could ever again be whole.

And yet, just weeks before last Christmas, my world changed again. The children and I arrived home after tramping through the woods of a Christmas tree farm looking for the perfect balsam for our living room. We walked in with our prize, exuberant from an afternoon outdoors. Julie lay stretched on the floor, whittling a project for art class. She had tossed the mail onto the carpet next to her, and I began to sift through the assortment of bills and Christmas cards. Suddenly I noticed a return address from a Wisconsin adoption agency, but I dismissed it as a plea for a donation. I opened it anyway, disinterested. I read only the first sentence: "A search application has been filed by your adult adoptee . . ." I burst into tears and lowered myself onto the sofa, unable to continue. Julie took the letter from my hand, read it, and looked up confused. She and Laura had known about their half sister for years. "Mom, why are you crying? Heidi is looking for you. Aren't you happy?"

After twenty-two years, my firstborn was reaching out to me. For the next few days, I felt the elation I had experienced when I discovered I was pregnant with Julie. But one question gnawed at me: did she understand that adoption had been the best thing for both of us at that time? My fears that she might resent me after all these years vanished with her first letter to me, dated January 1987:

> To sum up my feelings I have held for you since I can remember, is gratitude. If I were allowed to tell you one thing, it would be "Thank You." Thank you for being unselfish, for giving me the benefit of the doubt and letting me live. Although I've never met you, you have greatly influenced me by teaching me the value of a human life.

Through misty eyes I searched the enclosed photographs for the face of the infant I had known so briefly. I reread her letter and thanked God and her parents for the person Heidi had become. She had been raised a wonderful, sensitive, mature daughter.

We met eight months later; the moment is something I will never be able to describe adequately. I received a letter from her shortly thereafter in which she wrote: "It was important to me that you are a kind person. You fulfilled that hope beyond any expectations. You are unselfish, open, caring, and kind. I love and respect you for those qualities. It's the most I could hope for in a mother." The daughter who had been lost to me for so long had given me the ultimate gift. Our new, close relationship continues to add new dimension to my life.

Because of that reunion, I am filled with a serenity at last that Justin and I will be reunited—that someday we, too, will know one another. By giving Heidi back to me, God has given me that hope.

On October 15, 1987, I entered the Rayburn House Office Building in Washington, D.C. as a member of the National Coalition Against Surrogacy. I had been asked to testify in favor of Congressman Thomas A. Luken's bill to ban surrogacy on a commercial level.

I stopped at the doorway of the hall momentarily, awestruck by the formidable power suggested by the room—its dark, rich wood and imposing American flag. Oliver North had held the nation spellbound at that very table only weeks before.

A tall, dark-haired man stood in the room with his back to me. It was Dr. Richard Levin. I found myself saying his name and walking toward him. I had often visualized the moment, wondering how we would react to one another. I had hoped that in those seven years he would have aged, but when he turned toward me, it was evident that Mother Nature had been kind. The years had only served to enhance his good looks.

Within seconds, we were exchanging kisses on the cheek. I had never imagined that when we met again it would be in the halls of Congress with reporters, his wife, Pam, and his four lovely daughters cataloging the exchange.

"You look wonderful, Rich," I blurted. As glad as I was

to see him again, I trembled inside, knowing he would disapprove of the things I would say today.

When he motioned for me to sit with him to chat, I declined. I had to return to the waiting room to make the last page of my testimony legible. But I had been told that the baby brokers would not be present while the surrogate mothers testified. Was this to be our only contact after seven years? Only a few brief moments in the public eye?

Within a short time, the members of our coalition solemnly filed into the hall. I stood near the table, searching for name cards, then froze. Richard had pulled a chair directly in front of the card reading ELIZABETH KANE. I knew exactly what he was trying to do. Surely he wouldn't be allowed to breathe down my neck during my testimony! Somebody would notice and ask him to leave. I was sure of that. I wriggled sideways to slide into the small space he had left for me. My peripheral vision allowed me to see his hands resting on his outstretched legs. His presence loomed until I could think of nothing else. My throat closed in alarm.

I can't do this, I thought, looking for help from the coalition's strong supporter, Jeremy Rifkin. I nearly stood up and asked to be excused, but the sound of Jeremy's voice beginning his testimony stopped me. Leaning forward to glance at all the members of our coalition, I remembered I was not alone. We were there to tell Congress about the business of buying and selling human beings, and to reveal our personal distress at having been part of that business.

When it was my turn to speak, I did so unwaveringly, and Richard's intimidating presence receded, shrank to nothing. I ended with a plea that Congress put a stop to the pain caused by surrogate parenting.

A recess was called, and I turned to leave with the others, but Richard blocked my way. In his face I saw nothing but scorn.

"Why don't you tell them about the adoption, Mary Beth?" He was referring to Heidi. I remembered all the times he had told me never to reveal the illegitimate birth to the press.

"I will, Rich. When I'm ready." I said it softly, wishing he would step aside.

His voice grew louder, more insistent. "No, Mary Beth. I think you should tell them now. It's important for Congress to know you had a baby and gave it up with no apparent problems."

For a split second, I almost responded in the familiar pattern: appeasing his wrath by pleading with him and making excuses for myself. I watched as a controlled rage filled his face; we were both barely aware of the people milling nearby. So. Not one thing had changed in seven years. He still had the ability to control me. In that split second, I separated myself from him. I drew up, tall. With me in my three-inch heels, we were eye to eye and I held his gaze.

"I will tell them in good time." I felt the anger rise with new strength. "You cannot tell me what to think or say any longer, Richard."

The invisible string had snapped. I was free at last.